BUILDING LEARNING COMMUNITIES IN CYBERSPACE

BUILDING LEARNING COMMUNITIES IN CYBERSPACE

Effective Strategies for the Online Classroom

Rena M. Palloff

Keith Pratt

Jossey-Bass Publishers
San Francisco

Jossey-Bass books and products are available through most bookstores. To contact Jossey-Bass directly, call (888) 378-2537, fax to (800) 605-2665, or visit our website at www.josseybass.com.

Substantial discounts on bulk quantities of Jossey-Bass books are available to corporations, professional associations, and other organizations. For details and discount information, contact the special sales department at Jossey-Bass.

Manufactured in the United States of America.

Library of Congress Cataloging-in-Publication Data

Palloff, Rena M., date.
  Building learning communities in cyberspace : effective strategies for the online classroom /
Rena M. Palloff, Keith Pratt. — 1st ed.
    p. cm. — (The Jossey-Bass higher and adult education series)
  Includes bibliographical references and index.
  ISBN 0-7879-4460-2 (acid-free paper)
    1. Distance education—United States. 2. College teaching—United States—Data processing.
3. Computer-assisted instruction—United States. I. Pratt, Keith, date. II. Title. III. Series.
  LC5805 .P35 1999
  378.1'75—dc21
                                                                              98-58077

FIRST EDITION
PB Printing   10 9 8 7 6 5 4

THE JOSSEY-BASS

HIGHER AND ADULT EDUCATION SERIES

CONTENTS

PART ONE: THE LEARNING COMMUNITY IN CYBERSPACE

LIST OF FIGURES, TABLES, AND EXHIBITS

Figures

Tables

Exhibits

PREFACE

In computer-mediated distance learning, an instructor or facilitator delivers courses by communicating with students through the use of a computer network or the Internet. This method is a relative newcomer to education. The explosive growth of the Internet has contributed to the increasing popularity of this type of learning and has brought with it a set of issues and problems heretofore unexplored in education. According to a U.S. Department of Education study ("ED Study . . . ," 1997), about 90 percent of all higher education institutions with enrollments of ten thousand or more will be offering some form of distance education by the fall of 1998; 76 percent were offering distance education programs in the fall of 1995. Sixty-one percent of medium-sized colleges and institutions already offer distance education classes, and an additional 24 percent plan to add such courses. Not all distance education programs include computer-mediated course offerings; they may include video conferencing and other means of distance learning. Course offerings span all disciplines. Table 1 presents a sampling of some of the courses currently being offered by universities across the country.

Challenges of Computer-Mediated Distance Education

In this book we will be exploring computer-mediated distance education, along with the benefits, problems, and concerns inherent in it. The reader will note that

TABLE 1. A SAMPLE OF COURSE OFFERINGS.

University	Online Courses Offered
Texas State Technical College	Computer Science
University of Texas	Biology
British Columbia Open School	Accounting, Agriculture, Calculus, Art, German, Biology, Business, Drafting, Economics, French, Journalism, Physics
Rochester Institute of Technology	Statistics, Microelectronics, Chemistry, Bioethics, Computer Concepts, Earth Science, Energy Management, Hydrology, Psychology, Applied Mechanics, Environmental Management
Stanford University	Master's Degree in Engineering (beginning Fall 1998)
Pennsylvania State University	Commentary on Art
New Promise Internet University (a collaboration of approximately 90 institutions including Harvard, Indiana University, Michigan State, and University of Minnesota)	Aeronautics, Arts, Business, Composition, Computers, Economics, Education, Government, Health, History, Humanities, Languages, Law, Literature, Management, Mathematics, Science, Sociology

throughout the book we have used the phrases distance education and distance learning interchangeably. This reflects the current state of the field.

The shift to computer-mediated distance learning poses enormous challenges to instructors and their institutions. Many faculty members believe that the online classroom is no different from the traditional one—that the approaches that work face to face will work when learners are separated from them and from each other by time and distance. However, when the only connection we have to our students is through words on a screen, we must pay attention to many issues that we take for granted in the face-to-face classroom.

For example, how do we know when a student is engaged with the subject matter? How do we account for attendance and participation? How do we know if a student is having difficulty or is upset for some reason? Is it possible to read emotion into students' posts? How do we deal with students who are not participating? How can we recognize and deal with disagreement and conflict? Educators and trainers who are already familiar with computer-mediated education will find these issues relevant. They are derived from the relationship of the user to the machine, the relationships between the instructor or facilitator and the participants, and the relationships among the participants themselves. These relationships define such things as:

- Participation in the group or involvement with the subject matter
- The emotional state and availability of the participants
- Personality that is developed through this interaction

We will explore these and many other critical issues. This book will help faculty make the transition from the classroom to cyberspace and more fully understand the new approaches and skills they will need if they are to be successful.

Origins of the Book

The seeds for the book began germinating when we both were Ph.D. students at the Fielding Institute in 1993. The Fielding Institute is a distance learning program offering midcareer adults both master's degrees and Ph.D.'s in human and organizational systems, human development, psychology, and, most recently, in educational leadership and change and organizational design and effectiveness. Its more than eight hundred students are located all over the world; at the time, students were linked electronically through Fielding's own electronic network—the Fielding Electronic Network (FEN).

What we discovered as we participated in the virtual community formed by this network was that it seemed difficult to pursue and work out differences and disagreements online. We became interested in the benefits, issues, as well as the difficulties, involved with building a virtual community and the impact such a community can have on computer-mediated distance learning. We further noted that the human elements involved in electronic communication often seemed to be neglected in Fielding's electronic realm, leading to conflict and problems with decision making. We found this ironic in an educational community that is linked electronically and that prides itself on openness and on the acceptance of difference. Consequently, we opted to create a structure wherein a small group of Fielding students could explore topics electronically that would tap into the humanness of grief, conflict, and interconnectedness.

The electronic seminar we created was not driven by course content but was designed to explore the use of electronic communication as a means of delivering distance learning programs. As the eight-week seminar progressed, we lovingly named our minicommunity "The Cyberspace Sandbox," as we all felt like little children exploring and playing in unchartered territory. In many ways, the development of this sandbox community paralleled the development of most small groups or communities. The seminar group, composed of ten doctoral students in various phases of their work, moved through an initial phase of testing the waters; it then moved rapidly into a conflict phase, then into a phase of intimacy and work, followed by termination. It was fascinating to us that, even with the brief nature of the experience and minimal-to-no "human" interaction, all phases of group development appeared and were worked through. The relationships formed through this interaction were strong and continue to the present in the form of friendships that are maintained both through e-mail communication and periodic face-to-face contact.

The majority of the core group of participants were people with many years of technical experience. Several times during the seminar they stated online that they had never had an electronic experience like that one. Never had they experienced such intimacy and trust on an electronic bulletin board. Participants also commented on the differences in their behavior online and off—a subject we have researched and will discuss in this book. We conclude, based on this work, that the anonymity and perceived safety of the medium allow participants to explore and experience components of their personalities that they might not otherwise access. Additionally, participants have the luxury of time; they have time to give more thought to their contributions to discussions.

This first seminar created, for us, the beginnings of a framework for effective distance education. This framework includes deliberate attempts to build community as a means of promoting collaborative learning. Embedded within community building are the active creation of knowledge and meaning and the purposeful empowerment of participants to become experts at their own learning. We have concluded through our work in this medium that the construction of a learning community, with the instructor participating as an equal member, is the key to a successful outcome.

Since our first seminar, we have continued to teach using a computer-mediated approach and have begun to add elements to the framework we are developing for successful distance learning. What is most effective about our approach is its simplicity and the fact that it does not depend on any one form of technology. It is about using our best practices as educators and applying them in a completely different environment. Tried and true techniques used face to face in the classroom sometimes do not work when the classroom is virtual.

Although computer-mediated learning is currently under study in many venues, very little scientific research has been conducted regarding the efficacy, benefits, or pitfalls of a computer-mediated approach to education. Within the next few years, the results of studies should become increasingly available. In the meantime, much of what is written about and shared—including what is in this book—is anecdotal and based on the experiences of instructors and students.

This book is based on our own experience, which is considerable. How to develop online learning communities has been the focus of our work since we delivered our first online seminar in 1993. More and more often, we are asked to consult to educational institutions where distance learning programs have been implemented but do not have successful outcomes or are not satisfactory to those involved. Many institutions are lured by attractive software packages or by the prospect of reducing costs and increasing their student population through the use of distance education—which can certainly be benefits. However, focusing on these elements and ignoring what it takes to learn in this environment can be expensive mistakes.

This book, then, is the sharing of our framework—and of our successes and our difficulties—with our colleagues who wish to deliver distance learning programs more effectively. It is designed to be useful to anyone engaged in the process of online work, be they academics, group facilitators, or those working in networked organizations or delivering corporate training programs online. It is written both for faculty who have been teaching online and wish to discover new ideas to incorporate into their practice and for those who are embarking on this journey. Others who will find the book useful are department chairs and deans responsible for the development and delivery of online offerings, those responsible for faculty and instructional development, and designers who are working with all of those groups in order to make the transition to online work.

This book is not about technology. Neither is it about the use of computer-assisted instruction, wherein a student interacts only with a software package installed on a computer. We are concerned with software and hardware only as vehicles in the creation of an environment that is conducive to learning. The process of teaching and learning through the creation of an online community is our concern. We have gleaned from our experience a number of techniques and approaches that work well in this environment, which we now apply in every class we teach. We will present these techniques, along with examples and questions to consider, to help with their implementation. Because we teach in the social sciences, our examples and cases emerge from that discipline. However, we encourage readers from other disciplines to seek out colleagues across the country who are teaching classes online. Instructors using this medium frequently make their materials available on the Internet, welcoming comments and questions about their courses and experiences.

As academic institutions are moving rapidly toward the use of the Internet to offer courses and programs, as well as to develop virtual universities, instructors must be trained and supported as they move into this arena. We cannot assume that all faculty, regardless of how well they perform in the classroom, will be able to make this transition easily, just as we cannot assume that all students will fare well. This book will make a significant contribution to the discussions and struggles that frame the transition. We offer suggestions that can help pave the way to well-planned and effective computer-mediated distance learning.

Organization of Contents

The book is divided into two parts. Part One is designed to lay the foundation for our distance education framework. Chapter One begins to explore the issues involved in teaching and learning when learning leaves the classroom and moves into the online environment. Chapter Two looks at the essence of our framework—the importance of building community in the online environment. In so doing, the chapter differentiates for the reader a traditional model of pedagogy from a model that will lead to success in the electronic classroom. Chapter Three explores in more detail the issues that we have discovered to be key and needing attention in the electronic classroom. They have emerged from our seminar work and, consequently, we include bits of dialogue from those seminars to illustrate each issue. Chapters Four and Five tackle some of the more concrete issues of time, group size, and technology as they pertain to online teaching.

In Part Two we provide an experiential guide to the creation of an electronic learning community leading to effective distance learning. Chapter Six shows how to make the conversion from the traditional classroom to cyberspace. Chapters Seven through Ten provide practical applications of the framework. More specifically, Chapter Seven offers suggestions for creating an appropriate syllabus, setting objectives and learning outcomes, negotiating guidelines, setting up the course site online, gaining participation and student buy-in for the process, and accounting for presence in the online classroom. Chapter Eight provides practical techniques for stimulating collaborative learning among participants. Also presented are ways to promote and facilitate relationship building and personal process, thus humanizing what can be viewed as a nonhuman environment. Chapter Nine explores a critical component of online learning—transformative learning—which is learning about how we learn through the use of technology, learning about the technology itself, and most important, learning about ourselves. The chapter shows how to incorporate this process stream into the context of the online course. Chapter Ten focuses on an important concern of most educators—how to evaluate results. This chapter discusses student assessment, appropriate assignments for evaluation purposes, and course and program evaluation. Finally, in Chapter Eleven we summarize and review what we consider to be the keys to successful online learning. In addition, we discuss the ramifications of this work for teacher training. The case examples, vignettes, and questions for consideration in the chapter will help readers bring the material alive and apply it successfully in their own computer-mediated classes.

Included throughout the book are student posts to various types of discussions in online courses. We have deliberately left them untouched. Except for paring them down to manageable size, we have not edited them for grammar and have asked the publisher to refrain from doing so. We have found in our experience of online teaching that commentary on or editing of student posts creates a type of performance anxiety that results in reduced participation. Just as most instructors would not think to correct the grammar of a student who is verbally contributing in a face-to-face class, we would not correct the spelling or grammar in a post, as this is the equivalent of speaking in class. Because an instructor who is venturing into this arena needs to be prepared to receive unedited posts from students, we have deliberately chosen to leave the ones we present as they are. This shift in thinking represents but one of the numerous shifts instructors need to make as they enter this arena.

Computer-mediated distance education is dynamic and ever-changing. In this book, we have captured and discussed the issues as they exist today. Advances in technology will bring new challenges to an evolving field. This book, however, should help instructors face today's challenges more effectively.

January 1999

Rena M. Palloff
Alameda, California

Keith Pratt
Ottawa, Kansas

To Gary and Dianne for your infinite patience,
the Fielding Institute for giving us our start,
and all of our students—past, present, and future.

ACKNOWLEDGMENTS

A book such as this one, which describes a collaborative learning process, could not have been completed in isolation. Consequently, we wish to acknowledge a number of people who contributed to the development of our work. We are deeply grateful to the Fielding Institute—its faculty, staff, and students—for starting us down this path. Not only did we begin our collaboration there but we were supported in beginning our research into this new territory while the institute worked to gain a more solid footing in the distance-learning arena. Most of all, we wish to thank Don MacIntyre, president of the Fielding Institute, for his vision, friendship, and unwavering support.

We wish to acknowledge the "pioneers"—the Elcomm group—who were the first contributors to our research in the area of building community online. We also thank our students from the California Institute of Integral Studies, John F. Kennedy University, and Ottawa University for their enthusiastic participation in our online classes, their willingness to allow us to use some of their posts in this book, and mostly for teaching us more than we could ever hope to teach them. Thanks to our good friends and colleagues, Charlie Marshall and Alpha Sarmian, for reading the early drafts of the book and giving us feedback and encouragement. A special thanks to Alpha for his assistance with the graphics and his ideas, which will definitely take us further into this journey than we had ever anticipated. We are grateful to Gale Erlandson and David Brightman of Jossey-Bass for their assistance and support, and for taking on this project in the first place.

Finally, and definitely far from least, we wish to acknowledge and express our gratitude and love for Gary Krauss and Dianne Pratt. Thanks to both of you for putting up with both of us. We could not have done this without you.

THE AUTHORS

Rena M. Palloff has been managing and supervising both hospital-based and private, nonprofit treatment programs for twelve years. She consults to addiction treatment programs in the areas of program development and marketing, as well as in the development of service delivery systems that are sensitive to the managed care environment. She has been working extensively in health care, academic settings, and addiction treatment for the last twenty years.

Palloff is an assistant professor at John F. Kennedy University, teaching students in counseling psychology in the Graduate School for Holistic Studies. She is also an adjunct associate professor in the Chemical Dependency Studies Department at California State University–Hayward. In addition, she is a faculty member at the Fielding Institute in the Organizational Design and Effectiveness Program, which offers a master's degree completely online. She teaches classes on organizational behavior and on management and leadership on an adjunct basis for the International Studies Program at Ottawa University in Ottawa, Kansas, in various sites throughout the Pacific Rim. She teaches both online and face to face in the Organizational Development and Transformation and Master of Arts in Business programs at the California Institute of Integral Studies in San Francisco.

Palloff received a bachelor's degree in sociology from the University of Wisconsin–Madison and a master's degree in social work from the University of Wisconsin–Milwaukee. She holds a master's degree in organizational development and a Ph.D. in human and organizational systems from the Fielding Institute.

Keith Pratt began his government career as a computer systems technician with the U.S. Air Force in 1967. He served in various positions, including supervisor of computer systems maintenance, chief of the Logistics Support Branch, chief of the Telecommunications Branch, and superintendent of the Secure Telecommunications Branch. After leaving the air force, Pratt held positions as registrar and faculty (Charter College), director (Chapman College), and trainer and consultant (The Growth Company).

As an adjunct faculty member at Wayland Baptist University and at the University of Alaska, Pratt taught courses in communications, business, management, organizational theories, and computer technology. He is currently an assistant professor in the International Studies Program and chair of the Management Information Systems Program, main campus and overseas, at Ottawa University in Ottawa, Kansas.

Pratt graduated from Wayland Baptist University with a dual degree in business administration and computer systems technology. He has an M.S. in human resource management (with honors) from Chapman University, an M.S. in organizational development, a Ph.D. in human and organizational systems from the Fielding Institute, and an honorary doctorate of science from Moscow State University.

Palloff and Pratt are managing partners in Crossroads Consulting Group. Since 1994 they have collaboratively conducted pioneering research and training in the emerging areas of electronic group facilitation, face-to-face and electronic community building, distance learning, and management and supervision. In addition to their work in the development and delivery of effective distance education, their consulting work has centered around team building and team effectiveness, conflict resolution, program planning and development, and community building. They tailor training to organizational needs, offer management support and development in dealing with the aftermath of change efforts, and facilitate the development of effective internship programs. They are also providers of continuing education, offering courses online to assist professionals in completing their continuing education requirements.

BUILDING LEARNING COMMUNITIES IN CYBERSPACE

PART ONE

THE LEARNING COMMUNITY
IN CYBERSPACE

CHAPTER ONE

WHEN TEACHING AND LEARNING LEAVE THE CLASSROOM

Today's academic institutions are in transition. Much of the change we are seeing is due to economic pressures from mounting costs and demands by the business world for graduates with the ability to function well in a knowledge society; greater diversity among the students who are choosing to attend school is also a factor. Although colleges continue to attract 62 percent of high school graduates onto their campuses immediately following graduation, larger numbers of so-called nontraditional students, as defined by age and life situation, are seeking degrees (Hammonds, Jackson, DeGeorge, and Morris, 1997). It is estimated that fewer than one-fourth of the students on college campuses today are between the ages of eighteen and twenty-two and attending full-time—our definition of a traditional undergraduate (Twigg, 1994b).

How are universities responding to these changes and demands? Institutions of higher education are, with increasing frequency, turning to the use of the Internet to deliver courses to students at a distance, as well as to enhance educational programs that are delivered on campus. Some institutions view this as a way to attract students who might not otherwise attend classes; others use it as a way to begin meeting the needs of a new population of students: "Universities are feeling the pressure to control costs, improve quality, focus directly on customer needs, and respond to competitive pressures. Information technology (IT) has the potential to solve many of these problems. It can change the roles of students and faculty, facilitate more learner-centered, personalized education, save money through improved business processes and distance education, and expand the scope and content of the curriculum" (Horgan, 1998, p. 1).

As technology comes into greater use, faculty and students alike are grappling with the changes it brings to the educational environment. Courses and degree programs are being offered over the Internet. Virtual universities are being constructed, such as the Western Governors' University and the California Virtual University, where students can apply for admission, register for courses, purchase books, and attend classes without ever visiting a physical place called a campus. Several educational programs have been developed that involve students interacting with a piece of software on a computer, with no interaction occurring among groups of learners. This is known as computer-assisted education or computer-based training. Other programs are more interactive, allowing students to post comments to a discussion area on a website, which is known as *asynchronous discussion*. Participants in this form of computer-mediated learning can read and comment on the topic under discussion at their leisure. Yet another way to teach online is to use *synchronous discussion*, or chat, wherein all participants log on to a course site at once and interact with each other in real time.

Regardless of which instructional method is used, a transition must be made from the typical campus classroom to the classroom in cyberspace. Instructors and students behave differently in the two types of classrooms; learning outcomes are different as well. Computer-mediated courses and programs have been appearing so rapidly that little thought seems to have been given to the possible impact of the delivery method—either educationally or socially. Nor has much thought been given to the need to modify the educational approach; traditional teaching methods are being attempted in a nontraditional environment.

What happens when instructors and their students never meet face to face but are connected only through text on a screen? How does that change the transmission of knowledge, the nature of the learning process, and the relationships among the people who are interacting online? We will be tackling these questions and more in this book, with the hope that academic institutions and their faculties might pause just a bit in the development of online options and consider the important issues and concerns that should be a part of the development of the online classroom. The nature of teaching and learning does change when it leaves the classroom—sometimes dramatically.

Defining Computer-Mediated Distance Education

The emergence of computer mediation for the purpose of education has created a redefinition of what is meant by *distance education* and *distance learning*. The website of the California Distance Learning Project (1997) presents a number of definitions of *distance education,* generally referring to the provision of learning resources to remote learners and involving both *distance teaching* (the instructor's role in the process) and *distance learning* (the student's role). The project proposes the following defining elements as key to distance learning:

- The separation of teacher and learner during at least a majority of each instructional process
- The use of educational media to unite teacher and learner and carry course content
- The provision of two-way communication between teacher, tutor or educational agency, and learner
- Separation of teacher and learner in space and time
- Volitional control of learning by students rather than by the distance instructor

These elements begin to reveal the development of a new paradigm of education. In the online arena, the instructor may continue to define course content and drive the course. However, there is a great deal of room for students to explore the content collaboratively or to pursue their own, related interests. No longer is there a unidirectional imparting of knowledge by an "expert" on a particular topic. No longer is there a necessity for courses to be place- or time-based. In fact, many institutions are struggling with fitting distance education courses into the usual eleven-week quarter or fifteen-week semester and finding these arbitrary measures of time confining to a distance learning process. However, even this attempt at redefinition omits an extremely important element that sets computer-mediated distance learning apart from the traditional classroom setting: *Key to the learning process are the interactions among students themselves, the interactions between faculty and students, and the collaboration in learning that results from these interactions.* In other words, the formation of a learning community through which knowledge is imparted and meaning is co-created sets the stage for successful learning outcomes.

Certainly, we see these elements in a number of college classrooms today. And we continue to learn more about how people learn. A recent study (Twigg, 1994b) indicated that many students are concrete-active learners, that is, they learn best from concrete experiences that engage their senses. Their best learning experiences begin with practice and end with theory (Twigg, 1994b). Many instructors, seeking to improve their practice and the learning outcomes for their students, have incorporated active learning techniques such as working collaboratively on assignments, participating in small-group discussions and projects, reading and responding to case studies, role playing, and using simulations (Myers and Jones, 1993).

These practices transfer well into the online classroom. However, instructors need to be diligent and deliberate in ensuring their success. When learners cannot see or even talk to each other, the use of collaborative assignments becomes more challenging. (We offer suggestions for implementing collaborative learning techniques in the online classroom in Chapter Eight.)

Learning in the distance education environment cannot be passive. If students do not enter into the online classroom—do not post a contribution to the discussion—the instructor has no way of knowing they have been there. So students are not only responsible for logging on but they must contribute to the learning process by posting their thoughts and ideas to the online discussion. Learning is an active process in which both the instructor and the learners must participate if it is to be successful. In the process, a *web of learning* is created. In other words, a network of interactions between the instructor and the other participants is formed, through which the process of knowledge acquisition is collaboratively created. (See Chapters Eight and Nine for a discussion of collaborative learning and the transformative nature of the learning process.)

Outcomes of this process, then, should not be measured by the number of facts memorized and the amount of subject matter regurgitated but by the depth of knowledge and the number of skills gained. Evidence of critical thinking and of knowledge acquired are the desired learning outcomes. Consequently, cheating on exams should not be a concern in an effective distance-learning environment because knowledge is acquired collaboratively through the development of a learning community. (The evaluation of student performance in this environment is discussed in Chapter Ten.)

Institutions entering the distance learning arena must be prepared to tackle new issues and concerns and to develop new approaches and new skills in order to create an empowering learning process, for the creation of empowered learners is yet another desired outcome of computer-mediated distance education. Successful online distance education is a process of taking our very best practices in the classroom and bringing them into a new arena. In this new arena, however, the practices may not look exactly the same.

Take, for example, a recent discussion with a professor in a small college where a distance delivery model was being implemented for a master's degree program. A software program was chosen and a consultant hired to install it on the college's server. There it sat for almost a year until the college decided to begin using it more extensively. Because of our expertise in faculty training and development for the delivery of distance education programs, we were consulted about the best way to improve a program that was not working very well. The professor informed us that the software had been used by a couple of instructors for a couple of courses. However, with further inquiry, we discovered that a course syllabus had never been posted online in any of these courses; nobody knew that an extensive faculty handbook for course development and delivery was embedded in the software. All they had been doing was using this potentially powerful software package as an e-mail system rather than for creating a distance learning environment. Was distance education and learning really happening here? No, of course not. So what does it take to make the transition from the classroom to cyberspace and to do so successfully? What are the differences we face in this new environment? And finally, what issues do we need to be concerned with? We answer the last question in the next section through a discussion of the new issues and concerns related to distance education. The answers to the other questions follow in subsequent chapters.

New Issues and Concerns

When instructors begin to use electronic communication for education, they experience a whole new set of physical, emotional, and psychological issues along with the educational issues. The new issues include the physical problems that can be experienced as the technology is used extensively, such as carpal tunnel syndrome, back problems, headaches, and so forth. Psychologically, students and faculty can become addicted to the technology. They can begin to fantasize and experience personality shifts, and their minds can drift. We have not had to address these issues in the traditional classroom, but we must do so as we move into using this medium because they affect the ways learners interact with each other and with course material. In the traditional classroom, if a student experiences mind drift it may not be noticeable to the instructor or to the other students in the class. The student may be physically present but psychologically absent. In the virtual classroom, however, if a student drifts away, that absence is noticeable and may have a profound impact on the group.

We are also bringing, with the advent of distance learning, a whole new set of issues and problems into academics; as a result, we must become more flexible and learn to deal with these problems. Professors, just like their students, will need the ability to deal with a virtual world in which they cannot see, hear, or touch the people with whom they are communicating. Some participants may even adopt a new persona, shifting into areas of their personalities they may not have previously explored. For example, an instructor, like a student, who suffers from performance anxiety in the face-to-face classroom may be more comfortable online and more active in responding to students. A colleague of ours who has wanted to teach for several years and who feels that he has a contribution to make is very nervous about entering a classroom and facing a group of students. He has been offered several opportunities to teach because of the expertise he would bring to a learning situation, but he has resisted. When offered an opportunity to teach online, however, he accepted readily, acknowledging that the relative anonymity of the medium feels more comfortable for him. The idea of being able to facilitate a discussion from the comfort of his home office was very appealing to him, whereas doing the same thing face to face was intimidating. But just as not all instructors are successful in the classroom setting, not all will be successful online. It takes a unique individual with a unique set of talents to be successful in the traditional classroom; the same is true for the cyberspace classroom. The ability to do both is a valuable asset in today's academic institutions.

Students in Cyberspace

Some attributes make students successful online when they are not in the face-to-face classroom. For example, what about the introverted student? Will such a student, who does not participate in the face-to-face class, blossom in the virtual classroom? Research conducted by one of the authors indicates that an introverted person will probably become more successful online, given the absence of social pressures that exist in face-to-face situations. Conversely, extroverted people may have more difficulty establishing their presence in an online environment, something that is easier for them to do face to face (Pratt, 1996).

The California Distance Learning Project (1997) reviews some of the research on successful students in distance education programs and suggests that students who are attracted to this form of education share certain characteristics. They

- Are voluntarily seeking further education
- Are motivated, have higher expectations, and are more self-disciplined
- Tend to be older than the average student
- Tend to possess a more serious attitude toward their courses

Nipper (1989) describes the successful learner in a computer-mediated environment as a "noisy learner," one who is active and creative in the learning process. As these characteristics suggest, distance education has been applied to and seen as most successful in the arena of adult education. However, more universities are using this delivery method with all groups of students regardless of age or level of educational experience. Should we expect that all students will succeed in this environment? Although a student who is unsuccessful in the face-to-face classroom may do well online, it is unrealistic to expect that all students will do well. When a student does not perform well, as evidenced by lack of participation, he or she should be given the option of returning to the face-to-face classroom. This should not be considered a failure but simply a poor fit. Changing is not usually an option in the face-to-face classroom; there may be no other alternatives. The online classroom, then, provides an alternative that may be useful for some students.

In our experience, computer-mediated distance education can successfully draw out a student who would not be considered a noisy learner in the traditional classroom. It can provide an educational experience that helps motivate students who appear to be unmotivated because they are quieter than their peers and less likely to enter into a classroom discussion. Take the example of an Asian student, Soomo, who participated in one of our online classes on the topic of management and organizational theory. He introduced himself to the group in the following way. We have not changed his writing; we wanted his struggles with language to be apparent.

And one of my problems, it's my responsibility, English is not my native language so I'm still struggling with learning English. I'll try hard but everyone's consideration will be appreciate regarding this matters in advance. I'm also see myself with introvert style. And feel uncomfortable to talk by on line.

By his own admission, he was generally a quiet member of face-to-face classes. Although he wanted to share, his struggles with English and the extroverted nature of his classmates left him silent, though actively listening to discussion. As our online course continued, his posts to the discussion were frequent and indicated a depth of thought. The following is his contribution to a discussion of Bolman and Deal's (1991) *Reframing Organizations:*

My understanding for the human resources frame is that this frame focuses on the fit between individual and organization. In this point of view, I can think about the "manager's job and the organization theory." The potentially disastrous consequences can be avoided, however, if the manager commands a sound knowledge of the organization theory. This theory can help him or her make quality decisions and successfully influence others to carry them out. It can help improve decision quality by making the manager aware of the various components of organization theory. To understand how they fit together as an explanation of the activity of the organization provides a perspective for seeing a decision's consequences. . . . Better quality decisions coupled with more effective implementation through better understanding of individual and group behavior can bring improved performance to the organization. I think it's important that a manager (management group) ensure that its members have exposure to organization theory.

Personally, I don't like the word "Frame". Because it means, in other words, "easy to break". Some organizational changes are incremental. They entail incorporating new technologies with existing missions and strategies. Organizational growth and redirection may also be incremental, but not necessarily. Other organizational changes are frame breaking. The risks are high, and events happen quickly. This usually means a change in the organization's goals and operations. Organizational start-ups and mergers are likely to be frame-breaking experiences.

Most of this student's contributions to the discussion throughout the course were of this nature. He received feedback from other students regarding the thoughtfulness of his contributions and his ability to help them look at ideas in another way. Generally quiet and concerned about his language skills in a face-to-face classroom, this student was able to overcome all of this in the online environment and make significant contributions to his own learning as well as to that of his student colleagues.

Making the Transition

The following is from a graduate student.

I am quite uncomfortable on-line. It is interesting to me that while I seem to be outspoken in person, I am finding that the depth of my contributions are not satisfying . . . for me. But I'm working on it. It's fascinating being in this program . . . moving around, trying to find good fits and observing all the different lenses at work. I am happy with this class' dialogue on-line and appreciate all the effort to contribute. *Tonia*

This quote, posted by a graduate student to an online course, is representative of some of the struggles that may occur as the transition is made from the face-to-face classroom to an online environment where interactions among learners are expected. When teaching and learning leave the classroom, many elements are left behind.

Picture a classroom on a college campus. As the time for class approaches, students begin to gather. They may arrive individually or in small groups. They begin to talk to each other, possibly about the class or about activities, friends, and life outside the classroom. When class ends, students gather again in the hallways, on the grounds of the campus, or in the student union in order to make personal connections, create friendships, and simply to socialize. In the computer-mediated classroom, as it is configured currently, instructors and students are represented by text on a screen. We cannot see the facial expressions and body language that help us gauge responses to what is being discussed. We cannot hear voices or tones of voice to convey emotion. As Tonia indicated in her post, it is difficult for some students to establish a sense of presence online. Instructors and their students become, in effect, disembodied. In a face-to-face situation, we are able to convey in a multitude of ways who we are as people. How does one do that online? How do we help the other participants get to know us; likewise, how do we get to know them so that we have a sense of the group with which we are communicating? How does an instructor actually teach in this environment? How do the participants in the online classroom become reembodied?

The following are web pages from an asynchronous, four-week continuing education course offered online to addiction treatment counselors. The pages provide one example of how an online course might look, along with instructions to the participants as to what is expected of them and how they are to interact with the material. To participate in the course, students entered a discussion forum by simply clicking on the title and posting a message to that discussion. The result is what is termed a *threaded discussion*—a series of posts displayed in outline form. The example in Exhibit 1.1 serves to illustrate the somewhat disembodied nature of online learning and the consequent need to use techniques to personalize and humanize the course as a result.

Although the graphical interfaces contained in current software packages devoted to online distance education are helping to create a more interesting and stimulating environment in which to work, current distance education programs are predominantly textual. Writers about distance education have expressed concern as to how one makes more "human" connections while continuing the learning process. Nipper (1989), a relatively early writer in the area of computer-mediated distance learning, discusses the need to create a sense of "synchronous presence" and reduce the social distance between all participants. Even though in most computer-mediated distance learning courses students have the luxury of logging on to the course site whenever it is convenient for them (asynchronous communication), Nipper is suggesting that it is important to somehow create the sense that a group is working together in real time. Rarely will that group of people be online at the same time unless the software being used for the course allows for synchronous communication (chat). However, an attempt to form connection and community online allows participants to feel, when they enter a discussion forum in a course site, that they have entered a lively, active conversation.

Nipper notes that the need for social connection is a goal that almost supersedes the content-oriented goals for the course. Students need to gather in cyberspace, just as they do on the campus of a university. To accomplish this, they need to establish a sense of presence online; that allows their personality to come through to others in the group. This may create a sense of freedom, allowing otherwise unexplored parts of their personality to emerge. Such exploration can be fostered by encouraging students to post introductions along with their fears and expectations for the process or, when possible, to create a homepage that others in the group can visit. Some courseware applications allow for the creation of a homepage, complete with graphics and links to other sites on the Internet that are

EXHIBIT 1.1. EXAMPLE OF AN ONLINE COURSE.

Chemical Dependency CDC1 (section S1)—Summer, 1998

Managing Managed Care

Instructor: Rena M. Palloff Ph.D.   E-mail: rpalloff@ix.netcom.com

Class Info

Announcements

Schedule

Students

Learning Links

Help/Utilities

Summer, 1998—Chemical Dependency CDC1—Section S1

Course Info

Instructor: Rena M. Palloff Ph.D.   Email address: rpalloff@ix.netcom.com

Goals and Objectives

Policies and Procedures

Required Texts

Web Links

Goals and Objectives

This 4-week class will explore the issues currently facing Chemical Dependency Counselors as they work with managed care. The goal is to develop more effective strategies in working with managed care entities so as to maximize benefits for clients.

At the conclusion of this class, participants should:

1. Understand the nature of managed care entities and case management.

2. Understand the ASAM Criteria and its usefulness in working with managed care to achieve maximum results for clients.

3. Be able to develop and implement effective treatment strategies and treatment plans consistent with the ASAM criteria dimensions.

4. Be able to effectively challenge and appeal managed care decisions affecting good client care.

Policies and Procedures

In order to successfully complete this course and receive 4 hours of continuing education, participants are expected to:

1. Log on to this course site at least twice weekly for the duration of the class, read what has been posted by both the instructor and other participants and post a substantial response or begin a new topic. This is meant to be an online discussion, so please respond to one another, debate ideas, and also have fun!

2. To complete the class, please post a reflective piece in the "Electronic Reflections" section of the discussion forums. Your reflection should be a couple of paragraphs describing what you've learned and what an online learning experience was like for you.

3. Complete the course evaluation which will be e-mailed to you.

4. Once the reflection pieces have been posted and the course evaluation returned via e-mail, a certificate of completion will be issued.

Required Texts

There are no required text books for this class. Information will be posted in the form of weekly lessons for participants to read. It is strongly recommended that participants order copies of the ASAM Criteria from the American Society of Addiction Medicine.

Web Links

Summer, 1998—Chemical Dependency CDC1—Section S1

Class Schedule

Week One   Week Two   Week Three   Week Four

Week One

Begin by introducing yourself to the group by creating your own homepage. The utility to create your homepage can be found by clicking on the button marked "?" or "Help/Utilities" found on the course homepage. Please include in your introduction

(Continued)

EXHIBIT 1.1. Continued.

your experience in the field of chemical dependency and your experience in working with managed care. Also, please include your hopes and expectations for this course.

After you have introduced yourself, read the brief introduction to managed care located in Lesson A and respond to the question posted in Discussion A.

Week Two

Read the material about the ASAM Criteria posted under Lesson B and answer the questions in Discussion B.

Week Three

Read the case posted under Lesson C and then begin a discussion about an appropriate treatment plan for this client under Discussion C.

Week Four

Read the material on dealing with denials under Lesson D and the case update. Collaboratively create an appeal for the case you read in Lesson C through Discussion D.

Summer, 1998—Chemical Dependency CDC1—Section S1

Learning Links

Discussion Forums

Discussion A—What is Managed Care?

Discussion B—The ASAM Criteria

Discussion C—Effective Treatment Planning

Discussion D—Dealing with Denials and Appeals

Electronic Reflections

Lessons

Lesson A—What is Managed Care?

Lesson B—The ASAM Criteria

Lesson C—Effective Treatment Planning

Lesson D—Dealing with Denials and Appeals

Note: The webpage was created using Web Course in a Box™; copyright © Virginia Commonwealth University, 1996, 1997, 1998.

favorites of the person who created the page. This is a wonderful way for students to let others in the group know who they are and how they might connect.

As computer-mediated communication deprives us of some of the physical cues of communication and allows for increased self-generated cues that affect our behavior, it also adds dimensions that otherwise would not be present (Pratt, 1996). For example, the availability and number of personal interactions using computers is limited only by time and access, not by distance or social class. We can create, cultivate, and maintain social relationships with anyone who has access to a computer. Connections are made through the sharing of ideas and thoughts. How people look or what their cultural, ethnic, or social background is become irrelevant factors in this medium, which has been referred to as the great equalizer.

The relationships formed may, in fact, be more intense emotionally as the physical inhibitions created by face-to-face communications are removed. Social psychologist Kenneth Gergen (1991) believes that these interactions can continuously alter who we are. He states: "One's identity is continuously emergent, re-formed, and redirected as one moves through the sea of ever-changing relationships" (p. 139).

In the traditional face-to-face classroom, the quality and intensity of social relationships is simply not as much of an issue. The traditional model of pedagogy allows for the instructor as expert to impart knowledge to students, who are expected to absorb it. How students interact socially is not a concern. Certainly, many instructors have begun to realize that the traditional lecture model is not the model of choice for today's more active learners and have begun to adapt their teaching methods to accommodate this, including techniques such as small-group activities and simulations. Campuses are working to develop learning communities because of the power they hold in facilitating a culture of lifelong learning (Fleming, 1997). In the online classroom, it is the relationships and interactions among people through which knowledge is primarily generated. The learning community takes on new proportions in this environment and consequently must be nurtured and developed so as to be an effective vehicle for education.

The Search for Knowledge and Meaning in the Online Classroom

Young children today are being weaned on interaction with various forms of media. Involved in everything from video games to the Internet, our youth are coming to expect more active ways of seeking knowledge and entertainment. Adults, including educators, however, are for the most part newcomers to this technological arena. As a result, something of a technological generation gap is emerging. Writers examining this gap note that the technological changes sweeping our culture have left education largely unchanged. A rift has opened between how education is viewed and delivered in the classroom and how we are beginning to obtain knowledge in our society (David, 1990; Kolderie, 1990; Strommen and Lincoln, 1992). We have not yet begun to tap the power and potential of technology in the educational arena.

Recent theories in educational circles that attempt to bridge this gap, such as constructivism (Brooks and Brooks, 1993; Cranton, 1994) and active learning (Myers and Jones, 1993), posit that learners actively create knowledge and meaning through experimentation, exploration, and the manipulation and testing of ideas in reality. Interaction and feedback from others assist in determining the accuracy and application of ideas. Collaboration, shared goals, and teamwork are powerful forces in the learning process. Group activities, simulations, and the use of open-ended questions are but a few of the activities used to achieve these goals. Learners, then, interact with knowledge, with the learning environment, and with other learners. The instructor acts only as a facilitator of the learning process (Brooks and Brooks, 1993; Cranton, 1994; Myers and Jones, 1993; Strommen and Lincoln, 1992; Wright, 1993). This is the essence of self-directed learning, as it empowers learners to follow those interactions wherever they may lead and are not dependent on the instructor. Jonassen and others (1995) discuss the outcome of this form of teaching and learning. They note that the facilitation of learning environments that foster personal meaning-making, as well as the social construction of knowledge and meaning through interactions with communities of learners, is preferred to instructor interventions that control the sequence and content of instruction. In other words, the educational process is learner-centered, with the learners taking the lead and determining the flow and direction of the process. Figure 1.1 illustrates this model of education. As we can see, we are beginning to fit together the pieces of a puzzle, which make up a new paradigm of education. This more active model of education is directly transferrable to the online environment.

Let us reconsider the definitional elements of online distance education:

- Separation of instructor and learner in time and place for a majority of the instructional process
- Connection through educational media
- Volitional control of the learning process resting with the learner

It becomes clear that a more active learning model is the model of choice for the online distance learning environment. Given the limitations of access to the student population, as well as such elements as time and distance, the instructor cannot be in control of how or what is being learned. And because they are left to some degree to their own devices, it is up to the learners to make sense of the body of knowledge associated with the course being delivered. The instructor sup-

FIGURE 1.1. THE NEW PARADIGM FOR LEARNING.

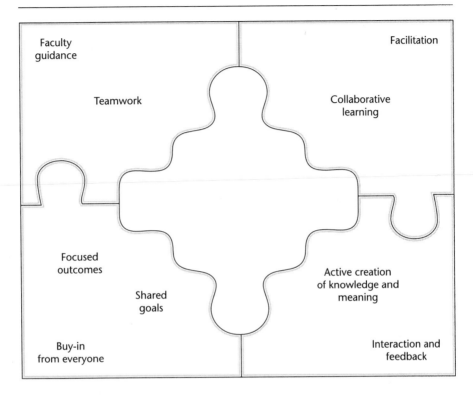

Faculty guidance

Facilitation

Teamwork

Collaborative learning

Focused outcomes

Active creation of knowledge and meaning

Shared goals

Buy-in from everyone

Interaction and feedback

ports this process through the use of collaborative assignments, facilitation of active discussion, and promotion of the development of critical thinking and research skills. The outcome is an environment rich in the potential for collaborative learning and the social construction of meaning (Jonassen and others, 1995).

New Approaches, New Skills

What, then, leads to successful outcomes in online classes and seminars? Is it the mode of teaching or facilitation? Is it the norms established or the guidelines for participation? Is it the level of education of the group? Is it the relative absence of faculty-facilitator input during the process? We believe that all of these factors come together to create success in this medium. When teaching and learning leave the classroom, it is up to the instructor to create a container within which the course proceeds by posting goals, objectives, and expected outcomes for the course, initial guidelines for participation, thoughts and questions to kick off discussion, and assignments to be completed collaboratively. Then it is time to take a back seat and gently guide the learners in their process by monitoring the discussion and entering it to prod participants to look at the material in another way or to gently steer the conversation back on course if it should stray. This is not a responsibility to be taken lightly and requires daily contact and presence with the learners online. The instructor, then, incorporates peer feedback on assignments into the evaluation of student progress, which can later be figured into a grade.

What we are suggesting is a *new paradigm* for an electronic seminar or course. In our observation, many seminars run electronically are typically content-and faculty-facilitator-driven, just as they are in the face-to-face classroom. In many ways they perpetuate an old model of teaching and learning, wherein participants are producing pieces of work that are to be evaluated and commented on by an expert. There is discussion and feedback, but it relates to the work that has been presented. The framework we will present in this book, by contrast, is free-flowing and interactive. Participants generate the bibliography of readings, negotiate the guidelines, and create the structure, venturing into areas previously unexplored. The work that students create in the process may be shared online and peer feedback on the work encouraged. This is truly an empowering mutual learning experience, akin to the synergy that can occur in the classroom when an instructor energizes students by allowing them to fully immerse themselves in content and follow the resulting paths wherever they might lead. The sections to follow show what a framework for successful online teaching should contain.

Access to Technology

In order to successfully conduct classes, meetings, workshops, or seminars in this environment, participants must have access to and familiarity with the technology to be used. Comfort with the technology (both hardware and software) contributes to a sense of psychological well-being and thus to a greater likelihood of participation. Additionally, wherever computer-mediated distance learning is incorporated into the curriculum, it is important to pay attention to the learning curve involved in the use of the technology by participants as well as faculty or facilitators. This should be incorporated into the learning process. (We will explore this more fully in Chapter Five.)

Guidelines and Procedures

Guidelines and procedures should be loose and free-flowing, and generated predominantly by the participants. Imposed guidelines that are too rigid will constrain discussion, causing participants to worry about the nature of their posts rather than to simply post. In larger classes, small discussion groups or work teams can be created wherein guidelines can be discussed and negotiated. Good, respectful "netiquette," however, should be encouraged. (In Chapter Seven, we will provide suggestions and examples for the development of this type of class, including sample syllabi that have been successfully used in this medium.)

Participation

Buy-in from the participants is essential. In order to conduct a successful class, meeting, or seminar online, participants must agree to participate in this medium and understand what they are committing to. Minimum levels of participation should be established and agreed upon in order to create a high level of discussion. Ideally, an initial face-to-face session will establish a sense of group and thus serve to support participation. When this is not possible, initial online contact must include attempts at group development before moving into content. For example, the instructor may ask that all participants post an introduction. This may be followed by the instructor posing open-ended questions, possibly around the establishment of guidelines. Continued attention to these issues must be included throughout the course. (We will continue our discussion of these issues in Chapter Two and throughout the book.)

Collaborative Learning

In order to be successful, classes, seminars, and meetings conducted in an online environment must create an equal playing field. In other words, there must be equality of participant-facilitator and participant-participant interactions. The most powerful experiences are those in which interaction occurs throughout the group instead of between one participant and the facilitator within a group setting. The best facilitation in this medium is by modeling the methodology, that is, by acting as a group member who is contributing to the learning process. (We will further discuss these issues in Chapter Eight.)

Transformative Learning *or* Learning About Learning, Technology, and Oneself

A critical component is attention to the learning that occurs through the use of the medium itself. Participants must be given the opportunity and space within the context of the class, seminar, or meeting to explore how this learning environment is different for them. They need to discuss the fears and insecurities, as well as the successes and surprises, this medium offers. (We will discuss this issue extensively in Chapter Nine.)

Evaluation of the Process

Finally, it is important to encourage participants to provide feedback to each other on an ongoing basis. Additionally, given the nature of this environment, it is important to pay particular attention to the issue of evaluation. How will student performance be evaluated? How do we evaluate the success of the course or lack thereof? Is the online program meeting the needs of the participants? Because we are promoting the use of a collaborative environment in the teaching process, collaboration must also be incorporated into the process of evaluation. And because we are attempting to create empowered learners as a desired outcome, self-evaluation is also an important component. (We will return to this important issue in Chapter Ten.)

Key Concepts

The keys to the creation of a learning community and successful facilitation online are simple. They are as follows: *honesty, responsiveness, relevance, respect, openness,* and *empowerment.* As we present our framework for distance learning in more detail, stressing the importance of the learning community as a central feature, the role and importance of each of these keys to success will become clear. When faculty create a container for participants in which these elements are present, group members can feel safe in expressing themselves without fear of how they will be perceived, allowing for active, rich discussion. The implications are that, as educators and facilitators, we must be able to create an atmosphere of safety and community in all of our learning settings, whether they are electronic or face to face. Students or participants need to be able to speak and debate their ideas without fear of retribution from any source and should be encouraged to explore and research topics that may not be an explicit part of the curriculum or agenda. Instructors and facilitators need to act as "playground monitors" or gentle guides while participants "play in the sandbox," developing the norms and rules as they go. Facilitators and participants need to become equal partners in the development of an online learning community, as it is the participants who are the experts when it comes to their own learning.

If we can facilitate this occurrence in the online environment, we will be well ahead of what has traditionally occurred in the classroom or meeting room. Ideally, this will encourage us to engage in best practices in both environments. Finally, many current models of distance learning maintain a traditional student-teacher relationship in interaction with a set curriculum. Our experience of electronic facilitation shows us how much further we are capable of traveling into the unknowns of cyberspace to explore new worlds of electronic learning. The development of community as a part of the learning process helps to create a learning experience that is empowering and rich. It is essential to impart the importance of this process to faculty in order to maximize the use of the electronic medium in education. Without it, we are simply recreating our tried and true educational model and calling it innovative, without fully exploring the potential this medium holds.

CHAPTER TWO

DEFINING AND REDEFINING COMMUNITY

To know someone here or there with whom you can feel there is understanding, in spite of distances or thoughts expressed, can make of this earth a garden.

GOETHE

Howard Rheingold wrote in an article in June 1992: "Computers, modems, and communications networks furnish the technological infrastructure of computer-mediated communication (CMC); cyberspace is the conceptual space where words and human relationships, data and wealth and power are manifested by people using CMC technology; virtual communities are cultural aggregations that emerge when enough people bump into each other often enough in cyberspace" (p. 1). Although a fairly simplistic look at a developing concept, this reasoning seems to indicate that there are, in fact, such things as *electronic community* and *virtual community.*

In the past the concepts of *differentiation* and *membership* were relevant factors in the development of community. People seeking commonality and shared interests formed groups and communities in order to pursue the interests that distinguished them from other groups. In addition, communities were generally considered to be place-based. The small town or neighborhood in which you lived was your community. Adherence to the norms of that community allowed you to maintain membership. Expressing your uniqueness as a person was at times problematic because of the need to adhere to those norms (Shaffer and Anundsen, 1993). Because community is no longer a place-based concept, we are redefining what community is and is not.

Community in Cyberspace

With the advent of electronic communication and virtual reality, it has become difficult to determine exactly what is meant by the word *community*. Communities have spun off into many types, with many varied attributes. Entry into the virtual community and maintenance of membership in that community entails a very different process and may, in fact, be more difficult for some people to achieve. Steven Jones (1995), in his book *Cybersociety*, states: "The extent to which people use CMC as a means to invent new personas, to recreate their own identities, or to engage in a combination of the two and the ways which they do so are issues central to the construction of a computer-mediated social world" (p. 156).

Jones is describing what has been termed *the electronic personality* (Pratt, 1996)—the person we become when we are online. Our work has shown that for this electronic personality to exist, certain elements must manifest themselves:

- The ability to carry on an internal dialogue in order to formulate responses
- The creation of a semblance of privacy both in terms of the space from which the person communicates and the ability to create an internal sense of privacy
- The ability to deal with emotional issues in textual form
- The ability to create a mental picture of the partner in the communication process
- The ability to create a sense of presence online through the personalization of communications (Pratt, 1996, pp. 119–120)

Thus the person creates a virtual environment that allows his or her electronic personality to emerge. People who are introverts are more adept at creating a virtual environment because they can processes information internally and are less outgoing socially. It is more comfortable for an introvert to spend time thinking about information before responding to it. It is more difficult—but not impossible—for extroverts to interact this way, perhaps because they have less need to. Extroverts tend to feel more comfortable processing verbally and in the company of others. "Extroverts choose higher levels of noise in a learning situation and perform better in the presence of noise, while introverts perform better in quiet" (Ornstein, 1995, p. 57). Consequently, the introvert may have less difficulty entering the virtual community, whereas the extrovert, with a need to establish a sense of social presence, may have more trouble doing so (Pratt, 1996).

Coalescence in these communities can be virtually instantaneous, but for a coalesced community to be functional and exist for any extended period of time, that coalescence must also take place over a period of time. Linda Harasim (in

Shell, 1995) feels that the "information superhighway" terminology used to refer to the Internet confuses people about what it is. She believes that the Internet is a place and is more like a community, as we have been defining it, rather than a thoroughfare or network of routes to information as its name implies.

It really is up to those of us involved with the use of this technology in education to redefine community, for we truly believe we are addressing issues here that are primal and essential to the existence of electronic communication in the educational arena. Even in this virtual or electronic community, educators must realize that the way the medium is used depends largely on human needs, meaning the needs of both faculty and students, and that these needs are the prime reason that electronic communities are formed. In some respects these educational communities may be more stimulating and interesting for those involved with education because they bring together people with similar interests and objectives, not just people who connect casually, as we find in other areas of cyberspace.

Our seminars offer a perfect example of geographically disconnected people becoming "connected" in a community with several purposes but with a shared interest. How connected were all of us as instructors and learners? We essentially conversed in ways we may not have tried before. As instructors, we interacted as peers, sharing information of a more personal nature than we might have in a face-to-face classroom. Our participants felt free to discuss ongoing life issues such as job and relationship difficulties, birth, and death. We did not have to worry about how we looked or how we were dressed. We connected, nonetheless, around common interests and a common subject matter, which we explored together.

Can the community-building process in online groups be complete without the group meeting face to face? Although face-to-face contact at some point in the community-building process can be useful and facilitate community development, that contact is not likely to change the group dynamic created online. It is possible, however, to build community without it. Shaffer and Anundsen (1993) feel that what they term *conscious community* can be created electronically through the initiation of and participation in discussion about goals, ethics, liabilities, and communication styles, that is, norms. Consequently, as norms would be negotiated in a face-to-face group or community, the same needs to occur online. In fact, in the online environment, those collaboratively negotiated norms are probably even more critical as they form the foundation on which the community is built. Agreement about how a group will interact and what the goals are can help move that group forward. In a face-to-face group, assumptions are made but not necessarily discussed, such as rules that one person will talk at a time and that a person should ask to be recognized before speaking. In an online group, we can make no assumptions about norms because we cannot see each other. Therefore, nothing should be left to chance, and all issues and concerns should be discussed openly.

The following excerpt illustrates how community can emerge in this environment. This particular group had no face-to-face contact until well after their class ended.

I have never seen anything develop quite like this. Endings, beginnings, break-ups, new-flowering love, blues, backaches, and the wonder of it all! I have been touched by so many of your messages and in such diverse ways that I confess to feeling unable to respond appropriately to each without risking the appearance of insincerity—or multiple personalities. Each response would seem to call for a different emotional driver. *Mel*

Or take another example:

As a book lover, on one level this seminar is like reading a favorite novel. Each day I pick up the book . . . and join the characters in the evolution of the story. Just as I become emotionally absorbed into the people and ideas of a good novel, I have become absorbed into the seminar. *Claudia*

Numerous discussions and sites on the Internet are related to the virtual community—how it is formed and the elements that comprise it. Many agree on some basic steps that must be taken in order to build such a community:

- Clearly define the purpose of the group.
- Create a distinctive gathering place for the group.
- Promote effective leadership from within.
- Define norms and a clear code of conduct.
- Allow for a range of member roles.
- Allow for and facilitate subgroups.
- Allow members to resolve their own disputes.

Taking these steps can foster connections among members that are stronger than those in face-to-face groups. The following excerpt from one author's dissertation journal gives credence to the quality of relationships that can be formed online when this does occur. This was written following a face-to-face session concerning the development of a dissertation proposal.

As I continued to struggle with my concept, I found myself directing my comments, discussion, and attention increasingly toward Marie. It wasn't that she, above the rest, understood my concept any better. It was that I felt confident that she really understood *ME* based on our previous on-line connection. That gave me comfort and the confidence to struggle on.

Redefining Community

From our discussion thus far, it is clear that the growth of the Internet and its increasing popularity are having a significant impact on the ways people interact, as well as the ways they define and redefine notions of community. Societal and scientific advances and discoveries, along with technological development, have given us different approaches to issues that are deeply embedded in our attempts to interact. Also embedded in the process of communication is the fact that we live in and search for community. In fact, our attempts to communicate are attempts at community building. Our basic need to connect on a human level has not only affected the development of electronic communication but has conversely been affected by it. Our relationships are far more complex due to our increasing network of associates and enhanced by postmodern technological developments. Our communities and neighborhoods are now virtual as well as actual, global as well as local. Our technology has helped to create a new form of social interdependence enabling "new communities to form wherever communication links can be made" (Gergen, 1991, p. 213).

Linda Harasim (in Shell, 1995), a professor of communications and writer in the areas of computer-mediated communication and distance learning, states that the words *community* and *communicate* have the same root, *communicare*, which means *to share*. She goes on to say, "We naturally gravitate towards media that enable us to communicate and form communities because that, in fact, makes us more human" (p. 1). Certainly, computer-mediated communication is one such medium. It has helped to shrink the globe while dramatically expanding the parameters of what we call our communities. It is important, at this point, to begin to discuss what is meant by community and why this is important to the process of education and learning online.

The Importance of Community

Carolyn Shaffer and Kristin Anundsen (1993) talk about our human yearning for a sense of belonging, kinship, and connection to a greater purpose. Changes in the makeup of our families, neighborhoods, and towns have increased that longing, as we are not as easily able to identify with something we can call a community. Our communities today are formed around issues of identity and shared values; they are not place-based (Palloff, 1996).

Shaffer and Anundsen (1993) define community as a dynamic whole that emerges when a group of people share common practices, are interdependent, make decisions jointly, identify themselves with something larger than the sum of their individual relationships, and make a long-term commitment to well-being (their own, one another's, and the group's).

Some people fear entering into a community because they think they must submit to the will of a group in order to do so. Through this definition, however, it seems that the need for connectedness—for community—does not necessarily mean giving up autonomy or submitting to authority in order to become part of a group. Instead, it is a mutually empowering act—a means by which people share with each other, work, and live collaboratively. In the past, involvement in community was assumed by where you lived (your home town or neighborhood) or determined by your family or religious connections (identification with a country of origin or religious organization). Involvement in community today takes a conscious commitment to a group. Shaffer and Anundsen refer to this as *conscious community*—meaning community that emphasizes the members' needs for personal growth and transformation, as well as the social and survival aspects of community.

The social-psychological literature is full of material about group development. The literature about the development of community shows parallels to that process. Writers in the areas of group and organizational behavior have referred to these stages as forming, norming, storming, performing, and adjourning (Tuckman, 1965). First, people come together around a common purpose. This is the forming stage. Then they reach out to one another to figure out how to work toward common goals, developing norms of behavior in the process. It is not uncommon as this occurs for conflict to begin as members grapple with the negotiation of individual differences versus the collective purpose or objective. However, in order to achieve group cohesion and to perform tasks together, the group needs to walk through that conflict. If attempts are made to avoid the conflict, the group may disintegrate or simply go through the motions, never really achieving intimacy. Just as in face-to-face groups, the conflict phase is an essential element that the group must work through in order to move on to the performing stage. Our work with online groups has shown us that these groups go through the same stages as face-to-face groups and communities, even if they do not work together face to face. But how do online groups deal with these phases without the benefit of face-to-face contact?

Sproull and Kiesler (1991) talk about the difficulties that distributed work groups have in achieving consensus when no face-to-face contact occurs. They state: "When groups decide via computer, people have difficulty discovering how other group members feel. It is hard for them to reach consensus. When they disagree, they engage in deeper conflict" (p. 66). They seem to be suggesting that the conflict is a bad, undesirable thing. Ian Macduff (1994), in his article on electronic negotiation, states that there is greater potential for conflict to emerge in electronic discussion than in face-to-face discussion due to the absence of verbal, facial, and body cues and to difficulty in expressing emotion in a textual medium. However, he sees great potential in the resolution of conflict through the use of electronic media, especially if norms and procedures for conflict resolution are established and used.

So if conflict is not such a bad thing, and if it is necessary in order to achieve group cohesiveness and intimacy, why do so many fear it and attempt to avoid it, especially in this medium? And how do we as educators establish norms and procedures for resolving conflict in this virtual community of online learning?

One of the concerns about conflict in this medium is that with the absence of face-to-face contact and cues, many people feel less socially constrained. In a face-to-face situation, people tend to choose a number of options for dealing with conflict. They may avoid it or confront the situation directly. Although this may be done in anger, it is best done within the confines of what we would consider to be socially appropriate behavior. We see the same conflict choices being made online, but because the conflict is being handled through the transmission of written messages, with the possibility of timing and sequencing becoming a problem, resolution of conflict in this medium takes patience and work. In an online classroom, another member of the group may step in as a mediator to facilitate this process.

In one of our earliest online seminar experiences, which was devoted to exploring the topic of creating online community, conflict occurred between two members of the group, mainly due to the sequencing and timing of messages. Communication was out of sync, which led to a flaming incident, that is, an angry message was sent. One of the group members involved in the conflict responded as follows:

When I read that last message, my heart sank. That's it. I'm sorry. I can't go on. This is one of those places where this medium simply hasn't sufficient dimensionality for me to express what I want and to feel comfortable that my meaning has gotten across. I feel the need for those subtle physical and psycho-social signs that are so much a part of face-to-face communications. *Mel*

He was opting to pull away from and avoid the conflict. However, another group member stepped in to mediate and offered the following:

I'm having a hard time understanding all the heat around defining community. . . . I realize that the purpose of this seminar is to debate issues around community and to define what the intersection is between the "human" and "virtual" communities. I also realize that we will disagree on what those elements and definitions are and that sometimes that disagreement will get heated. That's fine with me. But can we agree to establish a norm that we won't make it personal? I think that if we can, we may move through some of the conflict into some really important ideas about what comprises community. *Claudia*

The working through of this conflict helped to create an extremely strong connection among the members of the group, leading to a positive learning outcome. In a face-to-face classroom, conflict may emerge as a part of a disagreement over ideas. Generally, opening the classroom environment to the debate of ideas is seen as positive; it provides evidence that students are engaging with the material. And although conflict can become heated and in need of intervention on the part of the instructor, for the most part it is manageable in the classroom context. However, conflict is not considered part of a community-building process in a traditional classroom. Although it can contribute to learning outcomes, it is not a critical component of the learning process.

In the online learning community, conflict contributes not only to group cohesion but to the quality of the learning outcome. Therefore, instructors in the online environment need to feel comfortable with conflict; they may actually need to trigger it or to assist with the facilitation of its resolution. And they should applaud its appearance.

However, there is a danger in unresolved conflict in this medium. If an instructor fails to intervene or fails to support the attempts by other students to resolve a conflict, participation in the online course will become guarded and sparse. Additionally, the direction of communication will change, with students directing their posts to the instructor and not to the other members of the group. We experienced this in one of our online seminars. A participant became angry about what she perceived to be a lack of participation by the other group members. This was not revealed online but was told to one of us in a phone conversation. Very quickly we noticed that this student's posts were being directed toward us, with no comment or feedback being directed toward the other participants. Without naming anyone in the group, we simply restated the group guideline that all students should provide feedback to each other online. The result was a rather surprised message from the student in question containing an apology to the group for not being open with them about her concerns and for withholding feedback from them. Given this unique aspect of the virtual community, let us turn now to a discussion of its importance in online education.

The Importance of Community in the Electronic Classroom

What does all of this have to do with education and online learning? If we reconsider our discussion in the previous chapter of the new paradigm for learning, which involves a more active, collaborative, constructivist approach, the link becomes clear and the missing piece of the puzzle falls into place. The principles involved in the delivery of distance education are basically those attributed to a more active, constructivist form of learning—with one difference: *In distance education, attention needs to be paid to the developing sense of community within the group of participants in order for the learning process to be successful.* The learning community is the vehicle through which learning occurs online. Members depend on each other to achieve the learning outcomes for the course. If a participant logs on to a course site and there has been no activity on it for several days, he or she may become discouraged or feel a sense of abandonment—like being the only student to show up for class when even the instructor is absent. Without the support and participation of a learning community, there is no online course. This difference is illustrated in Figure 2.1 by a modification of the learning model presented previously.

New-paradigm teachers promote a sense of autonomy, initiative, and creativity while encouraging questioning, critical thinking, dialogue, and collaboration (Brookfield, 1995). In a face-to-face learning situation, this can be accomplished through the use of simulations, group activities, and small-group projects, as well as by encouraging students to pursue topics of interest on their own (Brooks and Brooks, 1993). A sense of community in the classroom might be helpful to this process but is not mandatory to its success.

Students in a face-to-face classroom see each other and work together, getting to know each other better through that process. How, then, can we make that happen when all contacts consist of text on a screen? In fact, we cannot make it happen instantaneously. It must be facilitated. One way community can be developed is through the mutual negotiation of guidelines regarding how the group will participate together. Beginning a course by posting introductions and encouraging students to look for areas of common interest is a good way to start. Instructors in this medium need to be flexible—to throw away their agendas and a need to control in order to let the process happen and allow for the personal agendas of the learners to be accommodated. This may mean that the discussion will go in a direction that does not feel completely comfortable to the instructor. But rather than cut it off abruptly, the instructor should gently guide that discussion in another direction, perhaps by asking an open-ended question that allows the learners to examine that interaction.

We need to be able to make space for personal issues in an online course. This must be done deliberately and fostered throughout the course. If this space is not created, it is likely that participants will seek out other ways to create personal interaction, such as through e-mail or by bringing personal issues into the course discussion. Some participants, however, when finding the personal element missing, may feel isolated and alone and, as a result, may feel less than satisfied with the learning experience. We frequently set up a space in the structure of our electronic classrooms to enable this to happen, which we will explore further when we discuss techniques for building foundations for the course in Chapter Seven.

FIGURE 2.1. FRAMEWORK FOR DISTANCE LEARNING.

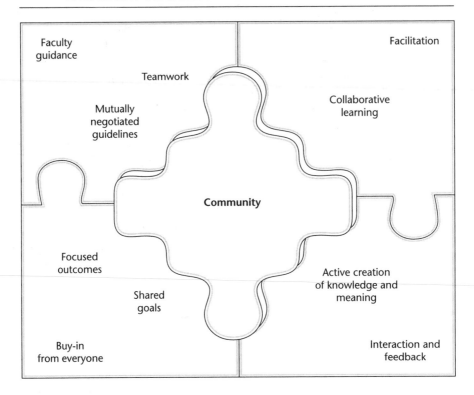

The development of community, then, becomes a parallel stream to the content being explored. It is given its own equal status and is not seen as something that "mucks up" or interferes with the learning process. Harasim, Hiltz, Teles, and Turoff (1996) state:

> Social communication is an essential component of educational activity. Just as a face-to-face school or campus provides places for students to congregate socially, an online educational environment should provide a space, such as a virtual cafe, for informal discourse. . . . The forging of social bonds has important socioaffective and cognitive benefits for the learning activities. The virtual cafe should be primarily a student space and not be directly tied to the curriculum [p. 137].

But are all electronic classrooms active, constructivist learning environments? Do all distance education programs use active and collaborative tools and approaches to learning? Unfortunately, the answer is no. We have seen many distance education programs in which the instructor posts lectures and attempts to control the learning outcomes by directing and dominating the process. We have also seen many instructors who continue to use multiple-choice and true-false exams as measures of learning. Many of these instructors are forced to bow to pressure from their universities, which are unwilling to let go of old methods of pedagogy or do not understand how that could be done. Many of these universities are also facing pressure from accrediting agencies that do not understand the forms of teaching and learning that work best in this environment. We have heard many online instructors complain about the absence of interaction among their students or about the lack of response to questions they posed online. With further exploration, we usually find that either these instructors were posing closed questions that did not stimulate discussion or the instructors were dominating the discussion, thus not allowing the process to be learner-focused. (We will discuss the differences between forms of questions in Chapter Eight.)

Given all of these issues and concerns, what constitutes effective teaching in an online classroom? What is the role of the learner in this process, since we are describing an interactive process? And what constitutes positive learning outcomes? In the next section, we will briefly review the answers to each of these questions.

Participation and Desired Outcomes in the Electronic Classroom

Clearly, an online learning community cannot be created by one person. Although the instructor is responsible for facilitating the process, participants also have a responsibility to make community happen. We have already established that the learning process in the electronic classroom is an active one. Therefore, in order for students to be considered "present" in an online class, they must not only access the course site online but must make a comment of some sort. Instructors often establish guidelines for minimal participation, making it more likely that students will engage with their colleagues and facilitating the community-building process. This expectation of participation differs significantly from the face-to-face classroom, where the discussion can be dominated by one or more extroverted students, giving an illusion that the class is engaged. The ability to think before responding and to comment whenever the student wishes helps to create a level of participation and engagement that goes much deeper. As one of our students describes it:

It seems that we as students have been more willing to talk and discuss the issues at hand than we probably would inside the classroom. I feel this is so for two reasons. One is that we have time to concentrate on the question and think, whereas in the class you are asked and immediate response is in need. Two, we can discuss openly and not have to worry about failure as much. If you post something that is not right, no one has said this is wrong but instead we give encouragement and try to guide each other to find the right answer. *Brandi*

Additionally, because we are working in a text-based medium and in the absence of visual and auditory cues, participants focus on the meaning of the message conveyed. As a result, ideas can be collaboratively developed as the course progresses, creating the socially constructed meaning that is the hallmark of a constructivist classroom in which an active learning process is taking place. This ability to collaborate and create knowledge and meaning communally is a clear indicator that a virtual learning community has successfully coalesced.

Some of the desired outcomes, then, indicating that an online community has been forming, are as follows:

- Active interaction involving both course content and personal communication
- Collaborative learning evidenced by comments directed primarily student to student rather than student to instructor
- Socially constructed meaning evidenced by agreement or questioning, with the intent to achieve agreement on issues of meaning
- Sharing of resources among students
- Expressions of support and encouragement exchanged between students, as well as willingness to critically evaluate the work of others

It is certainly possible, in this environment, to foster the development of a community wherein very little learning occurs but strong social connections exist among members. It is for this reason, among others, that the instructor needs to remain actively engaged in the process in order to gently guide participants who stray; they must be coaxed back to the learning goals that brought them together in the first place. It is the development of a strong *learning community* and not just a social community that is the distinguishing feature of computer-mediated distance learning.

We have been describing what the electronic learning community looks like and how it functions, as well as its importance in the online learning process. We have also discussed the importance of the instructor's facilitating the community's development. However, we have not yet discussed the numerous issues that are likely to surface as that community is forming; neither have we described the need for instructors in this environment to be aware of those issues and to facilitate the discussion about them once they emerge. In the following chapter, we explore these topics in detail, along with the contribution each makes to the development of the online learning community.

CHAPTER THREE

WHAT WE KNOW ABOUT ELECTRONIC LEARNING

E lectronic communication comes in several forms, including e-mail, public electronic forums, bulletin board systems, pay-for-use services, and electronic network chatting within and outside of an organizational structure. These forms of communication share several core issues that run throughout the medium and seemingly invade every type of electronic communication. Additionally, they pertain to the face-to-face communication that occurs as we attempt to build community. Because we are concerned with humanizing a nonhuman environment and creating a learning community in the process, human issues will emerge, whether we expect them to or not. In a traditional classroom setting, an instructor may not know that a student is struggling with the end of a relationship or a chronic illness in the family unless the student volunteers that information. In the virtual classroom, however, in order to create community it is critical to make room for the personal, the mundane—that is, everyday life.

The following issues are the ones we deal with over and over again as we build learning communities while delivering classes online: (1) virtual versus human contact, connectedness, and coalescence; (2) shared responsibility, rules, roles, norms, and participation; (3) psychological and spiritual issues; and (4) vulnerability, privacy, and ethics. It is critical to pay attention to these issues in the electronic classroom, whereas it may not be so important in the face-to-face classroom. The excerpts of dialogue that follow the discussion of the issues are pieces written by our participants as they were dealing with the issue being discussed.

Virtual Versus Human Contact, Connectedness, and Coalescence

Sproull and Kiesler (1991) state: "When people perceive communication to be ephemeral, the stakes of communication seem smaller. People feel less committed to what they say, less concerned about it, and less worried about the social reception they will get. . . . By removing reminders of a possibly critical audience, electronic mail induces people to be more open" (p. 42). The up side of this is that "social posturing and sycophancy decline. The disadvantage is that so, too, do politeness and concern for others . . . reduced social awareness leads to messages characterized by ignoring social boundaries, self-revelation, and blunt remarks" (p. 39). Craig Brod, a psychologist, takes a particularly pessimistic view of the impact of electronic communication on a social-psychological level. He feels that as our computer use increases, we are "diminishing and altering our sense of self and of others, creating new barriers to what we long for: intimacy, continuity, and community" (Shaffer and Anundsen, 1993, p. 133). As we previously established, however, direct attention to community building online can break down these barriers, allowing for a new sense of intimacy and connection.

It is difficult but not impossible to convey feelings online, especially anger. Depending on the kind of community developed and whether it involves both human and virtual contact, expectations about how messages are received are somewhat different. In other words, because participants assume that people know them in a different context, they believe others will understand the intent behind their words in exactly the way they mean them to be understood. So to some degree, participants are less cautious about what they say because they think everyone "knows" them. That delusion can cause pain and conflict, as it is impossible for people we have met only briefly or virtually to truly know us and what we stand for unless a deep level of connection is promoted and sustained.

Virtual contact offers many advantages to the shy, reclusive person, who can sit at the computer and interact with people without all the hassles of making physical or visual contact. People desiring virtual isolation can simply refuse to respond or interact with other participants. Certainly, this can become a problem when options for socialization are limited to contacts made through the Internet. However, we have found that our students who are shy in social settings learn something about social skills by interacting in an electronic course. We have seen that begin to carry over to face-to-face classrooms. One of the authors had the experience of working with a student both in an online and a face-to-face class during the same academic term. Describing herself as shy and reclusive to the online group, the student also noted that it was becoming easier for her to interact with members of the group when she met them in other social or classroom situations. Her participation in the face-to-face class increased as she continued to interact with the online group and receive positive feedback for her contributions to the course.

Virtual Versus Human Contact

The notion of virtual as opposed to human contact in electronic communication sets up an artificial dualism. Because people generate communication, even if it is textual, virtual communication *is* human. The removal of context cues in this form of communication can be both beneficial and detrimental. Textual communication is a great equalizer and can prompt us to be more thoughtful about what we say online. The issue of isolation is also a factor when communicating electronically. Although we create connection while online, the risk of isolating ourselves from face-to-face contact in the process does exist.

I "hear" "tones of voice" in messages I read, from either strangers or friends who communicate in this medium. In some case they are remembered tones of voice (those I "know"), in other cases they are imagined tones of voice (those I don't know). *Mary Ann*

Connectedness and Coalescence

As we have discussed, the need for connectedness does not necessarily mean giving up autonomy or submitting to authority. Instead it should be a mutually empowering act. This sense of connectedness and coalescence can lead to an increased sense of knowing one another through the shared experiences of struggling with course material and the medium together; connectedness also comes through conflict and through learning to learn in a new way.

I'm not someone who connects easily with "strangers". Small talk is my downfall. I wrote in my article "An Introvert's Guide to Networking" that I need a reason to call my mother. So I find reasons. I suppose in some ways you could say I have a phobia about face to face contact. Until I have some reason to connect, something to connect about. I may have passed each of you in the [university] "halls," but without SOMETHING that connected us, probably just said hello. Now we have a common experience to talk about. *Theresa*

Shared Responsibility, Rules, Roles, Norms, and Participation

It seems that by looking at the issue of community and how it develops, we are beginning to explore the topic of shared responsibility, rules, roles, and norms. We share the responsibility for the development of the group through participation. The rules need to be fluid, and in fact, there should be few rules. The only real discussion many of our groups have had around rules was regarding participation and norms, meaning how much and how often. Our groups did not always agree on this. It seems, at times, that we as facilitators have different expectations for participation than the group does. Consequently, it is important to openly discuss these issues when the group first convenes.

Roles

As for roles, the designated facilitator serves a number of functions, from organizer to cheerleader to imparter of information. Participants, too, take on roles. The literature on work groups interacting through technology suggests that task and process roles do emerge in these groups (McGrath and Hollingshead, 1994). We have found in our groups that there is always a participant who attempts to keep things moving when the discussion lags, or one who attempts to mediate conflict or who looks for other members when they have not been present in the discussion for a few days. The emergence of these roles is an indicator that community is developing, that members are beginning to look out for one another and to take care of the business of the course as well. Certainly, in the traditional classroom, leadership will emerge from one or several students in the group. This, too, represents a way in which students connect and look out for each other.

I can see how the groups in this virtual class are being created already. Of course, we have our formal groups but certain informal groups are being formed. We have all started to develop roles, too. Who are the ones that have a lot to say, who are the ones that just comment on what the other people say and add insight, who are the ones that get a lot out of the book, or the ones that have personal experiences? *Carmen*

Norms, Rules, and Participation

Norms emerge in these groups as the process moves along. Frequently, we find groups discussing issues of openness, honesty, and safety as norms we commonly hold and ones that need to be reinforced. As a group, we may also discuss our goals, communication styles, and the liabilities of this type of communication. These discussions help to create a community that evolves emotionally and spiritually and that provides a safe, intimate, and cohesive space in which we can openly share our thoughts and feelings while learning from each other. Few norms are established at the beginning of our seminars; participants usually agree to norms of openness and honesty. Norms around levels of participation emerge as the group progresses.

Communicating interactively needs tools, processes, and roles/responsibilities to synthesize a variety of opinions, to seek out the silent voices, and to keep it all moving. It has been a challenge for [our university] as it seeks to do more [electronically]; it is a challenge for business; it will be a challenge for our towns and government. *Claudia*

It is very important to establish a virtual environment with norms, purpose, and values. In that sense I don't think it is any different from establishing a healthy human environment. It needs to be seen as safe for everyone to enter and participate. The voices must be heard, the individuals respected. *Claudia*

Increasingly, it is expected, even mandated, that students entering a university program open an e-mail account when they enroll, the expectation being, of course, that they will use it. However, having an account does not mean that students will be involved, because so many students are reluctant to use this medium; some even claim to be technology-phobic. Additionally, having a mailbox does not guarantee that people will respond to the mail they receive. How many messages have all of us sent and received no response, even when those messages were cries for help or assistance of some sort. Sometimes this may be due to information overload. However, it is easy in this medium to send messages into what seems to be a black hole.

The same happens in an electronic seminar. We have had at least one student who posts an introduction and then we hear nothing further, leaving the other students wondering what happened. One student, who dropped out of a seminar with no explanation, finally contacted us to say that her expectation after she posted her introduction was that the others would respond to her personally and make comments about what she had said about herself. When that did not happen, she became discouraged and disappeared, reluctant to respond even to our inquiries about her intent to continue.

Interestingly, the same phenomenon occurs in groups in real life. People simply drop out or away for whatever reason, and a core group continues. Usually in a group situation, although perhaps not in a classroom, people who leave are asked to come back and say goodbye to the group. The physical presence or absence of someone in a face-to-face group is noticeable, whether they participate verbally or not. In this electronic setting people can disappear more easily; their absence is noticed but is easier to ignore than an empty chair would be. It is also easier to be a silent member in a face-to-face group. People know that you are present even when you are not speaking. In our electronic groups, silent members just are not there.

When members do not participate or respond to messages-it might be they are too busy, overwhelmed, ambivalent, apathetic, or whatever, but it can be construed as a mode of control in the sense that we don't know why they aren't joining us. *Cyd*

It is important for instructors to pay close attention to which students are posting messages and which are not. Because the success of the seminar depends on participation by all members, instructors need to remind students about their responsibility to participate, either by posting messages to that effect on the course site or through individual contact.

We have been in electronic situations where people were "listening in," whether or not they made their presence known. Participants simply ignored their presence, which is easier to do when the listener is unseen. An observer in a classroom is noticed by the students attending the class; an observer in an electronic classroom is easily ignored. Interestingly, we have found that even when students know they are being observed in the virtual classroom, their willingness to share on a deeply personal level is not affected. It is important, however, for instructors to provide an explanation to participants when someone will be listening in but not participating in the discussion and to allow discussion of this issue if it makes anyone uncomfortable.

Participation is essential if we are to learn of and from each other. It isn't simply a matter of arbitrarily choosing to participate or not-this is a collective, or better collaborative, effort REQUIRING conversation and reflection. To be truly collaborative, we must all participate. *Cyd*

Psychological and Spiritual Issues

Discussions about psychological and spiritual issues are often considered controversial and even volatile when they occur in a face-to-face classroom or situation. In presenting the psychological and spiritual issues embedded in the online community, we are not suggesting that instructors need to become counselors or spiritual advisers for their students. We are suggesting, however, that our participants' attempts to connect in the online arena will cause these issues to surface. We need, therefore, to acknowledge and recognize psychological and spiritual issues when they emerge, as they are core issues in the formation of community.

We value rugged individualism in our culture. Our intense holding of this value is a piece of what can cause us emotional and psychological distress (Peck, 1993; Ornstein, 1995). So our search for community and the solace we find there is in part our need for connection, interdependence, intimacy, and safety— psychologically speaking (Shaffer and Anundsen, 1993; Walker, 1993; Whitmyer, 1993). Fear is what keeps us from experiencing a high level of psychological connection with others—fear that we will lose ourselves in the process, fear that we will be rejected, fear that we are fakes, fear that we are just not good enough. Our isolation is a major contributing factor to psychological unease or illness (Peck, 1993). Connection, through community, friendships, therapy, and so forth, is the means to achieve psychological well-being (Shaffer and Anundsen, 1993). Being accepted and supported for who we are, no matter what that means for us as humans, is the psychological benefit of community.

Psychological Issues in the Virtual Community

Certainly, community can provide all of those psychological benefits just mentioned. But speaking from a Jungian perspective, community also has a shadow side—elements that are "buried" and unconscious—elements we do not want to face. Some of those are a tendency to promote "groupthink," that is, the subtle and not-so-subtle pressure to conform in thought and in action. This kind of oppression can be devastating on a psychological level. When one is experiencing that kind of pressure, the result can be feelings of unease, not belonging, not feeling safe—feelings of being an outsider. There is a tendency to keep quiet and just feel uncomfortable when a loud, vocal group is speaking for the community or group. After awhile, one may speak out and risk ostracism or leave. If this is occurring in an online classroom, students who are uncomfortable will simply drift away and possibly drop the course. It may be difficult for an instructor to reengage students who feel they cannot share their thoughts with a very vocal group. When this occurs, it is important for the instructor to intervene and make space in the process for more silent members. Just as an instructor may call on a quiet student in a face-to-face setting, the same may be necessary in the online group, particularly to support a student with a dissenting opinion.

The psychological issues from a technological point of view depend on the hardware and software environment. If the person feels comfortable with those two components, then the environment is safe and secure. But the opposite could be true if the hardware or software environment changes or is difficult to navigate. This can also cause physiological problems such as eyestrain, back problems, headaches, and stress. All of these can have psychological results. We have experienced class or seminar participants who, because of the hardware or software being used, felt frustrated and unhappy with the entire online experience.

Risk taking for the purpose of connecting appears to be the main psychological issue facing those in communities, whether electronic or face to face. Consequently, instructors must be cognizant of the psychological issues that could affect the success or failure of an online class. Just as in the traditional classroom, attention must be paid to students who seem overly stressed or who express a significant degree of painful emotion in their posts. Certainly, instructors want to encourage students to take risks and to post ideas that might be considered different or controversial. However, it is important to strike a balance and to intervene if a student appears to be in psychological trouble.

I find myself now part of the [group] and psychologically involved. And yet, I feel the walls and bounds between us. Out of courtesy and respect, we don't probe each other too much. We often take safe positions. I read that some of you are going through some pain, yet I don't know how to reach out through this medium. I feel safe in communicating with you all, yet I do not (yet) feel a strong individual connection with any one of you. I know you are out there and willing to support. But, we each have to be responsible for taking the first step – to ask for help, to share a problem or an achievement. I suspect inclusion and a psychological connection come only when we each decide to jump in and get involved. There are some interesting questions here about personal responsibility in community. *Claudia*

Ritual as the Psychological Expression of Community

Phil Catalfo (1993) writes regarding his experiences on the WELL (Whole Earth 'Lectric Link). He talks about an interview with John Barlow, who is the lyricist for the Grateful Dead. Barlow was apparently doing an interview on "small towns, real and virtual" and said that "cyberspace villages like the WELL would never become real communities until they could address sex and death in ritual terms. Marriages and funerals are the binding ceremonies in real towns . . . but they have a hard time happening among the disembodied" (Walker, 1993, p. 169). Phil Catalfo disagreed and so do we.

On more than one occasion we have had to deal with the death of a faculty member or student as an electronic class was in progress. Participants have created a mourning ritual that included a forum through which to share feelings and memories. Through these forums, we clearly celebrated in ritual terms what it means to be human. The following was posted in response to the death of a faculty member:

The night I read about Ari's death, I sat and stared at the computer while tears flowed down my face. His death came less than a week after I lost a close colleague. It hit me hard. I felt a sensation of disbelief flow through me like a lightening bolt. Though I will later suggest that computers themselves do not embody a spirit, they certainly did during that mourning period. I could not have gotten through Ari's death without the [electronic] "memorial." *Theresa*

As a result of the sudden death of a student participant at the start of one of our classes, we created a memorial forum online. The posts were printed and read at the student's funeral by one of the authors and were given to her family, who were amazed at the depth of feeling being expressed by her student colleagues. The following is an example of one of the posts to the memorial forum:

For the past week or so, I have contemplated how the loss of one of my classmates will affect me or if it even would. I have a hard time dealing with death whether it be somebody I never met before or someone that was extremely close to me. I lost my father a year ago and one of my best friends in August. I'm not sure if these have an effect on the way I feel about the loss of Pam or not but this is how I feel. . . . Pam was a challenge to me. She was not a student that accepted what a professor said and took it as the truth. She challenged every idea to the fullest. I remember that in most of my classes if we were discussing something then Pam would always bring in articles from the Wall Street Journal or somewhere that she had read about the issue. I can only imagine how hard it is to try and be a non-trad student, to get along with all of these teenage or older kids that try and blow everything off (the things that seemed so important to Pam). Although I never tried to reach out and meet Pam, I learned two things that I feel were very important to her. First of all, I truly learned how important Pam's degree was to her. Especially from the lecture our class got the first day in HR Admin. and the way she applied herself to everything, I knew that Pam was proud of the fact that she was at school and accomplishing something that she wanted to do for herself. Secondly, Pam lived and loved for her daughter. There were many times in classes that she discussed something about her daughter or just related about her in a story. She posted about her in her biography in this class. I could just tell that she was always thinking about her and cared for her so much. Death is a tragedy no matter how it occurs. I am saddened by the loss of a classmate that I had in all four of my classes this semester and thankful for the simple lessons that my short occurrences with her taught me. God works in mysterious ways and although sometimes his plans confuse me, I am going to bed praying tonight that Pam rests in peace happily by his side. Who knows, maybe she is meeting some of my past and learning something about me. Rest in Peace, Pam. *Carmen*

It is also important to celebrate accomplishments and positive occurrences in ritual terms. For example, we had members of the university's track team participating in one of our online courses. When they won a significant victory, we celebrated online by acknowledging the win and encouraging others to do the same.

Spirituality in the Virtual Community

The discussion of the importance of ritual in an online class leads to thoughts about spirituality because part of the expression of the human spirit is through ritual. When we first thought about spirituality and electronic communities, it almost seemed like an oxymoron. However, we do feel that spirituality enters the electronic community in more than one way and thus enters the electronic classroom.

First, if we have established (and we think we have) that electronic communities are essentially human, then they are also essentially spiritual. One of the key words here is *essentially*, as we feel that the spirit is the essential energy that drives and connects us all. It is an unseen force that is greater than all of us and works through us. Everything we do as humans, including our interaction with technology, is spiritual. John December (1997), in a special focus issue of *CMC Magazine* devoted to spirituality online, stated that "if we confine our study of CMC [computer-mediated communication] to only a perspective which assumes a technological, social, or cultural basis for phenomena [we] will miss part of the essence of human experience online" (p. 1).

Spirituality and consciousness are closely intertwined. Our spirituality helps to increase our level of openness and awareness. The increasing openness with which participants communicate in an online class is spiritual. We find the power of groups, whether face-to-face or electronic, intensely spiritual. It goes back, then, to connectedness. The connection between people, however that may happen, touches the spiritual core. So regardless of its faults, the electronic community is a spiritual community.

This seminar will be long over and we will all be off onto other tasks. It feels sad to me. If part of being in community is a sense of caring and interest in each other, then, for me, a piece of that is already here. I may not have a visual picture of all of you to draw on, but after reading several messages from each of you, there is a sense of personality and spirit that comes through. *Claudia*

Again, it is important for instructors to make room for the spiritual in an online course. Students frequently express a sense of wonder and amazement at the depth and nature of the interaction that occurs online. Some students become so comfortable and feel so accepted by the online group that they begin to discuss their religious beliefs in the context of a course. We had one student who began to quote from the Bible to support his posts in a class. As an instructor-facilitator of this process, it is important to accept and accommodate this as a dimension of the spirituality of the medium and the online group.

Vulnerability, Privacy, and Ethics

Any social interaction—any attempt at connection—involves making ourselves vulnerable. We risk rejection, pain, and misunderstanding when we reach out to others. But as we have established, the benefits of connection far outweigh the risks. Issues of privacy are major in community. How much do we need to share about ourselves in order to connect, and how much can we legitimately retain without jeopardizing the essence of community? Privacy issues emerge in community in other ways. For example, in face-to-face or telephone interaction, we can have relatively private conversations. We can also feel somewhat sure that a message sent directly to someone's mailbox in e-mail communication is relatively private. However, there are no assurances of privacy when we communicate in the virtual classroom. Several writers have noted that people communicating on bulletin boards frequently act as if their contributions are private and are shocked and hurt when they discover the reality. It is similar to holding a private conversation in a public place. We never know who might be listening.

Ethics

The question of ethics opens an area of discussion that is frequently controversial. Because this area is so new, the ethics around how communication happens and is used are still being debated. There are many places, both in the electronic classroom and around the Internet, where the notion of ethics comes into play. Those who have used e-mail systems at work probably have many stories about both ethical and unethical uses of the medium. Increasingly, we see articles appearing in journals, newspapers, and on the Internet discussing this subject. Additionally, university administrators are being pressured to confront these issues and set standards around them as unacceptable, even illegal, uses of e-mail on campus increase (McDonald, 1997). Mary Sumner (1996, p. 1) categorizes the new social and ethical problems in this medium as abuse of public computing resources, including tying up open-access workstations, disk space, network printers, and other shared resources; invasion of privacy, such as gaining unauthorized access to other people's electronic mail by breaking passwords or spoofing; and improper use of computer systems, including harassment, commercial use of instructional facilities, and misrepresentation of user communications.

Sexual issues are another unavoidable concern in electronic communication. Common experiences in this area may include posing as a person of a different sex, sexual innuendos in textual communications, and sexual harassment. One instructor reported to us some of her experiences with electronic seminars, one of which was interrupted by a "peeping Tom." Students who were participating and sharing some fairly personal material were angry and felt violated when this person revealed himself to the group in an inappropriate way. Although course sites are generally password-protected, it is possible for an intruder to enter. Despite the fact that observers may be present or others may be able to access the site, the group constructs an illusion of privacy, allowing them to continue to share openly with one another (Pratt, 1996).

No electronic classroom is truly private. Usually, system administrators have access to the site in order to work with technical problems that may arise. As part of a peer review system or training program for new faculty who want to teach online, many institutions have asked faculty to shadow one another in an online course. Finally, another student can hack into a course, as the student just mentioned did. Consequently, instructors and students need to think carefully about what to share or encourage in this medium. The goal should be to establish a balance between open dialogue and caution. If an instructor feels that a participant's posts are too personal or too open, it is important to contact that student confidentially to discuss the issue. Additionally, it is important for instructors to report any breaches of security in the system immediately, so that the integrity of the course is maintained.

Privacy

Privacy is virtually impossible to be sure of in electronic communications. The encryption of messages is the most reliable means of privacy, but it is rarely employed in an academic setting. Messages can be read, even if the reader is not physically present in the room. When the issue of privacy is addressed directly, the vulnerability of participation in this medium becomes evident, as there is uncertainty about how and whether contributions will be used by others. Although this should not stop instructors and students from using this medium for educational purposes, it raises fairly significant issues that must be addressed as a virtual community is developing. Members must know that their communications are not secure and that they must use good judgment in what they share. Boundaries, therefore, may be more important in this medium than they are face to face, and they must be adhered to and enforced.

Guidelines for the appropriate use of course material should be posted at the beginning of the course with a request for clarification and discussion to ensure that participants understand the importance of this issue. Inappropriate use of the medium must be addressed by instructors quickly and directly so as to maintain the norm of safety and acceptance within the group. If an instructor or a participant becomes aware that information posted to a course site has been quoted elsewhere without permission, for example, this must be directly confronted. If it comes to the instructor's attention that a member of the group is being stalked by another member, this must also be confronted and stopped, even if it means removing a student from the class. If a student drops the class, access to the course site must be denied through de-activation of his or her password. These are concerns we rarely have in a face-to-face classroom situation, but they become critical to the creation of a safe course site that facilitates the development of an electronic learning community.

Privacy is an interesting topic to me. I am a very private person in person. Yet I have been conversing with you about my fears and insecurities and life choices. And though I do intend my words for those who have been responding, I am aware that this is a public place where there are silent readers who now may know me a lot more than I know them. *Theresa*

Final Thoughts

It should be clear at this point that distance education requires more than a software package that allows an institution to offer coursework online. In any setting, whether academic, organizational, or corporate, it is critical to remember that *people* are using the machinery that makes the course go. The human element, therefore, will inevitably play a role in the electronic classroom.

Human concerns should be welcomed into the classroom, not feared, and should be worked with as they emerge. The human issues in a developing electronic learning community create a level of challenge to the instructor that might not be present in the face-to-face classroom. The physical distance between members in the community pushes instructors to be creative in the ways they cope with difficult students who are not participating or those who are violating the privacy of the group. The fact that the course is being conducted online does not limit the instructor to resolving all of these issues online. All means of communication, including the telephone and face-to-face meetings, need to be employed in order to address concerns and deal with problems. The lack of face-to-face contact means that the sense of group in an online learning community can be fragile, especially as it is forming. The group can disintegrate quickly when problems occur. Consequently, what is most critical for the instructor, even when playing a facilitative and nondirective role in the learning community, is to stay abreast of developments within the group and to act decisively and quickly when necessary. In the next chapter, we consider two more elements that affect the people and the work of online distance education: time and group size.

CHAPTER FOUR

TIME AND GROUP SIZE

In the previous two chapters, we discussed some issues that arise as we form an electronic learning community in cyberspace. However, as an electronic approach to the creation or facilitation of a class, meeting, or seminar is considered, additional factors must be taken into account if the class is to be successful: time and group size. The success or failure of an online endeavor depends on getting these right.

About Time

Concerns about time relate primarily to the amount of time required for participation on the part of both students and faculty. In this section, we discuss several of the concerns related to time: asynchronous and synchronous environments, time offline versus online, time constraints, and time management.

Asynchronous and Synchronous Environments

Electronic classes, meetings, workshops, or seminars can be conducted either synchronously (real time or chat) or asynchronously, meaning that postings are staggered. Our preference, based on our experiences with online teaching, is for the asynchronous environment. It is the creation of community in that environment to which all of our previous discussion relates. The asynchronous environment allows participants to log on to the class or discussion at any time, think about what is being discussed, and post their own responses when they wish.

The challenge of conducting a synchronous meeting or seminar is to coordinate time with a dispersed group and to facilitate in such a way that all "voices" are heard. Although many groups ask for the ability to have synchronous discussion (chat capability), we find that it rarely allows for productive discussion or participation and frequently disintegrates into simple one-line contributions of minimal depth. It can replicate the face-to-face classroom in that the participant who is the fastest typist will probably contribute the greatest amount to the discussion, thus becoming the "loudest voice" in the group. Additionally, contributions may end up out of sync; a participant may respond to a comment made several lines earlier but be unable to post that response immediately due to the number of people posting or the speed of the connection to the discussion.

If the group is internationally distributed, time differences become critical, as does the impact of culture on communication. The use of synchronous communications is becoming more popular with those who need to conduct meetings with distributed work teams, and we were asked to consult to a human resources staff person for a large multinational company using a distributed team format. The manager of an internationally distributed team within the company was baffled when a Japanese member resigned. Upon investigation, she discovered that the team member was required to drive for two hours in the middle of the night in order to get to the office to participate in a synchronous team meeting. However, because it was not appropriate for him to complain to a superior, given his cultural background, he felt that his only option was to resign. As computer-mediated distance learning programs increasingly attract an international market, educators will need to consider the impact of time and cultural differences on the conduct of courses.

The managers of an educational program being conducted almost completely over the Internet told us recently that they were resisting the addition of chat capability for their students due to concerns about time. Because the students in the program were globally distributed, theirs was a logistics concern. How would they be able to conduct a class meeting synchronously, given that their students were all over the world? On whose time schedule would these meetings be conducted? Would the schedule be determined by the instructor? The students? Whose time zone would win out? Although these may seem like small, petty issues to some, they become critical when an instructor or a participant is asked to get up in the middle of the night to participate in a class discussion. Certainly, this would reduce the quality of participation and thus erode a developing sense of community in the group.

Another concern in synchronous communication is the ease with which members can become confused and overloaded if guidelines for participation are not established at the start. As discussion occurs in real time, members may not be able to keep up with the pace established. In an attempt to deal with this problem, many software applications for synchronous communication include ways to signal for recognition—much like raising a hand in the face-to-face classroom. Although this helps create order out of possible chaos, it does not help stem a sense of overload as the discussion proceeds.

We do not mean to completely condemn synchronous communication, however. It can be a dynamic and challenging setting in which to meet and can be especially useful in facilitating brainstorming and whiteboarding sessions. (*Whiteboarding* is writing or drawing on a shared screen.) It can be a useful adjunctive tool in a computer-mediated class, but for it to be successful, the number of students participating should be small, the concerns and time zones of all participants must be considered, and guidelines for equal participation must be established in advance.

In asynchronous meetings or seminars, members have the luxury of time. Postings can occur at the convenience of the participants, allowing them time to read, process, and respond. However, because participants can take their time, asynchronous meetings or seminars need to take place over a much longer time period, which should be factored into the planning. What might have been a weekend workshop may need to be stretched over one or two weeks to allow for full participation. The amount to be discussed in one week during a semester course may need to be pared down to manageable size in order for all participants to have an opportunity to read and respond.

I really enjoy being able to do my work whenever I want to. Along with the flexibility it also gives me a sense of responsibility. *Jason*

Time Offline Versus Time Online

As we conduct our seminars and workshops about online teaching, one reaction is always expressed by a member of the audience: surprise about the amount of time it takes to teach a course online. Many instructors and institutions mistakenly believe that this mode of teaching and course delivery is easy. We have found the opposite to be true. An instructor for an online course cannot simply post material and walk away for a week. If that happens, the instructor may log on to find a flurry of posts and questions and may have difficulty appropriately reentering the conversation. We find that we need to check the course site at least once a day, if not more, in order to respond quickly to student posts, offer advice or suggestions, or simply make our presence known and felt. Students also need to be responsive and involved, as we have discussed previously. As one of our students stated:

One thing I must say with this group as compared to my classes last quarter, you have to check in more than the required two times a week. . . . I found that when I came on-line there were so many long postings and so many rich thoughts that it was hard to respond to soooo much. So my answer is to try and come on-line more often. *Cindy*

Another student commented:

To some degree it's easier to drive to a class every Wednesday night for three hours or to spend all weekend in class. At least you know that the time is designated and finite. This class, on the other hand, goes on 24 hours a day, 7 days a week. This makes it so much harder to know when to "go to class" so to speak. I thought this would be an easier way to take class. I was wrong! *June*

Instructors in the online arena will find that the time needed to deliver this type of class is two to three times greater than to deliver a face-to-face class. Table 4.1 illustrates this difference. This is an accounting of time by one of the authors in the online delivery of one week of a class, Basic Addiction Studies. The class was a graduate-level class that normally met once a week for two and one-half hours. The instructor needed to cancel a class and could not reschedule it, so she conducted the class online for a week. The twenty-three students participating were divided into four discussion groups. All of the groups were discussing the same topic. Students had varying levels of comfort with technology, although the instructor was very comfortable with it. This was the first experience in online learning for most of the students; very active discussion ensued.

Although the amount of time involved with the delivery of one week of instruction may seem daunting, the level and quality of participation on the part of students helps to surmount any feelings of being overwhelmed that might result. There is nothing more exciting than to log on to a course site and see groups of students actively engaged with the material. We find it energizing and exhilarating, although the amount of work involved cannot be minimized.

Additional Time Issues

Increasing amounts of online time can contribute to noted issues such as addiction to being online and information addiction (Conrad and Crowell, 1997; Harasim, 1989; Harasim and others, 1996; McWilliams, 1997; Young, 1998). Frequently referred to as information overload or "infoglut," information addiction actually goes beyond what we ordinarily think of as overload. In an overload situation, students and faculty may be inundated with so much poorly managed information that they feel they simply cannot keep up. Harasim and others (1996) report on this

TABLE 4.1. TIME COMPARISONS OF AN ONLINE VERSUS A FACE-TO-FACE CLASS FOR ONE WEEK.

Instructor Activity	Face-to-Face Class	Online Class
Preparation	2 hours per week to: Review assigned reading Review lecture materials Review and prepare in-class activities	2 hours per week to: Review assigned reading Prepare discussion questions and "lecture" material in the form of a paragraph or two
Class time	2½ hours per week of assigned class time	2 hours *daily* to: Read student posts Respond to student posts
Follow-up	2 to 3 hours per week for: Individual contact with students Reading student assignments	2 to 3 hours per week for: Individual contact with students via e-mail and phone Reading student assignments
Totals for the week	6½ to 7½ hours per week	18 to 19 hours per week

Note: Time involved with online classes is related to a number of variables such as the number of students enrolled in the class, the level of comfort with the technology on the part of both the instructor and the students, the encountering of technical difficulties, the degree to which discussion is an expected part of class activity, and the types of activities in which students are engaged.

negative aspect of learning online and student reactions to it: "Students report information overload, communication anxiety in relation to the delayed responses in an asynchronous environment, increased work and responsibility, difficulty in navigating online and following the discussion threads, loss of visual cues, and concerns about health issues related to computer use" (p. 15). A typical reaction to overload is to retreat. If a student disappears from an online class, overload may be the culprit. This needs to be investigated with the student so that appropriate course management techniques can be implemented. Frequently, students who are new to the medium call us asking for assistance in taking in and responding to the amount of information being generated within a course. Providing tips on how to read and respond often helps.

With information addiction, however, the opposite occurs. Participants may begin to "binge" on e-mail exchanges or contributions to the course site. A sense of urgency develops, coupled with frustration when others do not respond in kind. Inflammatory messages may be the result. Participants experiencing information addiction may, but will not always, sense that they are somehow out of control. Their need to spend time online takes over and goes beyond what would appear to be the norm. They may ignore family, work, and classes to spend time on the Internet (Young, 1998). Frequently, as with any other form of addiction, they do not recognize the extent of their problem; the instructor may need to intervene and help them manage the time they spend online. Although this may seem far-fetched to some, L. Dean Conrad and Perry Crowell (1997), in their article "E-mail Addiction," describe this means of communication as both a blessing and a curse. If not properly managed, addiction to the medium can lead to becoming less effective overall. The American Psychological Association, in its 1997 annual conference, also recognized this problem by presenting a diagnosis based on research conducted by Kimberly Young (1998), which they term *pathological Internet use* or PIU. Those suffering with PIU are said to spend in excess of thirty-six hours per week online and to be experiencing some of the symptoms mentioned earlier.

Conrad and Crowell (1997) present a "12–Step Program" to regain control. Many of their suggestions would be useful to a participant in an online course who is struggling with these issues:

- Set a specific time each day to read and respond to messages rather than doing it throughout the day.
- Wait to respond to a message that upsets you and be careful of what you say and how you say it.
- Never say anything that you could not tolerate seeing in print on the front page of your local newspaper.
- Establish clear priorities for dealing with messages and categorize messages by importance and need to respond (pp. 4–5).

The instructor's response to all of this should be course management techniques, such as good organization of the course site and presentation of material in manageable pieces, along with sensitivity to the signals that students may be giving regarding their inability to keep up. Table 4.2 lists some of the time concerns that may arise and techniques for dealing with the concerns.

Instructors must be prepared to help students manage their time online to avoid both overload and the potential for developing addiction to the medium. On a more positive note, however, students who use the medium appropriately find that it can help them develop the research skills needed for other classes, become more responsible in their study habits, and be better able to manage their time overall.

I do spend a LOT more time on line. Not only for this class, but I find myself using the Internet more for my other classes as well. *Carmen*

TABLE 4.2. COURSE- AND TIME-MANAGEMENT TECHNIQUES.

Concern	Instructor Response
Minimal or no participation on the part of one or more students due to information overload	Make personal contact to determine cause. Suggest setting a daily log-on time in order to read only. Print messages from course site. Set two additional times per week to respond. Prepare responses on word processor and copy and paste to course site. Assist in management of outside reading for the course.
Information overload due to poorly managed or poorly organized information	Make sure students are posting to the appropriate discussion forums and correct if necessary. Add discussion forums if necessary to separate and organize material. Present outside reading in manageable amounts. If class is large, divide the group into smaller discussion groups. Establish time limits on discussion of topics (for example, one or two weeks per topic).
Communication anxiety	Make personal contact to reassure student. Give supportive response every time the student posts until anxiety is reduced. Ensure that student is comfortable with the technology being used. Encourage preparation of posts on a word processor and copy and paste into course site rather than posting on the spot.
Lack of participation due to technical difficulties	Make personal contact with student to provide instruction and coaching on the technology in use. Contact systems administrators to resolve technical problems that are out of student or instructor control. Make technical support available for participants.
Reduced participation due to concerns about privacy and exposure	Make personal contact with students to determine nature of concern and encourage participation. Offer supportive responses to student posts to reduce anxiety and encourage participation.

	Plug any security leaks immediately by working with systems administrators and changing passwords if necessary.
Excessive posting accompanied by irritation with others who cannot "keep up"	Make personal contact with student to assist with course management and provide feedback on participation. Suggest only one time daily for logging on. Limit posts to two per week. Limit length of posts.

Time Management

Clearly, the need to be involved to a greater extent in these classes creates a greater need for time management. Part of what participants need to learn from an on-line class is how to divide their time into tasks: reading the assigned material to prepare for the online discussion, reading the contributions of other students and preparing one's own, participating in small-group work, and completing the other assignments for the course. The instructor can assist with this process by assigning reading material in manageable pieces, attempting to enforce time limits on the discussion of a particular topic, and establishing participation guidelines. Additionally, student anxiety about the perceived need to respond immediately to course material can be minimized through good time-management techniques.

Some of the suggestions we have made to students who are having difficulty with time management and course management in general are as follows:

- Log on to the course site with the intention of downloading and reading only.
- Print new messages, if possible, to allow time to review them in a more leisurely fashion.
- Once messages have been read and reviewed, formulate a response to be posted. Do not feel as if an immediate response is necessary in an asynchronous environment.
- In order to be more thoughtful about responses, prepare them on a word processor and then copy and paste them to the course site. If hard disk space is at a premium or if a lab computer is being used, copy your responses to a floppy disk.

These suggestions tend to allay student fears about what constitutes good participation while providing them with a more organized and thoughtful way to approach the course. Also, they reduce some students' tendency to respond off the tops of their heads, which improves the quality of their responses; the possibility of conflict and flaming is reduced as well.

Time Constraints

A final consideration in the issue of time, as it relates to online courses, is time constraints. Frequently, because instructors are teaching online courses through institutional structures, they are expected to fit these courses into existing time frames, such as quarters or semesters. This can be somewhat constraining or inhibiting in that an online course frequently takes on a rhythm of its own. It may start out somewhat slowly, as students work out any technical problems they may be experiencing and begin to feel out the parameters of the course and begin to know each other. We then frequently see the course take off for a period of time, with students contributing at a very high level and responding to each other with great frequency. The course may then begin to wane, particularly as students begin to grapple with the expectations and demands of their other face-to-face courses. Consequently, preparation for exams and term papers may slow down the interactive process, forcing the instructor to take a much greater facilitative role as the quarter or semester progresses, when we would expect the opposite to be true. We may, then, see a flurry of participation at the end, as students post final assignments to the course site and are asked to process the experience as a whole.

Another unrelated but interesting time constraint is the expectation of many institutions that instructors maintain office hours. An instructor who maintains an office on campus and is teaching both face-to-face and online classes may not find this particularly challenging. But how is this accomplished when the office is virtual? If students are geographically dispersed, as many are in online courses, or the instructor is adjunct and not available on campus, this can be a challenging restriction. Certainly, it is important for instructors to make themselves available by phone to students in an online course. This is by far the simplest solution. The establishment of telephone office hours or telephone appointments can serve the same function as face-to-face office hours.

One instructor with whom we have worked came up with a particularly creative solution to this dilemma. She established online office hours. Although working in an asynchronous environment, she notified students that she would be checking the course site every few minutes on Monday evenings from 9:00 P.M. until 10:00 P.M. and on Thursday evenings from 9:00 P.M. until 9:30 P.M. The Thursday office hours happened to coincide with the time that the television show "Seinfeld" was on, and she told her students that she would be watching Seinfeld in between the times that she checked the course site. What quickly happened was that all of the students began watching Seinfeld, checking the course site, interacting with the instructor and also with each other, discussing what was happening in the television show in one area of the course site and posting questions for the instructor in another area. This served not only to create an opportunity to get questions answered by the instructor and serve as her office hours but also deepened the sense of community developing within the group. This was a particularly interesting and creative means by which to accomplish this, given that the course was a statistical methods course—a course that would offer a challenge in the creation of an online learning community due to the subject matter.

At a recent distance learning conference, a nursing instructor shared an interesting story related to time and time constraints. She found that her class time online was not being respected by others in her department. If she logged on to her course site while in her office at the university, others did not seem to respect that she was actually teaching a class. Colleagues would come into her office and ask to speak to her. Someone would interrupt her and ask her to do something or ask if she was interested in having a cup of coffee. Her eventual response to these interruptions was to close her office door and post a sign on it that read, "In class. Please do not disturb." Her colleagues respected the closed door, and she was able to have uninterrupted time in which to focus on her class.

What is most important in considering a means by which to hold "office hours" and have the dedicated time for an online class is that instructors delivering online courses do not have the luxury of going on vacation for a week or two. Their continuous presence, guidance, and availability to the participants is critical to successful course outcomes. These elements must be acknowledged and respected by administrators and colleagues in order to provide the support that instructors need to successfully teach in this arena.

Group Size

Closely related to time are issues of group size—issues of major importance in the online classroom that relate to the ability of the instructor to maintain some modicum of control over the process without subjecting participants to information overload.

If a synchronous meeting or seminar is being conducted, the group should be small enough to allow for full participation and to prevent information overload. Groups that are too large can be overwhelming for the instructor and the participants; five to ten is an ideal number. Asynchronous groups, however, can be much larger. As many as twenty or more participants can have a successful experience in an asynchronous setting. However, the success of a large group depends on the skill of the instructor as facilitator, his or her knowledge of the electronic medium, the content being discussed and explored, and the means by which that exploration occurs. If participants are expected to post papers for discussion, for example, a smaller number of participants or staggered posting dates would better facilitate that process. Additionally, a large group can be broken into small groups or teams for the purposes of completing assignments, having discussions, or conducting evaluations, thus promoting an environment in which collaborative work is necessary. Again, the nature of the course and the types of assignments given must be taken into account. Smaller groups are necessary if papers are to be written collaboratively or if online presentations are to be prepared, for example, for presentation to the larger group.

Creativity on the part of the instructor is necessary to promote the best use of group size. The educational level of the participants and the course content play a role here as well. In many of our graduate-level classes, we ask students to research and complete papers that are posted online. This creates the basis for discussion that allows the participants to go far beyond the designated course content. With an undergraduate course, however, we may stay closer to the textbook but create smaller groups or teams to complete projects and work together on case studies that may or may not be presented to the large group. Discussion takes the form of responses to questions posed to the entire group; questions are related to the material being read in the textbook.

Regardless of the means by which group management is attempted, issues related to group dynamics and the potential for unequal participation must be considered. Whether working in a large group or in smaller teams, the dynamics of the online group and the process through which it develops is similar to face-to-face groups. Therefore, the instructor needs to monitor that process and jump in as facilitator when necessary. When smaller groups are created within a larger class or group, each group should be asked to appoint a team leader. That person then becomes responsible for facilitating the interaction within the team, with the understanding that help can be requested from the instructor if that becomes necessary. In the guidelines that we create for our online classes, we always ask group members to be willing to work out any issues or differences online. We do this to minimize outside discussion that may be harmful to the development of a working group. If members are gossiping or having what we like to call "side dishes" or side conversations that may not be supportive of what is happening in the group, it frequently will show up in limited participation in the group and an unwillingness to work collaboratively.

It is important to stress that group members have a responsibility to each other; they also depend on each other for the successful outcome of the course. One means of ensuring that participants work together, as we have previously discussed, is to establish participation guidelines at the outset. This still may not solve the problem of unequal participation, however. Harasim and others (1996) describe the problem as follows: "A potential benefit of learning networks is that each student can participate equally in class discussions and activities; however, each student may not put in the same volume or quality of material. Differences based on student interest, ability, availability, or other considerations affect the upper and lower levels of participation . . . some students may dominate or others refuse to participate" (p. 228).

Because of the issue of unequal participation, it is important to include participation levels in whatever form of evaluation is undertaken to measure student outcome. We have had team members evaluate each other's participation and contributions to the class within guidelines. For example, the team leaders can assign a grade for participation each week to the members of their team. That grade is then reported to the instructor, who evaluates it for fairness and makes some modifications, with good reason.

Administrative Issues Related to Time and Group Size

Linda Harasim and her colleagues (1996), when discussing the online classroom, state:

> The change in the concept of time that an instructor spends with students will present an even bigger challenge for the administrator. The time and effort an instructor expends becomes a linear function of the number of students in a class. Administrators can no longer economize on educational effort by increasing class size. The instructor can no longer adapt to class size by allowing less time for individual interaction with the students [p. 232].

Clearly, the idea that the larger the class the greater the return cannot be applied to the electronic classroom. Given the amount of time needed on both the parts of faculty and students in order to make the class proceed successfully, limiting class size when delivering courses in this medium is the key. A recent survey conducted by RAND (reported in the *Economist*, May 10, 1997) indicates that courses delivered using the Internet can help to cut central administrative costs while reaching out to more students who are beyond the confines of the university. Given the lower costs involved in delivery, then, universities can afford to keep class sizes small without reducing revenues from these classes. The survey further suggests that offering these types of courses is having an impact on the way universities are organized.

This does raise a larger issue, then, regarding course fees and faculty compensation. Many universities are charging the same fees for both face-to-face and online classes. We have heard students complain about this, stating that because the course does not cost the university as much to deliver, their fees should be reduced as a result. Students do not see the costs involved with computer-mediated distance learning because they are not physically attending a class where the instructor is present. Consequently, students in this environment need to see a high degree of faculty involvement and presence in order to feel as if they are getting what they paid for. In addition, they need to have adequate technical support.

Some institutions pay faculty less for teaching online due to the absence of travel and designated class time, along with the smaller group sizes. However, when we have discussed this issue with faculty who are teaching online, the feeling is that because they are required to be available every day for a particular class and are actually doing more work in the preparation and delivery of the class, salaries for this form of teaching should be higher. A study regarding institutional support for distance teaching (Wolcott and Haderlie, 1997) reports that faculty are more motivated to participate in distance learning programs when this is included in their teaching load and not considered an add-on. Motivation also increased when faculty felt they were adequately compensated for the amount of work required. Faculty felt less motivated to teach in distance mode when they did not feel supported by the institution or recognized for their efforts in this arena. The study states: "The amount of work required, together with the time involved to adapt instruction for distance delivery and to learn new skills associated with the technology, posed significant barriers to participation when added to an already heavy workload" (p. 15).

In fact, the provision of distance learning options may not be less expensive for the institution. Although the institution saves money on the use of classroom space, the costs of the technology, transmission, maintenance, infrastructure, production, support, and of course, personnel all need to be factored into the mix. The Instructional Telecommunications Council of the American Association of Community Colleges completed a survey regarding faculty compensation in distance learning courses. What they found was a range of compensation formulae among the institutions surveyed from no additional compensation, to added pay after a seat maximum, to elimination of enrollment ceilings, to per-head compensation for remote students. Some institutions offered a stipend for course development, the addition of preparation pay for the first class, or reduced enrollment for the first class (Salomon and others, 1997). Again, given that this arena is so new for many institutions, it will take time to sort out a formula for appropriate fees and salaries. If the RAND study is correct and the very nature of our academic institutions changes as the result of the implementation of distance education, institutions will no longer be grappling with the issues of cost, fees, and compensation; they will become a way of life. As with the pedagogical methods we have discussed, old forms of determining fees and salaries must make way for newer ones that factor in time and group size—issues that are very much a part of the delivery of distance education.

We return to a discussion of administrative issues relative to the delivery of online courses in the next chapter, as we explore the technical issues involved with online teaching. The administrative issues yet to be explored are those related to the choice of appropriate technology, the development of an institutional infrastructure, and the support and maintenance of that infrastructure.

CHAPTER FIVE

MANAGING THE TECHNOLOGY

The technology available for conducting classes, meetings, and seminars online generally involves the use of software that is either intranet-based, meaning that students use software to access a closed network on a remote server, or Internet-based. Several types of meeting or conferencing software are currently available; they vary in terms of features and ease of use, allowing for anything from brainstorming sessions to long-term discussion, as well as the use of graphics, audio, and video. Desktop video conferencing is also a developing technology, creating the ability to hold face-to-face sessions over the Internet, thus adding real-time video to the mix.

Regardless of the technology used, the instructor needs to be knowledgeable about it and comfortable enough with it to be able to help with problems. The instructor should also be able to construct the online meeting or seminar site so that participants find it easy to use and logical in structure. The technology must be available to and useable by all participants. The most beautifully constructed site, complete with graphics, audio, and video, is useless to a participant working with older technology. According to Whitesel (1998), "Technology does not teach students; effective teachers do. A virtual learning space that is effectively created by a competently trained instructor can deliver on the promises educators make to their students. It can help us deliver our content to a growing number of learners over a widely diverse geographical area" (p. 1).

It is not our goal in this chapter to discuss the various forms of technology available and their uses in distance learning. We are more concerned with developing an awareness of the role technology plays in the delivery of a course. Most important, the instructor or facilitator in an online distance learning environment must be continuously aware that people are connecting with them through a computer and that these participants are developing a relationship not only with each other but with the technology itself. All of these relationships must be considered critical components of an electronic classroom.

The Relationship of Person to Machine

Many writers in the area of distance learning and educational technology discuss the various types of technology that are available and how to use that technology in the process of developing and delivering a course in distance mode. What they sometimes fail to consider, however, is that people are interacting with the hardware, the software, the process, and each other. These relationships create a continuous loop that embeds itself in and becomes part of the learning process. As a result of this loop, some of the participants begin to construct an alternate identity—the person they are when they are online—surrounded by a sort of impenetrable bubble. They create for themselves a sense of privacy that allows them to ignore the rest of the world (Pratt, 1996). This can be likened to new lovers out in public who have eyes only for each other. The rest of the world no longer exists for them.

Sherry Turkle (1995), in her book *Life on the Screen*, quotes a physics professor who describes this reality by stating: "My students know more about computer reality, but less and less about the real world" (p. 66). Turkle further states:

> When we step through the screen into virtual communities, we reconstruct our identities on the other side of the looking glass. This reconstruction is our cultural work in progress. . . . On the one hand we insist that we are different from machines because we have emotions, bodies, and an intellect that cannot be captured in rules, but on the other we play with computer programs that we think of as alive or almost-alive. . . . The Internet is another element of the computer culture that has contributed to thinking about identity as multiplicity. On it, people are able to build a self by cycling through many selves [pp. 177–178].

Although these statements may seem to represent this phenomenon in the extreme, we do see evidence of it in the electronic classroom. We have had students who have named their computers. Some have even spoken of sleeping with their notebook computers. More commonly, however, this attachment manifests itself through the alteration of human relationships, which include relationships with other participants in the course and with the instructor. Take the following bit of dialogue from one of our seminars as an example:

Here's a weird thought, but I just wondered if anyone else ever sensed it. Sometimes when I see some of the people out of this class I want to say something to them about the class or something but I feel like I can't because I need to e-mail them or put it in a forum. Is that totally dorky? Like, if I see Mason I am like so did you post, what did you think about this. But, if I see someone I don't really know like Mike or Rob, it is weird because I feel like I can only do it on-line. Is this just totally stupid or has anyone else experienced that? *Carmen*

Carmen I experience this a lot when I see you going into one of Mr. Schwartz's classes I want to have a long discussion with you, and sometimes we do when we are at practice during our free times. Yet I don't see hardly anybody on campus because I am not here! So the rest of you I could say I am not for sure how I would feel. *Stacy*

I know what you mean Carmen. I feel like the forums are a better place to discuss classroom things. I would feel kind of guilty if I only shared my thoughts with one person instead of posting it for everyone to see. Sounds strange, I know. *Jason*

This exchange illustrates how the attachment phenomenon relates to the developing sense of community in an online classroom. It represents the establishment of boundaries around a protected space, with the members of the group sharing a common experience within those boundaries. However, at this stage of community development, they are unclear about the rules governing their interaction outside of that space. This type of exchange can lead to a deepening discussion among the members about the rules and norms of interaction both online and offline.

This is not a phenomenon to be feared but one that should be expected and taken into account as the course proceeds. In fact, a separate space should be created to allow it to happen. We have used the Cybercafe or the Electronic Reflections section, which we create on a course site, as well as the course discussion forums, to encourage the exploration of these relationships. We have also promoted it by posing questions that allow participants to explore and discuss these issues without fear that they will be ridiculed. To illustrate this point, the example just presented occurred in response to questions posed regarding group behavior and team building in cyberspace as a part of a course in organizational behavior.

An instructor or facilitator in an electronic setting will not surface these issues unless he or she feels comfortable doing so and purposefully seeks them out. These relationships are an important element of electronic communication and can affect the outcome of the learning process positively when they are encouraged.

This exploration forms the basis of what we have termed a *double loop* in the learning process and is the foundation of a transformational learning process, which we will discuss more fully in Chapter Nine.

Double-loop learning is a term offered by Chris Argyris (1992) to describe processes of organizational learning. He defines the differences between single- and double-loop learning as follows:

> Most people define learning too narrowly as mere "problem-solving," so they focus on identifying and correcting errors in the external environment. Solving problems is important. But if learning is to persist, managers and employees must also look inward. They need to reflect critically on their own behavior . . . and then change how they act. In particular, they must learn how the very way they go about defining and solving problems can be a source of problems in its own right. . . . To give a simple analogy: a thermostat that automatically turns on the heat whenever the temperature in a room drops below 68 degrees is a good example of single-loop learning. A thermostat that could ask, "Why am I set at 68 degrees?" and then explore whether or not some other temperature might more economically achieve the goal of heating the room would be engaging in double-loop learning [p. 84].

How does this concept apply to the use of technology and the relationship of the user to the technology in distance learning? When students are engaging in a learning process through the use of technology, they are learning not only course material but something new about the learning process and about themselves. The question becomes not "What have I learned about this course material?" but "What have I learned about this course material, what it takes to learn about it through the use of technology, and about myself in this process?" The learning process, then, involves self-reflection on the knowledge acquired about the course, about how learning occurs electronically, about the technology itself, and about how the user has been transformed by their new-found relationships with the machine, the software, the learning process, and the other participants. The following example illustrates this point.

I have got to say that this class has given me the opportunity to experience a lot. I [did] not use the computer for much but games. Now I think about it in a much different way. It is a learning tool. I have been able to research and expand my own ideas on many things. I have been able to question my own thoughts about many subjects. The ability to weigh my morals and judgements in regards to future lifetime experience will give me a strong basis for making decisions. It seems to have allowed me to express my thoughts without the fear of ridicule (that's a strong word) maybe non acceptance to a face to face encounter. Those have always been a [dis]quieting experience. I find that by posting on the computer I am able to accept the constructive criticism without out the facial or body criticism. This has been a good experience in all ways of manner. I have found that I have used the forum to warm me up to meeting and talking on-line to people across the world. It has open my ideas about many parts of the world. There is one thing though that you get hooked on this form of communication and like the others I can't wait to get on-line to find out what's happening. But still got to have base-ball . . . that doesn't get put aside by the computer. Other things (maybe). *Mike T.*

Learning about the use of technology, then, becomes an important component of the learning process as well as an outcome that we work toward. (We will discuss the means by which to achieve this more fully in Chapter Nine.)

Technology as a Facilitative Tool

Unfortunately, many academic institutions are swayed by the bells and whistles embedded in a fancy software package and do not consider what the learner can receive and handle as part of the learning process. They want the ability to add audio and video to a course site. They want students to be able to engage in synchronous chat. They want to be able to use desktop video conferencing. The problem, of course, is that although these applications can be useful and greatly broaden the approach to a course, they are only good insofar as they can be used by the participants. Participants using older hardware or living in a remote area with a slow connection to the Internet may simply be unable to participate in a chat session or receive audio or video. We always need to take into account the person at the other end of the wire. The bottom line is that the technology should not drive the course. Instead, the desired outcomes and needs of the participants should be the deciding factors. Harasim and her colleagues (1996) state: "The real question . . . is not whether a course *can* be done online but what is the best media mix to achieve the goals of the course within the constraints of the available resources or geographic dispersion of the students. More fundamentally, how should the media be used? What approaches to teaching and learning are most effective in a computer networking environment?" (p. 24).

The issue, then, is how to use the software developed to deliver the instructional material, also known as courseware, or course-authoring software. When it is too complex, it can lead to frustration on the part of the user and frustration with the learning process. Additionally, a complex software package would require that faculty be trained well enough to be able to develop and deliver the course, as well as act as a support person for the participants. Consequently, the courseware that is used should be:

- Functional (posting course materials and creating discussion forums should be easy)
- Simple to operate for both faculty and participants
- User friendly, visually appealing, and easy to navigate

We will now explore these components in more detail.

Ease of Use

The software used for a course should be transparent. A participant should not have to spend time negotiating several steps in order to post a message or respond in a discussion. The software should be in the background, acting only as a vehicle for course delivery. Furthermore, if the focus stays on the software as a facilitative tool to reach the learner and to enable the learners to reach one another, then the type of hardware available should be irrelevant. In other words, the main concerns with hardware should be that the user has access to a computer, the ability to connect to the Internet, and a computer with enough memory to allow for contact with and navigation of the course site.

A means by which to evaluate the effectiveness of the courseware used is the absence of participant comments on the software. No comments in this area means that the goal of transparency has been achieved. We expect some problems in the beginning of a course as participants become acclimated to the software and hardware. However, they should become adept at using the courseware quickly so as to get on with the more important aspects of the course. We have had student evaluations in which participants commented on the barrier that the software played in creating a successful learning experience. The following are examples of feedback we do *not* want to receive at the end of a course. This particular course was taught through an academic institution choosing to use software that was far from transparent. Problems with the software continued throughout the course, not only for the participants but for the faculty as well.

In terms of electronic learnings, I have learned that things will not always go the way they should but one must not give up when they don't. If I would have let problems with [the software] stop me from taking this class, I would have been the one who lost out. I'm glad I stayed through the electronic problems, through the storm, and even through the small class size. There was a great deal to gain from this class and I am glad that I was able to gain some of it, I feel I am the better for the experiences it held, both positive and negative ones. *Sandra*

Regarding my perceptions of strangeness-it has to do with many things-my trying to understand what taking an electronic course is all about-how it differs from traditional classes in the way information is exchanged, and knowledge is transferred-how it would have worked if the class had had more people and there were more interaction,-how things would have been if we hadn't had system problems in the beginning and if Sandra and Greg hadn't had their own computer problems. *June*

Although these students experienced system and software difficulties that interfered with the learning process to some degree, it is clear from these comments that some double-loop learning was an outcome. Because of their difficulties with the software, these students were put in the position quickly of assessing the impact of learning with and about technology. They learned that this is not the easier way to learn. One was happy to have had this experience and the other was not so sure. Regardless, a learning goal was achieved, although with more difficulty than we, as the course faculty, had hoped for or anticipated. When the technology is truly transparent, this goal can be achieved with far less pain.

Visual Appeal

The ability to create a visually appealing site does create greater interest on the part of the participants. Furthermore, participants' ability to represent themselves visually on the course site allows them to express their personalities, ideas, and ideals. This can be done through the creation of student homepages or biographies, including pictures or some other graphic image that helps participants build an online presence. This also helps to construct the relationships we described earlier to the machine, as well as to the software, the process, and to each other; all this contributes to the community-building process. Exhibit 5.1 is an example of a student homepage created for an online course.

When the only contact participants have with each other is virtual, they begin to create visual images for themselves about the other participants that may or may not be consistent with reality. Some faculty and students have described the advantage of having photographs of the others involved in a course available at their work site while interacting online. It is difficult for people to relate only to words on a screen. Having photos or visual images available helps to embody others. The following examples describe this phenomenon.

I'm not sure what the part is that scares me the most. Maybe it is the working with other people that you don't know or know that you can rely on. Maybe it is the fact that they will be these things on the computer that all you know about them is what they put in their bio. It is different with us now because we still see most of each other anyway. The trust factor I think just comes with getting to know someone which I would rather do in person. It is easier for this classroom because I know everyone

EXHIBIT 5.1. STUDENT HOMEPAGE.

Mason Clark

Email: clarks@usa.net

Biography

I am a 20-year-old student here at Ottawa University and I am a sophomore. I play line-backer on our football team and work in the computer lab. I am originally from Atchison, Kansas, which is a small town about an hour and a half north of here. To continue in the tradition of a biography I am 5'8" 210 and I have a shaved head and brown eyes.

Special Interests

Some of my "Special Interests" are football, or sports in general, the computer and socializing. Beyond that I really don't have any interests other than to have fun in life because I only live once. Also being in class with my favorite teacher in the whole wide world, Dr. Keith Pratt, is something I love to do.

WWW Links of Interest

My favorite chat room.

The best place for sports information.

A great place for free email.

My favorite class taught by my favorite teacher in the whole world.

The homepage of the NAIA.

The greatest web page ever created.

---

already. (It's weird but it is really nice to see a picture of Dr. Palloff because then she is not just this complete stranger in the classroom.) *Carmen*

Psychologically [this class] has played somewhat of a mind game in the sense that is this the true person that is talking and not the person being stated. In this particular situation where I know most of the students it is easier to tell but I feel that if I did not know the students then I would have had a harder time understanding or maybe being so open with thoughts and ideas. *Rob*

Sometimes it is hard to deal with the idea of virtual people. I am glad that I know most of you so I can put a face with the posts. *Jason*

When a class involves both face-to-face and online contact, this issue diminishes. Participants are able to connect a face with the words appearing on the screen. However, face-to-face sessions are not always possible. Consequently, the ability to include pictures and visual images helps participants connect the words with a real human being, thus humanizing the process.

Excuse Us, We Are Now Experiencing Technical Difficulties

Because much of the software available for the delivery of online classes or meetings is new to many users, the possibility for encountering technical difficulties is very real. Many instructors have complained about the lack of participation among students, only to find that students could not access a course site. Although this can also be deemed a convenient excuse, technical support must be available to help students log on, use the software, upload and download files, and so on, as well as to help faculty who are experiencing their own difficulties and attempting to help students with theirs. Some of the types of difficulties that are beyond the control of a faculty member who has engaged in the best possible planning for a course are things such as the university's server going down, problems with an Internet service provider, and problems or "bugs" in the software that cause it to act in unanticipated ways. Problems that can be resolved by the faculty member or the institution need to be resolved quickly. Ideally, problems should be anticipated and resolved prior to the start of a course. When problems occur during delivery of a course, however, rapid response is essential so as to avoid serious participation problems.

We cannot assume that our students are adept to any degree with technology. One technical support person gave us an extreme example of this when she told the story of a student living in a remote part of Alaska who was working on a doctorate through a distance learning program. She was attempting to talk him through some of his difficulties in accessing an Internet-based course and began to explain a command that needed to be typed in both capital and lowercase letters. The student asked, "How do I make a capital letter with this computer?" Should students who have so little knowledge of and ability with a computer participate in an online course? We emphatically say yes. Their participation can only increase their knowledge of, ability with, and facility in using technology. Rather than becoming upset or frustrated with the lack of technical expertise on the part of a student, faculty must remain helpful and flexible in order to enable the learning process around the use of technology.

Students are drawn to this mode of learning because it transcends distance and time constraints. However, they may be entering a totally new area. We have had many phone conversations with students to enable them to become conversant with the software being used, as well as to allay their fears about participation in this medium. When students have never interacted in a course through the use of technology, they may hold some fears about how their messages are being received and interpreted by others. This, too, is an element of their developing relationship with the machine.

Psychologically, this class has been challenging. I am always worried about how my posts will be taken. Sometimes I worry so much about the syntax of my statements [that I also] worry about the context. *Jason*

Faculty need to be open to these questions and concerns and to regard them as opportunities for teaching. By doing so, faculty are enabling the double-loop learning process we have previously discussed; they are also encouraging new modes of expression and the ability to take risks in a new and sometimes intimidating environment. Our hope is that this type of learning will transfer into other learning arenas as well. But are students the only ones who experience technical difficulties and problems with this medium? Consider the following story:

We don't expect this to happen to us and become upset with our students who complain about technical difficulties. But, finally, it has happened to me. I had been traveling for 5 years with a workhorse of a 486 notebook computer. Its only problem was its weight and that it could no longer really keep up with the demands I was placing on it. So, 3 weeks ago, I bought a brand spanking new Pentium notebook with all the bells and whistles. So what happens? Three weeks after I buy it, I take it with me to Malaysia. I am in the beginning stages of facilitating an online discussion which I really want to stay on top of, in addition to several hot, work-related issues that I have promised to stay in touch on. I arrive at my hotel, plug in the computer, turn it on, and discover that I have no display. I panic. I plug it into several different outlets and get the same response. I pull out the manual and pray that the trouble-shooting tips work. They don't. I'm jet-lagged, exhausted, upset, and angry. I decide that my only option is to go to sleep. The next morning, I wake up and as I'm reading the newspaper, I discover that there's a dealer for my brand of computer in the city I'm in. I call them, and shortly thereafter, me and my sick computer are in a taxi on the way to the shop.

When we arrive, the staff begins to ask questions about warranty. Of course, I hadn't thought to bring the sales receipt with me and what ensues are several phone calls to the States to get documentation faxed to me.

Then, the internal politics take over. Since this is a branch of a larger company, headquarters, which is 120 or so miles away, decides that they are the only ones who can do the warranty work. So off my computer goes via courier to HQ. Again I panic. What if it doesn't return in time for my departure? What if they can't fix it? As it turns out, both fears were justified. HQ suggested that the computer was so defective that I needed to just take it home with me and get a new one. Meanwhile, it didn't get back to me until about 2 hours before my scheduled departure.

So, how did I do what I needed to without a computer? Not very well. I sent faxes like a mad woman in an attempt to let people back home know why I'd disappeared from the virtual world. I found a cybercafe, which allowed me to access my e-mail. Meanwhile, the discussion group back home simply faded away and I felt irresponsible and horribly inadequate.

This nightmare—a true story experienced by one of the authors—shows one of the down sides of computer-mediated distance education. Although it is clearly the wave of the present and future, and many of us are working hard to stay on the crest of that wave, the fact that we are dependent on sometimes faulty hardware and software can make the ride more difficult than we anticipate. Those words on a screen are currently our only connection to one another when using this medium. When we are unable to gain or maintain access, we lose.

On the up side, however, there is nothing more exciting than having the mobility that comes with this form of teaching and learning. One is not place-based. It is certainly possible to teach a class from halfway around the world and teach it well. The keys, however, are flexibility and adaptability. Institutions, faculty, and their students need to be willing to enter new territory and experience the unknown. They should not do so unsupported, however.

Institutions, like their faculty, must engage in good planning in the delivery of online programs and courses and be willing to provide the level of support necessary to make the programs and courses a success. Anything less results in frustration on the part of both students and faculty, as well as a loss of confidence in the process of distance learning on the part of both. If institutions and faculty are unable or unwilling to make the commitment necessary to provide quality distance learning, they should not enter this arena.

PART TWO

BUILDING AN ELECTRONIC
LEARNING COMMUNITY

CHAPTER SIX

MAKING THE CONVERSION FROM THE CLASSROOM TO CYBERSPACE

This chapter marks the transition from the theoretical to the practical. In the first section of this book, we presented background material that we feel is critical to the understanding and implementation of our framework for distance education. Figure 6.1 shows a visual model of the components of that framework.

We now begin to deconstruct the model in order to provide suggestions and examples to the instructor who wishes to explore for the first time, or to reexamine, ways that effective courses may be delivered using distance education.

Effective Teaching and Learning in the Electronic Classroom

Mauri Collins and Zane Berge (1996) categorize the various tasks and roles demanded of the online instructor into four general areas: *pedagogical, social, managerial,* and *technical*. They describe the pedagogical function as one that revolves around educational facilitation. The social function, which we have been describing, is the promotion of the friendly social environment essential to online learning. The managerial function involves norms in agenda setting, pacing, objective setting, rule making, and decision making. The technical function depends on the instructor first becoming comfortable and proficient with the technology being used and then being able to transfer that level of comfort to the learners. Let us now take a look at each of these functions, based on the experience of our classes and seminars.

FIGURE 6.1. FRAMEWORK FOR DISTANCE LEARNING (REVISITED).

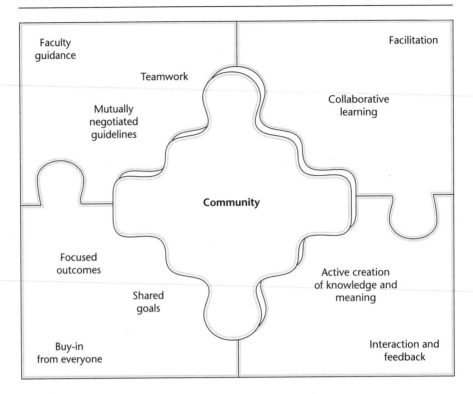

Educational Facilitation

Clearly, the role of the instructor, either in a traditional face-to-face or online setting, is to ensure that some type of educational process occurs among the learners involved. As we have discussed, in the face-to-face classroom that role is generally of the expert imparting knowledge to willing learners. In the online environment, the role of the instructor becomes that of an educational facilitator. As a facilitator, the instructor provides gentle guidance and a loosely constructed framework as a container for the course, thus allowing students to explore the course material, as well as related materials, without restriction. This is not done through the traditional use of lectures followed by some form of discussion. Instead, the instructor may provide general topics within the body of knowledge about which students together might read and make comment. Or the instructor may ask open-ended questions designed to stimulate critical thinking about the topics being discussed. Additionally, it is important for the instructor to make thoughtful comments on student posts, designed again to stimulate further discussion. As a part of this function, the instructor acts as a cheerleader, attempting to motivate students to go deeper and further with the material than they might in a face-to-face classroom. The following pieces of dialogue from one of our classes on organizational behavior demonstrate this function. The discussion was occurring around the reading of one of the books required for the course. A student comments on a number of other students' posts:

When you speak of common ground and getting as many constituents involved as possible I can't help but think of the appreciative inquiry model I am learning about now, it is very similar. [The author] comments on the power of getting folks involved. . . . Also the idea that the external environment helps shape the organization-everyone we have been reading as well as the appreciative inquiry model works with this concept. . . . In order to survive in this quickly changing market place now one must work with the external environment/forces. [The author] also speaks to this when she talks about designing the organization through the customers eye-and when she talks about the interdependence of competitors. *Cindy*

One of the authors, an instructor for the course, responds as follows:

I've done my review of [this book] and although I continue to be very impressed with her systems orientation, I'm going to do a little of my devil's advocate thing regarding her work. Quite honestly, it comes up a little short for me!! Does anyone else see her model as a little simplistic?? Although she asks great, wonderfully expansive questions on pages 60–64, the frameworks she presents on page 69 feel just as limiting to me as [some of the others we've discussed]. . . . The other concern I have is that I pick up a bit of Cartesian thinking throughout the book. The continuum model that she presents throughout the book . . . seems to contain a value judgement that fixed and adaptive organizations are not functional while only the inventive organization is. If this is the case, how then do fixed and adaptive organizations survive?? Additionally, I think it's a little naive to assume that adaptive organizations are political but that fixed and inventive organizations are not. Lastly, I have some difficulty with her definitions of power. [The author] seems to be indicating that Power With [or relational power] is the only acceptable source in an organization.

Another participant responds:

What great questions, reflections, and analysis. I mentioned once, I think, that I find myself easily seduced by structural — categorical — thinking and theory. It is so nice and easy to put things in boxes. And I find that I am just now able to let go of this comfort. So, personally, Cindy, I think that I am an example of what you are wisely suggesting — which is that we need to have a bridge to the new paradigm . . . (And, by the way, it occurred to me that [this author's] simplicity may serve as an easy introduction, a bridge, to change . . .). . . . We live in a sound-bit, speedy society where I think that it is easy to forget this and instead to hope that we will be able to facilitate a paradigmatic — or even an incremental change — in short order. Instead, I think that we have to de-velop strategic vision and be comfortable with short-term goals. *Judie*

As these bits of dialogue illustrate, the instructor as educational facilitator gen-tly guides the discussion by asking pointed, expansive, and sometimes difficult ques-tions and then follows the discussion wherever it might lead.

Community Building

As we have discussed in previous chapters, the instructor in an online class is re-sponsible for facilitating and making room for the personal and social aspects of an online community in order for the class to be a successful learning experience. Collins and Berge (1996) refer to this function as "promoting human relationships, affirming and recognizing students' input; providing opportunities for students to develop a sense of group cohesiveness, maintaining the group as a unit, and in other ways helping members to work together in a mutual cause" (p. 7). These el-ements are the essence of the principles needed to build and maintain a virtual community listed in earlier chapters. How, then, does an instructor go about build-ing this sense of group or community? Most online instructors begin their classes with the use of student introductions as a way to begin to know one another as people. Simply jumping into the course material without this creates an atmos-phere that is dry and sterile, devoid of any sense that there are people engaged here. Many instructors make use of designed group activities, simulations, and group projects as another means of facilitating a sense of being a group.

What we like to do in every one of our seminars and courses, is to create a space in the course site where everyone, instructors and students alike, can let their hair down and be comfortable with one another—a community space if you will. We may give it a title to begin with but are open to changing that title as the course progresses and students have input into what it should be called. It might be the Cyberspace Sandbox, the Coffee House, the Lounge, or simply Important Stuff. Certainly, some of the personal material will become mixed with the discussion of course material. However, we try to keep that space separate and sacred. The following fairly lengthy piece of dialogue is an example of how we kept track of the personal in a class on management and organizational behavior:

Rena: Hello All! I'm in a cybercafe in Malaysia and have found that Internet access is pretty easy and cheap here — only the equivalent of $2.80 for an hour! So I should be able to join you online at least twice a week while I'm here. I'm glad to see that many of you have posted your intro's. Hopefully, the discussion of [our first book] will start shortly and I'll be able to join that as well. Just a couple of quick words about Malaysia — a very interesting, and very HOT, HUMID place! Wonderful people and incredible food! Lots of American computer companies here, making for a fairly complicated multinational environment. Most are computer companies and Malaysia is being called "Silicon Valley East." As I learn more about management and organizations Malaysian style, I'll attempt to post my observations online, especially as they relate to our readings. More later. Hope you're all doing well!

Jennifer: Hi Rena, greetings to you in Penang. Yes I know exactly what you mean by HOT and HUMID. Singapore is 2 degrees above the equator and probably even a wee bit warmer than Penang (!) My father's side of the family is from Malaysia though they mostly live in the capital, Kuala Lumpur. However my mother used to have cousins in Penang, so I have been there a number of times as a child. Yes the food IS incredible. I am very proud of our food:) Having travelled this much now I can say without a doubt that we have the best combination of the different Asian foods and mix of East and West. As to Malaysia being called "Silicon Valley East", well, there will be many Singaporeans that will disagree and tell you that it is Singapore.

Keith: Hi Rena, Most of you probably don't know that I opened the center in Penang where Rena is now. Great bunch of people and some REALLY great food. I've tried Iguana, jellyfish, cuttlefish, rabbit, squirrel, etc. over there. Anyway yes the learning styles are different and I hope Rena will relate her experiences to us as they happen. For instance its very difficult to persuade the students to engage in a discussion with the Professor, because they've been taught that the professor is IT. The expert, so to get them to discuss issues and debate the relevance etc. is very challenging for the instructor, but I also find them more dedicated and motivated than my American undergradute students.

Judie: Oh, Jennifer. Thank you for joining in the discussion. You have so much to offer all of us. Please keep adding to our education. I am struck at how my thinking of management and organizational theory (and almost every other facet of life) has expanded because Rena is in Malaysia and is sharing her perspectives, responses, and questions. Jennifer, it prompts me to ask how you experience the Western concepts and how, and whether, they are in contrast to what you have experienced and learned. Singaporeans have, in some ways it seems to me, utilized some of "our" concepts and reshaped them. I particularly appreciate your vision and perspective that the conflict between Malaysia and Singapore will pass. What underlies your perspective? Thanks again to all of you for the richness that you are offering me.

Cindy: This is a very interesting conversation to me. I, on a much smaller scale, am experiencing a different culture. The VERY relaxed culture of Kauai. When Michael and I first got here we were running around trying to rent our car, get some food at the store and get to our cottage before it got dark. The woman who checked us out at the market said "you just got here hey?". And we said yes how can you tell, is it because we are so pale? And she said "no I know because you are in such a hurry." We laughed thinking to ourselves, hey this is our normal speed. Now mind you Michael and I run on some big energy, but being here shows us how driven we are. And the question is, is it the way to be? Hum??? Most folks here work two to three jobs to make ends meet, and a lot of them grow their own food. They just seem to make it financially, but they have a damn good life here. It makes you rethink our western drive to succeed, I have that western gene, or is it a cultural drive? Either one I am questioning it now, wondering why it is so hard to let go even for a moment??? Aloha!

In Chapter Three, we focused on all of the issues and elements embedded in this kind of interchange and the need to address them in some way in the creation of an online community. This bit of discussion further illustrates how these human elements inevitably emerge when human beings connect in this medium. The sharing of our lives, including our travels, our observations, our emotions, and who we are as people is deliberately brought into the classroom in an effort to promote group cohesion and connection. The dialogue presented definitely helped this group to begin to know each other as people, thereby increasing their level of comfort in working together. Just as a face-to-face group about to embark on a group assignment needs to get to know one another as a part of the process of developing trust in order to begin their work together, so does the online group need to develop this same sense of trust. The sharing of who we are as people begins to build that container of trust. As we have stated previously, it is this type of effort that is critical to the development of a learning community in the online classroom.

Administration

The instructor in an online course is also the course administrator, who posts a syllabus for the course, including assignments and some initial guidelines for the group to discuss and adopt or adapt; the instructor gently facilitates the flow of the course and evaluates the outcomes.

We generally post a syllabus, guidelines, and the accepted rules of "netiquette" at the beginning of a course. We then ask the participants to comment on all of this and to discuss their hopes for the course. What do they see as desired learning outcomes? What do they hope to gain by participating? All of this is open to negotiation within broad limits. For example, we generally set a minimum expectation of two substantive posts per week per participant. We would be unwilling to negotiate below that number, but we certainly are open to negotiating more participation if the group wants that, as many have. We are also willing—and we have done so—to renegotiate assignments if it becomes clear through interaction with the group that those assignments are not contributing to a positive learning outcome. (In Chapter Seven, we provide sample syllabi, guidelines, and assignments to further illustrate these elements.)

Evaluating outcomes, both in terms of the learning process and learner satisfaction with the course, is a more complex process in the online classroom. This is further complicated by the orientation or requirements of the host institution for particular outcomes. Some of these will be further discussed in Chapter Ten. Although some instructors prefer to continue to use examinations in this setting, and many software applications for distance education allow for that, we tend to lean toward the use of papers that may be individually generated or generated by a small group and posted online. Feedback on those papers is provided by all participants, thus promoting the development of skills in providing good feedback as well. In addition, we evaluate the quality of posts throughout the course in terms of evidence of critical thinking ability and the learner's ability to generate knowledge and make meaning of the course material. Evaluation, then, becomes a more qualitative process. Additionally, at the end of the course, we ask students to evaluate the outcomes based on their initial expectations. The following are two reflections on course content for a management and organizational behavior class we previously presented:

From all of the reading and discussion this quarter, I would have to say that the new paradigm is not clearly defined "out there" . . . I have gathered many new bits of information from our reading and discussion, and am working on synthesizing it all together to form my own definition of the new paradigm, or at least to clarify my thinking on what I would like to see occur in organizations. When thinking about this topic, I tend to go back to something we discussed earlier online; that whatever change will take place will have to start with each individual. As long as there are individuals in power within organizations denying that the old way is no longer working, and holding firmly to old scientific belief systems, the new paradigm cannot seep through. I guess I am trying to be realistic, since I have seen so many situations that totally kill any motivation and spirit within the company, but business goes on as usual without any major consequences as far as management goes.

The employees are suffering, and less effective in their work, but it doesn't get any notice from the "leaders". *Cindy*

I think that the definition of "new paradigm" in organization can be found where the organization standing on. That is to say, the level of the organization is different even the components of organization such as human resources or systems, policy and so on. . . . To recognize or reach to new paradigm, organization needs to be shifted to new world. In order to reach there, it is the essential things to change mindset of people in organization. I don't think that this concept is purely Westernized construct. Paradigms is always in everywhere and everyone. As we discussed on previous reading, we can closely connect the "new paradigm" to "metaphor". In order for managers to shift their paradigm is to imply a fundamental perceptions and profiles from the old paradigm. *Soomo*

Both of these examples indicate the evidence of critical thinking skills as well as an attempt on the part of the learner to "bring it all home," as it were, by articulating the meaning that has been derived from the exploration. They both indicate a positive learning outcome and successful completion of this learning experience.

Technical Facilitation

Collins and Berge (1996) discuss this function in terms of the instructor first becoming proficient and comfortable with the technology so as to ensure the comfort of the participants and to make the technology as transparent as possible. We find that this function goes well beyond this, as we described in Chapter Five. Certainly, faculty need to be competent enough with the technology to facilitate the course. However, we would hope that there is sufficient support available to them so that even a less proficient instructor could successfully run a course online.

Another more important function here is the ability of the instructor to create a double-loop in the learning process. In other words, because we know that instructors need to teach differently in this medium and that learners function differently, it is important to acknowledge that stream of learning in the overall learning process. The questions that arise related to this stream of learning are: How does learning and knowledge generation differ when we learn online? How does technology contribute to that? What do we learn about technology when we engage in learning in this way?

Just as we create a separate space for community in our courses, we also create a separate space to track our responses to these questions. We may title it, as we did in one course, something like, Electronic Learning and Other Friendly Stuff. What is important is that this stream become acknowledged and tracked. It is a place where participants can discuss their discomfort in interacting with technology as well as celebrate their successes in mastering it. Take the following examples of reflections on electronic learning:

Well hum, thought, thought, thought, hum. . . . (That is my brain in action.) This on-line component has been a big change for me. Although it isn't my style I see the great importance of the medium. The way I am dealing with this change is just making myself do it, and I must say I enjoy it more and more. I can just see it now, I will probably be one of those people who ends up loving on-line learning! Stranger things have happened— *Cindy*

In my case you are right about the curriculum and the learning being of interest. The online program was also exciting because it was a new challenge for me, and would help me to have the tools to move into the new millennium. I am, however, having difficulty getting accustomed to learning this way. I don't seem to learn as solidly through this type of free discussion as I do from a more direct outline format. I tend to get lost trying to sort out what is important when there is so much discussed. The reading online is very interesting, but deciding what to respond to seems to take more of my energy than actually learning and applying my learning. *Julie*

Learning through the use of technology, then, takes more than mastery of a software program or comfort with the hardware being used. It takes an awareness of the impact that this form of learning has on the learning process itself. Additionally, as this last bit of dialogue reveals, some students believe that online learning is not "real" learning. Another responsibility of the instructor, then, is to help contextualize this form of learning and facilitate a needed paradigm shift for the learner in order to allow this form of learning to have its greatest impact. (We discuss concrete suggestions for facilitating this shift in Chapter Nine.)

The Role of the Learner in the Learning Process

As we consider that learning process, what do we need to consider regarding the role of the learner? We have already stated many times that the successful learner in the online environment is active and engaged in knowledge generation. Let us now turn to the responsibilities of the learner in an online classroom. As we were able to categorize and thus more easily explore the roles of the instructor in the online classroom, so we are able to do the same with the roles of the learner. Although somewhat different from faculty roles, all of the roles are very much intertwined and interdependent. They are *knowledge generation, collaboration,* and *process management.* As we did with the roles of the instructor, we will now look at each of these individually.

Knowledge Generation

When we discussed the educational facilitation role of the instructor, we stated that the instructor serves only as a gentle guide in the educational process. What this implies, then, is that the recipient of that guidance—the learner—is responsible for using the guidance in a meaningful way. In the online classroom, this means that learners are responsible for actively seeking solutions to problems contained within the broad confines of the knowledge area being studied and raising the level of those solutions to one of more complexity. They are expected to view problems and questions from a number of perspectives, including the perspectives of the other learners involved in the process. They are expected to question the assumptions presented by the instructor and those of the other students, as well their own assumptions and ideas. In so doing, learners in the online classroom are generating the preferred learning outcome for this type of course: the construction of new forms of knowledge and meaning. By engaging in the learning process in this way, learners are learning about learning as well as gaining research and critical-thinking skills.

As we have seen in some of the course dialogue, learners should be able to critically evaluate their own learning style in addition to learning something about the area under study. As all of this is occurring, students should be gathering additional resources that are pertinent to the area under study and that go beyond the materials assigned. In doing so, their skills and their confidence as researchers should be developing; this development is considered to be a successful learning outcome.

Collaboration

Students in the online learning environment are not expected to undertake this process alone. The failing of many computer-mediated distance learning programs has been the inability or unwillingness to facilitate a collaborative learning process. In this environment, students should be expected to work together to generate deeper levels of understanding and critical evaluation of the material under study. In the process of seeking out additional materials for this purpose, students should be expected to share the resources they are finding with the other members of the group. Frequently, students will find an interesting website, article, or book that they become excited about sharing with others. In fact, this type of search and the reporting back to the group on the results can be an effective assignment leading to the expected learning outcomes of the course. We frequently expect students to generate a bibliography of readings. We get them started with a few suggestions, but it is up to the group to seek out and post other materials of interest in order to enrich the learning process for all group members.

This medium is perfect for the facilitation of this form of learning. In addition to meeting together at the course site, students with similar interests should be encouraged to "meet" in other ways and work together. They might exchange e-mail in order to further discuss a problem or to share information. They might also collaboratively prepare a report or paper to share with the others in the group. Additionally, students should be guided and encouraged in their ability to give each other meaningful feedback on their work—feedback that goes beyond giving one another pats on the back for good work; it should comment substantively on the ideas presented. All of this assists in the development of the critical-thinking skills necessary to effectively engage in the knowledge-generation role described previously.

Another means by which collaboration can happen is by facilitating dialogue *between* learning communities. By this we mean that instructors who are teaching similar courses, either in the same or different universities, can encourage and even facilitate discussion among participants in those classes. One group might research and prepare a presentation for another group, the outcome being the enhanced learning of both groups. This type of collaboration also increases the resources available to the participants as they explore areas of interest within the loosely defined boundaries of the knowledge area under study. Just the ability to study online can stimulate interest in collaborative work. As students discover that they are able to connect, using the Internet, with other universities and learning communities, their interest in doing so while working in other course areas also increases. Instructors can promote this type of activity through creative assignments that promote communication with other groups. (Further discussion of collaborative learning can be found in Chapter Eight.)

Process Management

The role of process manager is the one that most significantly sets this form of teaching and learning apart from the face-to-face classroom. As an active learner, students are expected to participate within minimal guidelines, interact and engage with one another, speak up if the course or discussion is moving in a direction that is uncomfortable for them in any way, and take responsibility for the formation of the online learning community. Take the following example of students speaking out in response to one of the author's posts as an instructor in the reflections on electronic learning section in an online course:

Most of you have mentioned that technology is the barrier or is at the very least uncomfortable for you. This is to be expected with any "new" medium of communication and learning, just as learning a new language is, but think what would've happened if we had given up on the telephone because it was uncomfortable. In this medium several things become magnified and several become almost nonexistent. For instance what you say online is recorded for people to read over and over again, no chance to change it once posted, just to clarify and explain. So people naturally spend more time formulating their thoughts and what they want to say before opening their "virtual mouth" (Except Rena and I). Rena and I often talk without having our brain connected to our virtual mouths' (keyboards). As you become more comfortable with the medium, this will likely occur for all of you. Physical cues such as touch, smell, body-language, etc. are missing leading to some difficulty, such as misperceptions, flaming, misunderstandings, etc. We learn to deal with this by inserting emotion (emoticons) into our writing. Emoticons are symbols that are used by the online community for emotion and expression such as :) (grin, smiling) ;) (wink) these are made by using the standard kybd characters. One of the surprising things I have found is that people with extraverted (British spelling) personalities have difficulty in online communication if they cannot quickly establish an online presence such as they do in social f–2–f settings. Once they discover that there is a lack of their presence they may even disappear (not participate) in online communication. Hence arrogant, egotistical people are somewhat disempowered and shun online communication and make excuses for not utilizing it. Offline introverts seem to thrive online. They have time to gather their thoughts before posting and seem to really enjoy the medium because they don't have to deal with the Physical presence of anyone. For instance I was conducting a seminar online and was impressed with the ability of one participant to continuously post incredibly wise quotes, until I discovered that this person was looking up quotes from old masters and posting them without giving proper credit. He didn't seek to deceive just to impress. Oh well enough of my ramblings, let me know what ya think!! *Keith*

A student responds:

Maybe we have an example of misunderstanding here and maybe not. Your assumptions about extroverted people seems odd to me especially after many have honestly stated their difficulty with on-line communications. You say about extroverts "arrogant, egotistical people are somewhat disempowered and shun on-line communication and make excuses for not utilizing it". Isn't this a bit harsh????? *Cindy*

And another student says:

Yes Keith I wonder too about your generalizations. I have always considered myself an introvert . . . but still am uncomfortable online . . . "arrogant, egotistical people . . . " seems to be harsh and to be oversimplified. *Tonia*

Keith's response:

Dear Group, I want to apologize for sounding so harsh in my last posting. I did not mean to insinuate that all extroverts are arrogant or egotistical or that all people who have difficulty utilizing the medium or getting used to the environment are making excuses to avoid exposure. What I meant to say is that in some cases this is true, especially in upper level management where the manager feels intimidated by the technology. I want to say that I respect and care about all human beings and would never stereotype or demean any group of people. I was just trying to make a point from observations I have made in my past experience. I have seen managers go crazy with the technology, insist on sending email when the workers are across the hallway. Sending warnings and establishing rules for sending email. I could go on and on, but I believe that our personaes do change online and sometimes radically. Please forgive me if I have offended anyone, that was not my intent and please accept my apology.

Clearly, this example shows the willingness of students to speak out in this medium when they are offended, uncomfortable, or simply have an opinion on something. The instructor's response shows the necessary willingness in this medium to leave behind the traditional power boundaries that exist between instructor and student to resolve the conflict and move the learning process forward. This medium has been described as the great equalizer, essentially eliminating the boundaries that exist between cultures, genders, and ages, and also eliminating power differences. Faculty must be able to relinquish their role of power within and over the educational process in order to allow the learners to take on their process management role. In fact, we frequently find that we learn as much from our students in an online course as our students learn from us. One author's response to a student post is an example of the ways in which this might occur:

Interesting thoughts, Cindy. You've made me look at Morgan's work from another angle! Frequently, I use his concept of metaphor and image to look at what already exists in the organization as a part of my assessment of it. And, in fact, Morgan in his application chapter suggests the same (ordering sort of hierarchically the metaphors in existence). I've not considered planful use of his metaphors in the creation of an organization, but I do think it has merit. Our discussion with [our guest speaker] on Sunday to some degree touched on this (I do hope you're able to get the tapes!). [He] talked about essentially doing a monthly "report card" in staff meetings where staff would each comment on how well the mission and vision of the organization are playing out in day-to-day operation. He felt that all "votes" would be equal in terms of looking at how well the organization is functioning, or not. If one area continuously shows up deficient, then they would need to strategize ways to improve it. When we discussed the need for consciousness in organizations . . . , I think this is what we may have had in mind as an example of at least attempting to be conscious about the business at hand. [His] is a small organization and can probably accommodate this kind of conscious evaluation process easily. In a larger organization it would be lots more difficult, I agree.

The ability, then, to remain flexible and open, and to relinquish control are characteristics that make not only for successful instructors in this medium but for successful learners as well. We must all maintain an attitude of being in this together and a willingness to adapt and adjust as we move along in the process. The ability for students to speak out in this regard, without fear of repercussion, must be there. Faculty must be able to communicate that this is not only acceptable but necessary in order for students to be able to take on the roles necessary to facilitate educational success in the online classroom.

Moving to Specifics

It is important now to turn to how these roles and functions are operationalized in a course. As we have presented sessions at conferences and workshops regarding teaching online, we find that instructors are always most concerned with such issues as:

- How do I convert a course to be effective online?
- Are there differences in the type of syllabus created?
- How do I learn to feel comfortable in this medium, and how do I get my students to overcome their fear of technology?
- How do I make this all happen and happen quickly?

In the next several chapters, we will devote our attention to the detail of course creation and maintenance in the online environment. We have included several examples of our own as well as those created by other instructors who are successfully teaching online. In addition, we have included questions for consideration that can help turn all of this into action. We hope this will help readers get their hands around the concept we call *electronic pedagogy* and begin to recognize that it is not course conversion that needs to occur but rather a paradigm shift regarding the way we view ourselves as educators, view our students, and view education itself.

CHAPTER SEVEN

BUILDING FOUNDATIONS

Up to this point, we have been describing the issues and elements that make up our framework for distance learning. For this and the next several chapters, we will move into the detail of how to create a successful course. In this chapter, we look at what is involved in the creation of an effective course: creating an appropriate syllabus for online teaching, setting objectives, negotiating guidelines, setting up the course site online, gaining participation and student buy-in, and accounting for presence in the electronic classroom.

As we present each topic, we include concrete examples from our courses as well as those of other instructors who have had positive outcomes in this medium. To delineate each piece of the process of building a good course foundation, the course syllabi have been broken into the components that correspond with the topic being presented. The examples presented are from the social sciences. However, many instructors from all disciplines are teaching a wide variety of courses online, including but not limited to English composition, humanities, hard sciences such as physics and engineering, computer science, and mathematics. (The complete syllabi are presented in Resource A.)

Creating an Effective Syllabus

Many instructors have mistakenly assumed that teaching online involves what is termed *curriculum conversion*. We argue that it is not the curriculum we are converting but our pedagogy. The creation of an effective online course involves a paradigm shift regarding the mode of delivery of the course material. Three basic steps are involved in creating an effective syllabus for an online course: (1) defining outcomes and objectives, (2) choosing appropriate reading material, and (3) establishing a topic-driven course outline.

Establishing Outcomes and Objectives

As with any good course, an instructor needs to begin with the end in mind. What do we want our students to learn as they interact with this course material? What skills and abilities should they be able to take with them at the end of the course? In the online course, the syllabus is deliberately left more open to allow students to develop new ideas, exercise critical-thinking skills, and develop research skills. Objectives, then, may be more broadly defined so that participants can take courses in unanticipated directions, based on their own interests and needs. However, in planning an online course, it is still important to consider expected outcomes as the course is being developed. Exhibit 7.1 shows examples of course objectives from several different classes to illustrate this concept.

As is evident through these examples, the development of course objectives for the online course does not differ much from the development of objectives for the face-to-face course. In fact, those presented would work as well in a face-to-face class as they do online; differentiation appears in the way the course is structured and presented through the course syllabus.

The Syllabus

Once the objectives have been determined, the next step is to create an effective syllabus, including topics for discussion, expectations for participation, and ways the class will be evaluated; a detailed outline describing the topics to be presented or discussed in each class is unnecessary. Instead, broad topic headings give students a general idea of what will be considered and discussed in the course. The syllabus in the online classroom should be more open, allowing students more leeway for exploration. We have found that the most successful classes are guided by a syllabus that is topic-driven. In other words, the weekly "schedule" for the class includes a discussion topic for the week, with readings geared to spark discussion of that topic. Another successful format is to structure the course around the required readings, allowing the material in the readings to create the discussion. Examples of both types of syllabi are given in Exhibit 7.2.

Courses like science, math, art, or music that do not lend themselves to the reading and discussion format may look very different. A science or math class,

EXHIBIT 7.1. SAMPLE LEARNING OBJECTIVES FOR ONLINE COURSES.

Management and Organizational Theory (Graduate Level Class):

Summary of Educational Purpose:

The purpose of this course is to introduce learners to post-modern philosophy as applied to management and organizations, to provide examples of new paradigm thinking in business, and to introduce one or more methodologies for applying new paradigm theories in the everyday, real world operation of businesses, non-profits, and government agencies. The course also provides a grounding in the history and theory of management and organizations in America. Finally, the course is intended to encourage learners to increase their exposure to and application of emergent management practices and organization designs that are humane, socially responsible, and ecologically sound.

Learning Objectives:

After completing this course, learners will be able to:

1. Understand the historical and cultural foundations of mainstream American management;
2. Articulate the strengths and weaknesses of the old paradigm;
3. Understand the historical and cultural reasons for a new paradigm;
4. Build awareness of what the new paradigm looks like and might include;
5. Appreciate when and how elements of the old paradigm need to be applied, and
6. Apply elements of new paradigm theory and practice.

Topics in Business Administration: The Search for Soul and Spirit in the Workplace (Graduate Level Class):

Introduction, Course Overview, and Objectives:

Writers in the area of organizational change talk about the constant change that besieges today's organizations as "turbulence" or "permanent whitewater." Rightsizing, re-engineering, and globalization are but a few of the changes having significant effect on the people who work in organizations. Jack Canfield and Jacqueline Miller (1996) in their book *Heart at Work* state, "The work environment in modern organizations leads to a parching of the human spirit. In reaction against this, people are speaking out for 'heart at work,' for 'spirit in the workplace.' We find a growing insistence that every part of society—especially the workplace where so many spend so large a portion of their lives—be conducive to the fullest development of the human being" (p. xi). Organizational writers have begun to pay attention to this growing demand and have begun to explore not only the importance of soul and spirit in the workplace, but also their implications for leadership and organizational transformation. This course will explore recent writings regarding the search for soul and spirit in the workplace, as well as how it impacts the notions of meaningful work, leadership, and organizational change.

Treatment and Recovery in Chemical Dependency (Graduate Level and Continuing Education Class):

(Continued)

EXHIBIT 7.1. Continued.

Goals & Objectives of this course:

At the conclusion of the course the student should:

1. Know the background of society's historical responses to abuse and addiction.
2. Identify the role denial plays in the assessment, intervention, and treatment process and can develop appropriate strategies to address this.
3. Know the probable effects of chemical dependency on the family system and can appropriately engage the family in the identification, intervention, and treatment process.
4. Know the basic approaches to identification, intervention, and treatment of chemical dependency.
5. Know the importance of the 12 Step programs in the recovery process for both the chemically dependent and their families.
6. Be able to identify the salient issues involved in chemical dependency treatment as they relate to issues of gender, lifestyle, culture, and life span.
7. Know case management principles, techniques, and standards of practice for the treatment of chemical dependency, utilizing the development model of recovery in social and/or medical settings.
8. Apply the essential elements of chemical dependency case management in assessment practices, treatment planning, progress documentation, discharge, and aftercare planning.
9. Know a variety of approaches and modalities effective in treating chemical dependency and its related problems, can implement preferred approaches, and apply appropriate counseling strategies and techniques.

Organizational Behavior (Undergraduate Level Class):

Course Description:

This course is designed as a study of human behavior in organizational settings; the organization's effect on employee perceptions, feelings, and actions; and the employee's effect on the organization. Emphasis is placed on the attainment of organizational goals through the effective utilization of people.

Goals and Objectives:

Upon successful completion of this course the student will be able to discuss, analyze and critically reflect upon:

Cultural influences on organizational behavior.

Group behavior and its effect on organizations and their structure.

Effective utilization of motivation and the theoretical constructs supporting it.

Team concepts within and outside the organization.

Processes and systems within and outside organizations that influence their structure and behavior.

The concept and constructs of organizational change and how to manage it.

Quantitative Methods (Graduate Level Class):

Course Description:
An examination of the formulation, use and interpretation of mathematical models for making sound business decisions. Models include linear programming, PERT/CPM, decision trees, inventory, queuing, and Markovian processes.

Course Objectives:

1. To help students formulate, use, and interpret mathematical models commonly used in business.
2. To see and use computerized models demonstrated in the text, software and others.

for example, may have a written "lecture" by the instructor to explain a procedure or theory. Students may be expected to complete problems on their own or in groups and submit the results to the instructor for evaluation. Discussion may take the form of questions about the material directed to the instructor or to other students to promote collaboration. Many science classes requiring labs make arrangements with remote facilities so that students can do their laboratory work. One instructor at Johns Hopkins University created a "virtual lab," where students could conduct simulated experiments on the World Wide Web (Kiernan, 1997). Some instructors provide supplementary material on video or CD-ROM, which students can then respond to online. Many art instructors scan artwork so students can view and discuss it online. Similarly, students can scan and upload their own artwork to complete assignments. Generally speaking, however, most online courses contain areas for presenting material to students, for asynchronous discussion, for posting assignments, and sometimes for taking exams; the ability to send e-mail is usually included. Some courseware also contains an area for synchronous chat, which can occur between two or more students or the entire group.

Course Guidelines

It is extremely important to begin the class with clear guidelines for acceptable participation. These guidelines are generally presented along with the syllabus and course outline as a means of creating some structure around the course. In addition, the guidelines can be used as a first discussion item. We have learned the hard way that if clear participation guidelines are not established, the course does not go well. What we assume is understood may not be as clear to our participants. For example, simply stating that participants must log on twice a week says nothing about what they are expected to do during that online session. One of our students

EXHIBIT 7.2. SAMPLE COURSE SYLLABI FOR ONLINE COURSES.

Syllabus for Management and Organizational Theory:

This is a graduate level class meeting both online and face-to-face. This syllabus illustrates organization of the course using the readings as an organizational tool.

Learning Activities:

Learning Activities	Percent of Class Time
1. Facilitation of and participation in online dialogue	30 percent
2. Experiential exercises and case studies	10 percent
3. Participation in face-to-face meetings	30 percent
4. Final integrative paper based on application of material generated in class to an organization in the community	30 percent

In general, learning activities consist of reading, learner reflections on the reading, discussion, experiential exercises, analysis of cases, application of the materials to an organization in the community, and integration through a final paper.

Readings: Learners will complete all reading assignments in timely fashion in order to facilitate group learning and discussion, which requires full and equal participation from each individual. Each learner will take responsibility for facilitating two weeks of the online discussion during the quarter, thus assisting the learning group in sharing the reading load. However, each learner is accountable for enough familiarity with the material to adequately reflect on the readings' impact on group discussion.

Learner Reflections: As learners complete the readings, they are expected to identify a list of key concepts, ideas, and questions. These should comprise the basis for online discussion. Learners may choose to enhance these thoughts and questions through reading additional material and sharing those readings online with the learning group.

Experiential Exercises/Cases: During the face-to-face meetings, learners will participate in exercises and will complete case studies designed to stimulate and enhance learning. These will be completed as a small group. In addition, each learner will be asked to write up and turn in two case studies. One will be due at the second face-to-face meeting and one at the last face-to-face meeting.

Final Integrative Paper: At the beginning of the quarter, learners will be expected to choose an organization in the community with which they wish to form a relationship and study. During the course of the quarter, students will be encouraged to visit the organization and explore the application of the concepts discussed through the readings, online, and in the face-to-face meetings with members of that organization. At the completion of the course, learners will write a 7–10 page paper integrating the readings, discussion, and the study of this organization, illustrating the presence or absence of new paradigm thinking within this organization.

Criteria for Evaluation:	Facilitation of and participation in online dialogue	30 percent
	Case studies and experiential exercises	30 percent
	Final integrative paper	40 percent

Required Texts:

Bennis, W., Parikh, J., and Lessem, R. (1995/96), *Beyond Leadership: Balancing Economics, Ethics, and Ecology.* Cambridge, MA: Blackwell Press.

Bolman, L. and Deal, T. (1991), *Reframing Organizations: Artistry, Choice, and Leadership.* San Francisco: Jossey-Bass.

Janov, J. (1994), *The Inventive Organization: Hope and Daring at Work.* San Francisco: Jossey-Bass.

Morgan, G. (1986), *Images of Organization.* Newbury Park, CA: Sage Publications.

Specific Assignments:

Specific assignments for this course will be posted online beginning the first week of the quarter. We will begin by reading Bolman and Deal's *Reframing Organizations* and discussing their ideas online.

Course Assignments (Posted online):

READING and OTHER ASSIGNMENTS

The following are the reading and written assignments for the quarter corresponding to the week they are due. I will create a separate discussion item for each book that we will be reading, but this will give you an overview.

April 7–April 13:	Introductions, check-ins, and expectations (Rena will facilitate)
April 13:	First face-to-face meeting (Agenda to be posted)
April 14–April 27:	Reading and discussion of Bolman and Deal, *Reframing Organizations*
April 28–May 11:	Reading and discussion of Morgan, *Images of Organization*
May 11:	Second face-to-face meeting (Agenda to be posted) **First written case study due**
May 12–May 25:	Reading and discussion of Janov, *The Inventive Organization*
May 26–June 8:	Reading and discussion of Bennis, Parikh, and Lessem, *Beyond Leadership*
June 9–June 15	What have we learned? Do we now have a holistic vision of organizations and management? What does that look like? How does it apply to the organizations we've studied? (Rena will facilitate)
June 15:	Final face-to-face meeting (Agenda to be posted) **Second written case study due** **Final integrative paper due and presented to the group**

Syllabus for Topics in Business Administration: The Search for Soul and Spirit in the Workplace:

This is a graduate level class with an initial face-to-face meeting and the remainder of the class occurring online. The course is organized around topics for discussion.

Methods to Achieve Course Objectives:

1. This course will be taught online. All students are required to participate actively in the online discussion. (*Please see the guidelines attached to this syllabus.*)

(Continued)

EXHIBIT 7.2. Continued.

2. Required Reading:
   Bolman, Lee and Deal, Terrence (1995), *Leading With Soul,* San Francisco: Jossey-Bass.
   Canfield, Jack and Miller, Jacqueline (1996), *Heart at Work,* New York: McGraw-Hill.
   Conger, Jay (1994), *Spirit at Work,* San Francisco: Jossey-Bass.
   Covey, Stephen (1990), *The 7 Habits of Highly Effective People,* New York: Simon & Schuster.
   Whyte, David (1994), *The Heart Aroused,* New York: Currency Doubleday.

3. Written Assignments:
   There are 3 written assignments for this course. They are:
   a. Visit a website devoted to issues of soul and spirit at work (there are many, trust us!) and write a brief paper evaluating the site and the information contained therein. This paper will be posted online by the due date contained in the schedule which follows.
   b. Complete a case study evaluation. The case will be provided by the instructors. Your evaluation will be posted online by the due date contained in the schedule which follows.
   c. Complete a final paper on one of the following:

   Write a 5 to 7 page paper on any topic related to soul and spirit in the workplace that has been touched on in this class. In order to complete this assignment, please read at least 2 additional sources besides those assigned in class.

   Complete an evaluation of the organization for which you work, addressing issues related to soul and spirit in the workplace. How are they manifested in your place of work, or are they absent? Please read at least 2 additional sources besides those assigned in class to support your work.

4. Attend one face-to-face meeting of the class. This will be held on Friday, January 16. The place of the meeting is to be announced.

Evaluation:

Evaluation of student performance in this course will be conducted as follows:

Number, content, and relevancy of online postings	40 percent
Website evaluation and case study	30 percent
Final Paper	30 percent

Please note: *Students will not be able to pass this class without participating in the on-line discussion. Consequently, if you are having technical or other difficulties with your participation, please contact the instructors immediately.*

"Schedule of Classes"

Please note that reading assignments are for the following week.

Week 1 (January 12–18):
• Students will post introductions online including hopes and expectations for the course
   Reading Assignments: Bolman and Deal, entire book

Week 2 (January 19–25):
- Soul, Spirit, Organizational Change and Transformation
  Reading Assignments: Conger, Chapters 1–3; Whyte, Chapters 1 and 2

Week 3 (January 26–February 1):
- Defining soul and spirit
  Reading Assignments: Conger, Chapters 4–6; Whyte, Chapters 3 and 4

Week 4 (February 2–8):
- Finding soul and spirit in the workplace
  Reading Assignments: Conger, Chapters 7 and 8; Whyte, Chapters 5 and 6

Website Assignment Due This Week

Week 5 (February 9–15):
- Leadership, motivation, soul, and spirit
  Reading Assignments: Canfield, Parts 1 and 2; Whyte, Chapters 7 and 8

Week 6 (February 16–22):
- Soul, spirit, and self-esteem
  Reading Assignments: Canfield, Parts 3 and 4

Week 7 (February 23–March 1):
- Soul, spirit, and the bottom line
  Reading Assignments: Canfield, Parts 5 and 6

Week 8 (March 2–8):
- Meaningful work
  Reading Assignments: Covey, Parts 1 and 2

Case Study Due This Week

Week 9 (March 9–15):
- "New paradigm" organizations and their relationship to soul and spirit
  Reading Assignments: Covey, Parts 3 and 4

Week 10 (March 16–21):
- Avoiding burnout through spiritual practice in the workplace

Week 11 (March 21–28):
- Summing up—What have we learned? How can we apply what we've learned?

Final Paper Due

Syllabus for Treatment and Recovery in Chemical Dependency:

This course is a graduate level course involving an initial and ending face-to-face meeting with the remainder of the course online. The course is topic-driven.

Course Structure:

The course will take place over the span of an academic quarter (11 weeks). It will be conducted completely online. Guidelines for participation and completion of course assignments will be posted online.

(Continued)

EXHIBIT 7.2. Continued.

Required Reading:

Perkinson, Robert (1997), *Chemical Dependency Counseling,* Thousand Oaks, CA:
   Sage Publications.

Evaluation:

Methods used to measure your goal attainment are:

A. Case studies:
   Students are expected to respond to 5 assigned case vignettes that will be
   posted online
B. Online participation
C. Brief report posted online regarding a visit to a chemical dependency treatment
   program
D. Completion of treatment planning simulation in online teams

The relative weight of these assignments is as follows:

Online Participation	(35 percent)
Case Studies	(20 percent)
Program Review	(20 percent)
Online Treatment Planning Exercise	(25 percent)

Discussion Schedule:

The instructor will introduce the topic of the week by posting some material regarding that topic. The following is the list of topics to be discussed:

Week 1:	The importance of treatment; the "Continuum of Care" concept; and outpatient vs. inpatient treatment
Week 2:	The developmental model of recovery; intervention-review of skills; and prospective patient placement
Week 3:	12–Step Programs; relapse, recovery, and aftercare; and treatment outcome
Weeks 4 and 5:	Adjustment of the family system to the crisis of alcoholism/ addiction; codependency; approaches to family treatment; adult children of alcoholics
Week 6:	Treatment issues and complications: Shame; grief; ambivalence, resistance, denial
Week 7:	Multimodal Care
Week 8:	Professional Ethics and Survival
Week 9:	Principles and practices of case management
Week 10:	Psychosocial assessment; treatment techniques
Week 11:	Work in online treatment teams to complete treatment plans for assigned cases; summary and wrap-up

Syllabus for Behavior in Organizations:

This course is an undergraduate course. Students were given an option of attending
the face-to-face section of this class or participating in the online class. Some attendance in the face-to-face class is mandated. The course is topic driven and based
around an undergraduate textbook.

Textbook: *Organizations: Behavior, Structure, Processes, by Gibson, Ivancevich, Donnelly, 9th Edition.*

Evaluation:

1. *Class Participation.* Assessment of the student's class performance will be based on the frequency, relevance, and quality of his/her participation in the discussion and other activities.
2. *Case Studies.* Each student is required to complete three case studies. These case studies will follow the format outlined in the attached guide (See Attachment A). Two case studies will be completed individually and one will be completed as a team project.
3. *Written Work.* The quality of written work, whether a case study or essay questions on an exam, will be graded according to content, context and spelling. All written assignments, with the exception of in class work, will be presented in typewritten form.

The students enrolled in the online version of this class will be required to be present in the classroom during the first week of class, a week (to be determined by the instructor) in the middle of the term and the last week of the class.

All students will be given the option of taking the mid-term and final exam either online or in the classroom.

Case studies will be assigned weekly on Monday or on the first day of class for that week. Response to these cases must be posted to the "Virtual Classroom" prior to midnight on Thursday. Students will be allowed to work on the case studies collaboratively and post their response as such.

Evaluation will be conducted in the following manner:

Number, content, and relevancy of postings — 20 percent
Case Studies — 30 percent
Exams, Quizzes and other written assignments — 50 percent

Grades will be assigned using the following standard:
    90 percent to 100 percent = A
    80 percent to 89 percent = B
    70 percent to 79 percent = C
    60 percent to 69 percent = D
    Less than 60 percent is an "F"

Spring Term Schedule for Behavior in Organizations:

Week One:	
January 14	Introductions
	Syllabus

Week Two:	
January 21, 23	Chapter 1: The Study of Organizations

Week Three:	
January 26, 28, 30	Chapter 2: Cultural Influences on Organizational Behavior

(Continued)

EXHIBIT 7.2. Continued.

Week Four: February 2, 4, 6	Chapter 3: Globalization Chapter 4: Individual Behavior and Differences
Week Five: February 9, 11, 13	Chapter 5: Motivation: Content Theories and Applications Chapter 6: Motivation: Process Theories and Applications
Week Six: February 16, 18, 20	Chapter 7: Rewarding Organizational Behavior
Week Seven: February 23, 25, 27	Chapter 8: Group Behavior and Team Work
Week Eight: March 2, 4, 6	Chapter 9: Intergroup Behavior, Negotiation, and Team Building
Week Nine: March 9, 11, 13	Chapter 10: Realities of Power and Politics
Week Ten: March 16, 18 March 20	Review for Mid-Term Exam Mid-Term Exam
Week Eleven: March 21–March 29	Spring and Easter Break

Week Twelve:
March 30
 	
April 1, 3
	Chapter 11: Leaders: Born, Made, or Responsive to
	   the Situation?
	Chapter 12: Leadership: Emerging Concepts and
	   Approaches

Week Thirteen: April 6, 8, 10	Chapter 13: Organization Structure
Week Fourteen: April 13, 15, 17	Chapter 14: Designing Productive and Motivating Jobs Chapter 15: Designing Effective Organizations
Week Fifteen: April 20, 22, 24	Chapter 16: Managing Effective Communication Processes
Week Sixteen: April 27, 29 May 1	Chapter 17: Managing Effective Decision-Making Processes
Week Seventeen: May 4, 6	Chapter 18: Managing Organizational Change and Development
May 8	Review for Final Exam
May 12	3:00 P.M.—Final Exam

Syllabus for Quantitative Methods:

This is a required graduate level course which is taught completely online. The course is organized around the teaching of models and skills.

COURSE REQUIREMENTS: Students must read the assigned chapters and complete weekly assignments. Homework will be collected for grading. Quizzes will be given online and will be based on material covered in the preceding week. These will be timed from when you download to when you send an answer. These can be taken at the JFKU campus instead.

GRADING CRITERIA:

Homework and computer problems	40 percent
Cases (2 written)	25 percent
Quizzes (at least 5)	25 percent
Participation online	10 percent

COURSE OUTLINE:

DATE	TOPIC(S)	READING ASSIGNMENT(S)
Week of Jan. 12	Introduction to course and probability concepts	Chapters 1, 2
Week of Jan. 19	Probability distributions, decision theory	Chapters 3, 5
Week of Jan. 26	Decision trees, utility theory, quality control	Chapters 6, 7
Week of Feb. 2	Inventory models	Chapters 8, 9
Week of Feb. 9	Linear programming and applications	Chapters 10, 11
Week of Feb. 16	Linear programming continued with sensitivity analysis	Chapter 12 (skim) Chapter 13 (skim)
Week of Feb. 23	Transportation models and assignment problems	Chapter 14 (sects 1–3, 7, 10, 12–15) and 15
Week of Mar. 2	Queuing theory, waiting lines, simulation	Chapters 16, 17
Week of Mar. 9	Continuation of simulation Network models	Chapter 18
Week of Mar. 16	Markov analysis; Wrap-up	Chapter 19
Week of Mar. 23	Case studies due	

Students should feel free to contact me if questions or problems arise.

who was not posting to the discussion felt she was fulfilling the guideline of logging on twice weekly because she checked the site and read what others had posted. We were able to track her presence on the site through the software being used and were able to verify that, in fact, she had been doing what she said. However, without making some sort of contribution to the discussion, it was difficult to give her a grade for participation in the course. Having learned from this experience, we now are explicit about what an online session consists of and what is expected of students when they post to the discussion. A post involves more than visiting the course site to check in and say hello. A post is considered to be a substantive contribution to the discussion, wherein a student either comments on other posts or begins a new topic. Exhibit 7.3 gives examples of guidelines from online seminars.

A final thought regarding guidelines is the need to take the educational level and setting into account, as we have illustrated with our examples. Undergraduates may need tighter guidelines than graduate students do. A course that is being taught with an option of online or face-to-face delivery may create an opportunity to move students to either option, depending on need and ability to work in one or the other setting. Regardless, the guidelines should act as an initial loose structure for the course and provide information to participants regarding expectations for participation and conduct in the course; feedback from participants regarding the guidelines should be solicited. This, along with the posting of participant introductions, should constitute the first week of discussion in an online class. We will return to this topic as we discuss what it takes to gain student buy-in.

Constructing the Online Course Site

Although the guidelines provide a framework from which to operate, the online course site provides the organizational structure through which participants can engage with the course material being investigated and with one another. It is, therefore, a critical contributing factor to an effective outcome. To some degree, the software used to deliver the course determines the ability to construct the site. Some software applications allow for flexibility and creativity on the part of the instructor; others are more limiting. As we discussed in Chapter Five when we looked at technology, the amount of flexibility desired in course construction should be one of many determining factors in choosing course software.

Regardless of the software application being used or the type of course being taught, we routinely build a number of elements into the course site, including:

- A welcome area, which includes a place for important announcements, guidelines, or questions that can be posted by any member of the group

EXHIBIT 7.3. ONLINE COURSE GUIDELINES.

Sample Course Guidelines for Graduate Level Courses:

Guidelines for online participation in "The Search for Soul and Spirit in the Workplace"

Co-Instructors: Rena M. Palloff, Ph.D., and Keith Pratt, Ph.D.

1. "Attendance" and presence are required for this class. Students are expected to log on at a minimum of twice per week and are expected to post a substantive contribution to the discussion at that time. Simply saying "hello" or "I agree" is not considered a substantive contribution. Students must support their position or begin a new topic or add somehow to the discussion when logging on.
2. Students cannot pass this class without participation in the online discussion.
3. Assignments, including case studies and papers, will be posted online. Students will be asked to comment on and provide feedback to one another on their work.
4. Although we strongly suggest that all issues, questions, and problems be dealt with online, students can feel free to call the instructors regarding these issues at any time.
5. Use good "netiquette" such as:
   a. Check the discussion frequently and respond appropriately and on subject.
   b. Focus on one subject per message and use pertinent subject titles.
   c. Capitalize words only to highlight a point or for titles—Capitalizing otherwise is generally viewed as SHOUTING!
   d. Be professional and careful with your online interaction.
   e. Cite all quotes, references, and sources.
   f. When posting a long message, it is generally considered courteous to warn readers at the beginning of the message that it is a lengthy post.
   g. It is considered extremely rude to forward someone else's messages without their permission.
   h. It is fine to use humor, but use it carefully. The absence of face-to-face cues can cause humor to be misinterpreted as criticism or flaming (angry, antagonistic criticism). Feel free to use emoticons such as :) or ;) to let others know that you're being humorous.

[The above "netiquette" guidelines were adapted from Arlene H. Rinaldi's article, *The Net User Guidelines and Netiquette,* Florida Atlantic University, 1994, available from Netcom.]

Guidelines for Quantitative Methods, a graduate level class taught entirely online:

Instructor: Suzanne Garrett, MBA

Cases will be assigned from the text or from supplemental materials found in the library. The homework problem assignments will be distributed online. Participation requires involvement in the discussions online and logging on at least twice per week. I will be online almost every day.

Sample Guidelines for Undergraduate Level Classes:

Guidelines for Organizational Behavior to be Taught Via Electronic Means:

Instructor: Keith Pratt, Ph.D.

(Continued)

EXHIBIT 7.3. Continued.

Participation/Attendance is mandatory for this class if you are participating in the online class. This means that you will be required to log on to the Virtual Classroom that has been setup a minimum of one time for each day that the class has been scheduled to meet. During each logon session the student is required to make a posting, message, interaction to the ongoing dialogue. This posting must be relevant and substantive. Logging on and just saying I agree or I concur is not acceptable, you must support your statements or begin a new dialogue or topic.

The students enrolled in the online version of this class will be required to be present in the classroom during the first week of class, a week (to be determined by the instructor) in the middle of the term and the last week of the class.

If participation according to these guidelines is not met over a two week period then the student will be required to return to the classroom to complete the course or will be asked to drop it.

- A community area where group members can interact on a personal level, apart from course material
- Course content areas, organized according to the way the syllabus was constructed
- An area devoted to reflections on learning through electronic means
- An area devoted to evaluation of the class, which can be posted initially or added to the course site as the course progresses
- A separate area for assignments and exams or for posting assignments as discussion items, depending on the course structure

Exhibit 7.4 shows an example of a course homepage using Web Course in a Box—a software application designed for Internet-based teaching. The setup of the welcome page is preset by the software. However, the graphics were selected by one of the authors, as the instructor for the course.

Exhibit 7.5 is a detail of the "Learning Links" section of the course site. The reader will note that the software allows the instructor to limit access to discussion forums. This is done to create privacy and confidentiality for a group of students; it also adds another level of security to keep those who may access the course site from entering into student discussions.

This example illustrates a course organized around weekly discussion topics, following the organization of the course text. A course that is organized around readings may have separate sections for each book being discussed. Yet another form of organization might be open-ended topics with no timelines attached. In more structured courses, such as courses in mathematic and scientific methods, the course might be structured around the specific skill set to be learned in a given period of time. The syllabus example, taken from Quantitative Methods, illustrates this type of organization.

EXHIBIT 7.4. SAMPLE WELCOME PAGE.

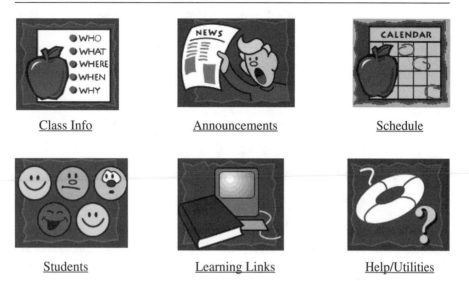

Class Info   Announcements   Schedule

Students   Learning Links   Help/Utilities

Regardless of the type of organization used, participants should be able to easily navigate the course based on the layout of the course site, which should reflect the organization presented in the course syllabus. The course site and the ability to navigate it with little or no difficulty should ease the burden of the participant who is learning to use the technology while participating in the course. Consequently, whatever limitations are present in the software must be taken into account in course organization. The author's example is illustrative of a web-based application that allows for the use of graphics. What does an instructor do, however, when the software is more basic? The example in Exhibit 7.6 is derived from an instructor's experience with a client-server software application that is organized into folders, or meetings. In this graduate-level class, the instructor posted a brief explanation of each folder in order to orient students to the course site.

The better the organization of the course site, the easier the use of technology will be for the participants. The less the participants need to worry about how to use the technology, the more likely they are to participate actively in the course. We now turn to more specific means of gaining student buy-in and participation.

If You Build It, Will They Come?

Many instructors have expressed frustration because they cannot stimulate participation in an online course. Some have described courses in which students

EXHIBIT 7.5. SAMPLE DISCUSSION FORUMS.

Spring, 1998—<u>Behavior in Organizations 30063</u>—Section OAD

Learning Links

Discussion Forums

<u>Pam Crosby Memorial Forum</u>

This Forum is being created in memory of "Pam Crosby" one of your fellow students.

<u>Distance Education (Access Restricted)</u>

<u>Week Three Discussion Forum (Access Restricted)</u>

Behavior and Motivation

<u>The "ACES" Team Forum (Access Restricted)</u>

This is the "Private" Team Forum for the ACES Carmen, Jason B., Mike Taylor, Michael Luarks. (Carmen is the Team Leader)

<u>"The RPM Team" (Access Restricted)</u>

Team composed of Rob Saunders, Pam Crosby (in absentia) and Mason Clark, Brandi Herron, Stacy Kroening. (Mason is the Team Leader)

<u>Week Five Discussion Forum (Access Restricted)</u>

Group Behavior and Team Building in "Cyberspace".

<u>Week Four Discussion Forum (Access Restricted)</u>

Rewarding Organizational Behavior "How Do We Compensate People"

<u>OBe Cafe (Access Restricted)</u>

The OBe Cafe is to be used for "Social Discussions" and things not particularly relevant to the text.

<u>Week One Discussion Forum (Access Restricted)</u>

This is the discussion forum for the first week of the class.

<u>Week Two Discussion Forum (Access Restricted)</u>

A discussion of "Globalization"!!!!!

<u>Reflections on the Class (Access Restricted)</u>

This is a forum for discussing what impact, issues, problems and concerns or any other idea relevant to how this type of class (electronic) is effecting you in any way.

<u>Week Six Discussion Forum</u> (Access Restricted)

    Intergroup Behavior, Negotiation, and Team Building<------HUH??????

Lessons

<u>First Weeks Assignment</u>

<u>Lessons for Week Two</u>

EXHIBIT 7.6. EXPLANATION OF THE USE OF "FOLDERS" AND "DISCUSSION ITEMS" IN A BASIC COURSE SITE.

This is the organization of a course site in Quantitative Methods, as taught by Suzanne Garrett, MBA.

Lecture Folder:

This is the meeting where I will post lecture notes, example problems, etc. I have some things in Power Point, Excel, and/or Word, all Windows-based. If anyone has a problem reading what is ever sent here, please let me know as soon as possible. Thanks.

Discussion Folder:

This is the place to ask questions and make comments—about the reading material, the lecture notes, examples, homework. That way, everyone in the course can discuss and see the response from everyone, including mine, just like in a classroom discussion.

Assignments Folder:

Please submit all homework problems to me individually, not to a meeting [folder]. If there are any questions, about the following assignments, please let me know. Thanks.

Week 1	Chapter 2 Supplement	Online Example Problems in Lecture
Week 2	Chapter 2	Problems 8, 11, 14, 19
	Chapter 3	Problems 13, 19, 24
Week 3	Chapter 4	Problems 11, 12, 13
	Chapter 5	Problems 17, 18, 19, 20, 21, 22
Week 4	Chapter 5 (continued)	Problems 25, 26
	Chapter 6	Problems 24, 27, 31, 33, 41
Week 5	Chapter 7	Problems 15, 17, 19, 21, 35 (write out equations—you do not have to solve them)
Week 6	Chapter 8	Problems 2, 3, 4, 5, 8, 10
Week 7	Chapter 10	Problems 12, 13, 18, 20, 23, 28, 33
Week 8	Chapter 11	Problems 15 (solve it), 17, 18, 23

(Continued)

EXHIBIT 7.6. Continued.

Week 9	Chapter 12	Problems 9, 12, 17, 18
	Chapter 13	Problems 16, 17, 18, 23
Week 10	Chapter 14	Problems 13, 16, 18, 27
Week 11	Chapter 15	Problems 14, 20, 25

Remember that many of these can be done using QM for Windows that came with your textbook. See Appendix 1 at the end of most of the chapters. You also can use Excel (or other spreadsheet program) by following instructions often found in Appendix 2 at the end of the chapters.

Good luck!

The following is the organization of a course site in Management and Organizational Theory.

Welcome to Management and Organizational Theory: A Global Perspective. It is my hope that we can explore these topics this quarter while keeping an open mind, inviting new perspectives, and avoiding dualistic thinking. There is no "right and wrong" way to view organizations and their managers. Although we're exploring what are termed "old" and "new" paradigm thinking, there is no value judgement implied. Instead, my hope is that we will develop a more holistic way of viewing organizations and develop an appreciation for all paradigms. So let's explore and have fun!

There are 10 discussion items in this conference.

1. Syllabus
2. Assignments
3. Guidelines and Other Important Stuff
4. Beginnings
5. April 21–May 4: Bolman and Deal
6. May 5–May 18: Morgan
7. May 19–June 1: Janov
8. June 2–June 15: Bennis, Parikh, and Lessem
9. Electronic Reflections and Other Friendly Stuff
10. Putting It All Together: Endings and Learnings

communicated with the instructor but not with each other. Others have described a complete absence of participation. We have discussed several strategies for securing student buy-in (willingness to participate in an online course) and then for securing ongoing participation as the course progresses. A summary of these strategies is as follows:

- Establish clear participation guidelines that the participants discuss and agree to.
- Be clear about how participation will be evaluated and how it figures into the grading scheme for the class.
- Create a clear syllabus and course structure that is easy to follow but allows for flexibility.

- Be clear about how much time is involved in participation in an online course so there are no misunderstandings about what it means to work in this medium.
- Create a course site that is welcoming, easy to navigate, and to which there is little difficulty posting messages.
- Be a good role model of online participation by being visible on a daily basis as the course progresses.
- Be willing to step in and set limits if participation is waning or is heading in the wrong direction.
- Be willing to make phone calls to people who are not participating to ask why and to draw them back in.
- Most important, strive to *create community* through inclusion of the human elements involved in the course.

When working to draw participants in and keep them connected, it is important to remember that real people are attached to those posted messages—people who have lives as well as human needs and expectations. It is important to use humor and to inject fun into the process. We tell jokes and get students to laugh in the classroom. The same is true online. Take, for example, the introduction to the online class, Human Behavior in the Management of Organizations, taught by Arlene Hiss:

WELCOME TO ORGANIZATIONAL BEHAVIOR
I hope that this will not only be a learning experience for you but will be FUN in the process. If you need to talk to me, you will find me at my desk during the day (Pacific Time). I'm usually teaching on-ground at night so it is a bit harder to catch me in during the evening. However, I have an answering machine and I will get back to you if I'm not in.

This course is going to cover such subject areas in organizational behavior as Theories of Motivation; Job Design; Group Behavior; Power, Politics, and Conflict; Leadership; Decision Making; Communication; Performance Appraisal and Evaluation; Rewards; Organizational Design; and Organizational Change, Employee Development, and Legal Issues and Current Trends.

Now for the SECOND week. . . . Just kidding. How's that for an action packed six weeks? So, hang on to your hats, grab your PC's and jump right in.

Arlene's welcome message is designed to draw students into the process and make it appealing; it also conveys who she is. It helps to develop interest in the class while indicating the level of work that will be involved. Here are Arlene's expectations for participation, drawn from her course syllabus, also delivered clearly and with humor and tact:

The student is expected to attend the virtual classroom by dialing in at least 5 out of 7 days of each week. The standard is that an average participant should "attend" class 5 of 7 days per week. This is measured by recording the date of each entry you make to the system—whether it be a response to one of the assignments, a comment on the work of another, or a question to the group or to your faculty. An absence does not excuse the student from the responsibility of participation, assigned work, and/or testing. Students may be dropped for poor attendance after two consecutive weeks of absences are accumulated.

It is extremely important to generate and participate in class discussion. The understanding and application of concepts is best reinforced by "lessons learned" of others. You should strive to participate in the meeting rooms and branches at least five out of every seven days. I would like to see you comment on your classmates' discussion questions, reports, and lessons learned. Besides commenting on other students' work, you will be given a final overall participation grade of 10 points. All discussion questions, comments to each other, or just plain 'ole rapping will be done in the Virtual Classroom. The Virtual Classroom is your "student lounge" so you should keep your "chatting" there. You may comment on each other's Reports, and Lessons Learned right in the same "Branch Meeting" where it was sent and this should all be topic related. I will be the observer/facilitator of this process and will be assessing your contributions to the topic related discussions. From time to time I will interject comments but for the most part, the discussions will be left to you. I will also be throwing out some "goodies" that you can hash over. I send handouts every day and you may comment on any of those. There will be plenty to talk about so you don't have to fear that you will run out of things to say. I would also like to mention that it is our online policy that you log on and *participate* 5 of the 7 days in the week minimum. Of course, since you will be so excited about this class, more than likely you will be logging on 7 of the 7 days;-). Remember that just logging on is not the same as logging on and *participating*.

This example also raises the issue of attendance. How does one account for attendance in the virtual classroom? Many software applications allow an instructor to track when and how often students log on. However, when that is not possible, the only means of tracking attendance is by monitoring the number and frequency of student posts on the course site. If a student logs on but posts nothing, their presence is not accounted for. Consequently, it is extremely important that this be clear to students from the outset. Some institutions are now requiring faculty to submit attendance reports along with grade reports at the end of a term. Creating those reports for an online classroom can be difficult when participation is low. When students are logging on and posting, however, accounting for attendance becomes a much easier task.

Final Thoughts

This chapter has focused on the organization and development of an effective online course. What follows are some guiding questions to allow the reader to consider the elements presented and apply them to the creation of a course of their choosing. In the next chapter, we turn our attention to another important element of participation: How does an instructor facilitate the collaborative learning process that is so critical to effective learning outcomes in this environment?

Guiding Questions to Assist in Building an Effective Course Syllabus

The following questions are designed to assist the reader with the development of an effective online course. Remember that we are not talking about course or curriculum conversion per se. Instead, this is an opportunity to reflect on teaching methods and how those might need to change as a course is being designed for online delivery.

What are the desired learning outcomes for this course? What do I want to accomplish?

What criteria must be included, as dictated by the institution (for example, disclaimers and office hours)?

Are there any unique requirements that my students need to be aware of such as methods to assess progress, desired outcomes, guidelines for participation, content, context, or the need to be aware of good grammar and punctuation?

What guidelines, rules, roles, and norms do I want to establish up front and stand firm on? Which can I be flexible about and negotiate? What do I let the participants decide?

How do I want to organize the course site? What are my options? How much flexibility will I have based on the software available?

How do I plan to assess the students? Are traditional means such as exams and quizzes adequate and appropriate? Or do I need to consider collaborative assignments, case studies, essays, and online exercises?

How do I address attendance requirements? Will I rely on the quantity, quality, and frequency of postings, or simply the number of log-ons and postings?

Do I want to establish "office hours" online? What times can I make myself available and be able to respond quickly to student concerns, questions, and ideas?

Do I want to offer face-to-face tutoring sessions, meetings, focus groups, and so forth? If so, what are the logistics of those?

CHAPTER EIGHT

PROMOTING COLLABORATIVE LEARNING

Throughout this book, we have been discussing the importance of collaboration in facilitating the development of a learning community and in achieving the desired learning outcomes for the course. The collaborative effort among the learners helps them achieve a deeper level of knowledge generation while moving from independence to interdependence. In their article, "Making Distance Learning Collaborative," Ellen Christiansen and Lone Dirckinck-Holmfeld (1995) postulate that the development of collaborative skills requires a means of study and an environment for study that "(a) lets a group of students formulate a shared goal for their learning process, (b) allows the students to use personal motivating problems/interests/experiences as springboards, (c) takes dialogue as the fundamental way of inquiry" (p. 1).

In this chapter, we further explore the concept of collaboration by suggesting ways to promote it. The skills necessary to promote collaboration are not necessarily imparted to us during our academic preparation, which takes place for the most part in classrooms promoting independent work. The skills of interdependence must be developed and taught through a process of active learning. Let us now explore the applications of these elements to the distance learning arena.

Formulating a Shared Goal for Learning

An important element of community, whether it is face to face or in the electronic realm, is the development of shared goals. Clearly, in the electronic classroom, those goals should relate to the learning process. An instructor can use a number of techniques to move students in the direction of embracing a shared goal, beginning with the negotiation of guidelines early in the course and continuing through an end-of-course evaluation of how well those goals were met. The following is a discussion of techniques that can be used, along with specific examples.

Negotiating Guidelines

We have discussed the importance of engaging the group in discussion of the guidelines posted by the instructor at the beginning of the course. But what form does that negotiation take? What does it look like? The following is an example of what we have been describing as the negotiation of guidelines. This online discussion took place in a graduate-level course in management and organizational behavior. It related to the discussion folders that had been created for the course and whether to separate our reflections on electronic learning into a separate discussion. One of the authors began the discussion by stating:

Maybe what would be a good adjunct to our learning would be to create a separate discussion item to process the learning experience as it happens—not the discussion of the books, but how we're experiencing this electronic component of the course. Is anyone game for this?? If so, I'll gladly create the item. But I'll wait to see if people think this is worthwhile.

A student replied as follows:

I think that you are right on target, Rena, suggesting that we share our experience, feelings, and process. How we do that is up to everyone. Last quarter people complained that there were too many folders and they wanted to limit them. Perhaps now — as experienced cyberspace journeyers — that is different . . . ? I can go either way with it. If we don't do that, I would encourage everyone to feel free to add bits of their process and their selves to our content discussion. Or, perhaps you could delegate some time at each monthly session to process. Again, you are getting a sense of me, I try to interelate things all of the time. I think that you are raising issues that arise in business. How do we create an environment that invites our staff to have a space to discuss their process, feelings, and issues? We get so immersed in task management that this (important) piece is often not tended to. *Judie*

Judie, Strange that you bring up the subject of "task management" vs "people/process management", that is the basis for Fiedler's theory of leadership and also part of a discussion that is continuing in my OB class now. How often we forget that there may be a time, place and situation that warrants one style or another. We often try to reach such a balance, but is it needed all the time?? *Keith*

As far as another place to chat, Rena runs a very tight ship and I think there would be room for one more section for that purpose. My only concern is that fatigue will get the best of us and the chat section will fall by the way side. Possibly making timely communication a bit uncertain. *Tonia*

I'm amazed that every time I join this conversation, more wonderful insights have been shared and there's more to think about. I agree with both Judie and Keith that there's time for balance and there are times when balance be damned contingent on the situation–thank you, Fiedler!! I also hear Tonia's concern that if I create an additional item, will people feel like they have the time to use it?? Or . . . we could just continue the conversation about process here along with task whenever that's appropriate. Obviously, I'm open to whatever!!! *Rena*

I think it would be interesting to have a special item to discuss online learning, although I see Tonia's point that it could be a bit too much. Maybe we could give it a shot and if it doesn't fly we will let it land where it will??? *Cindy*

Well let's try one more section. It seems this is a lively group. Will the addition be for online comments or other random friendly stuff? *Tonia*

How about an item for both reflections on our online learning as well as other friendly stuff. I'll create the item just like that and we'll see where it goes. We can also take time out of both of our next two f–2–f meetings to process our online learning. *Rena*

It is difficult to imagine a conversation like this one—about how to organize and contain the learning process—occurring in the face-to-face classroom. Although some may find this type of discussion tedious, it does not detract from the learning process; it contributes to it positively. The discussion allows participants to take responsibility for the way they will engage with the course and come to shared agreement about the ways they will interact with each other. This creates the first step in moving toward greater collaboration in learning.

Posting Introductions and Learning Expectations

It is important to begin the course with introductions. Students should be able to introduce themselves and begin to know each other. However, to achieve collaborative learning, an important addition to the process of getting to know each other is the sharing of expectations for the course. The following are the expectations shared by the same group studying management and organizational behavior. The discussion begins with the instructor modeling the process.

My hopes and expectations for this course are that we will engage in lively discussion about the topics of management and organizational behavior. I have chosen readings that I hope will spark this discussion and broaden our perspectives on these topics. My role in this, as I see it, is to act as a facilitator but not a director. I hope to see each of you taking a great deal of responsibility for making this course work. I am happy to share from my personal experience as appropriate, but I clearly don't want to impose that on all of you. Hopefully, you will all share your personal experiences in this area as well. *Rena*

In this class I hope to gain a solid foundation in management and organizational theory, as well as practical application. I hope to understand historical perspectives, and the results of applying one theory over another. *Julie*

My expectations and hopes for this class are that I would like to get more understanding of the theory and skills and knowledge through the discussion about the topics regarding Organization and Management. Also I'm interested in business organization consulting, so I'd like to share some information relating this with classmates. And one of my problems, it's my responsibility, English is not my native language so I'm still struggling with learning English. I'll try hard but everyone*s consideration will be appreciate regarding this matters in advance. *Soomo*

I am very interested in learning about various models of organizational management. I plan to eventually start my own company and would like it to be a sustainable organization and I therefore feel that this class will be very useful for me. I am very pleased to have met you all and I am looking forward to spending the next quarter with you. *Cindy*

I'm hoping to learn about Management in this course. For me it has been one of those oft bandied big words I've heard about a lot but never really known what it meant. *Jennifer*

I am really excited about expanding my understanding of management styles and theories so I can act in a meaningful way in the future. Thanks to all for your interesting personal info. I love biographies. *Tonia*

Asking participants to comment on expectations gives the instructor a process check, a means by which to determine whether or not we are all beginning this journey from approximately the same starting point. If congruence in expectations does not exist, this does not necessarily signify a problem. Instead, it allows the instructor an additional opportunity for negotiation. Given that we are creating and facilitating a learner-focused process, it may be the instructor whose expectations need to shift to correspond more closely to the needs of the learners. If conflict results from these negotiations, again this is not a problem. The handling and working through of that conflict can move the group closer to congruence in its expectations. The more closely we can achieve congruence in the area of expectations, the more likely it is that a collaborative learning process will be the result.

Encouraging Comment on Introductions

Frequently, students post their introductions and simply move on with the course. We have had the experience, however, of students feeling unrecognized when that happens. Our first encounter with this confused and surprised us. We were facilitating our first electronic seminar. Initially, ten participants posted introductions to the group, but one participant disappeared immediately thereafter. She rejoined the group later in the course, explaining that her absence had been due to the lack of comment on her introduction. She felt that she had shared quite a bit of herself and was hurt that none of the other group members had commented on any aspect of what she had written. We have learned from that experience and have since begun to model a way to respond to student introductions, which encourages other participants to do the same.

Not only does this practice enable students to begin opening up to each other but it begins creating a safe space in which they can interact. In Chapter Five we discussed the relationships that develop between the students and the instructor and among participants, as well as with the machine. The posting of an introduction is the first step in revealing who one is to the remainder of the group. Because participants feel more comfortable revealing parts of themselves in this medium that they might not reveal elsewhere, it is critical that they feel acknowledged so they can continue to do that safely throughout the duration of the course. This is the first point of connection—the point where these important relationships begin to develop.

The following are a few brief examples of the type of acknowledgment that can be helpful. They are taken out of context and are not meant to represent the threads of a conversation.

As I suspected, I'm learning more about all of you than we had time for in our face-to-face meeting. I'm impressed with the scope of your previous experiences and look forward to seeing you apply them as we discuss the readings in this class! *Rena*

Welcome Keith! I don't know Jim from Florence, but we will have to talk sometime to see if we have any acquaintances in common. I actually didn't grow up in Florence, (it was just Home Base) since my father was a career Army Officer. As you probably guessed, being from Columbus, he was stationed at Fort Benning several times during his career. I went to the 4th grade in Columbus! *Julie*

That was deep! I'm so glad you're joining us, Joyce! *Jennifer*

All of us need acknowledgment and need to feel welcomed into a new situation. The promotion of human connection allows students to begin forming the relationships that are the basis for collaborative learning. The bits of dialogue presented illustrate attempts to reach out to one another and connect. They indicate that this group is at the formative stage. Acknowledgment of contributions at this stage is particularly crucial due to the fragile nature of this stage of development.

Forming Teams and Posting Guidelines for Their Performance

Another means by which to deliberately promote collaboration in the electronic classroom is to create teams for the purpose of small-group discussion, completion of group assignments, and engagement in small-group activities and simulations. This can be particularly useful when working with a large group or when a group needs an extra push in working collaboratively. Teams can be formed by the instructor or through a directive to the group to form teams of their choosing. The latter option can be time consuming and may result in teams that lack heterogeneity. Therefore, it is advisable to provide some guidance to students in team formation and to establish a deadline by which the group must form itself into teams or lose the element of choice. If students can meet face to face, the formation of teams may optimally occur in that setting. We have found that team formation can be difficult in the asynchronous online environment because potential team members are logging on at their convenience and may not receive or respond to a request to join a team immediately. Encouragement and reminders from the instructor can help students move beyond this barrier.

When teams are formed, it is important to post guidelines and expectations for the performance of that team. How that team should connect and relate to the overall learning goals of the class should also be posted. The following is an example of guidelines that were posted by one of the authors in an undergraduate class in organizational behavior.

1. Each team will designate/elect/appoint a team coordinator/leader.
2. The leader will remain the same throughout the course unless replaced by a majority vote of the team or by the professor.
3. The team leader may make a decision unless overruled by a majority.
4. Any project assigned to the team will receive a grade that applies to every member of that group.
5. The team leader will have the final authority to modify any team member's grade up or down (except for his/her own).
6. The instructor will have the final say in all cases where the team cannot reach a decision.

Embedded in these guidelines is an expectation that team members will evaluate each other's work, participation, and contribution to the collaborative product that ensues from their work together. Some writers in the area of collaborative education have argued that this practice instills a sense of competition in the group rather than cooperation (Felder and Brent, 1994). However, we have found that in the online environment, when students may not be in contact except through that course, this can serve as an incentive to promote collaboration as well as to equalize the work load involved. Team self-evaluation may also promote the desire to become part of an actively working team.

Problems, Interests, and Experiences as Springboards for Learning

In order to actively engage learners in the online learning process and to facilitate the meaning-making process that is a part of the constructivist approach through which this learning occurs, the content of the course should be embedded in everyday life. The more that participants can relate their life experience and what they already know to the context of the online classroom, the deeper their understanding will be of what they learn. The process of connecting the learning gained from everyday life to the learning of the course not only creates a deeper sense of meaning for the participants but it validates them as people who possess knowledge and who can apply what they know in other contexts.

As we consider collaborative approaches, it makes sense for participants to connect around shared problems, interests, and experiences. The instructor can use group exercises and simulations to encourage connections; using questions that relate to the lives of the participants outside the classroom is useful. Connection can also occur naturally as the discussion evolves. In the next section, we examine approaches through which collaboration can be facilitated in online learning.

Encouraging a Search for Real-Life Examples

The types of questions asked to kick off the discussion of a topic within a course can encourage students to bring their life experiences into the classroom. Also, we often ask students to relate course material to what they see happening in the online classroom. When we ask students to process the work of the online group as they see it occurring, the same purpose can be served. Some examples of questions are:

As we consider the topic of leadership, think of someone who you feel displays good leadership qualities. Describe those qualities, and tell us why you think this person is a good leader.

What phase of group development would you say our group is displaying? How would that be different (or would it?) if we were meeting face to face?

Based on this experience, what do you feel are the issues involved with the development of distributed teams (that is, teams in which the members are physically separated and do their work using e-mail, teleconferencing, computer chat sessions, and so forth)?

Describe an organization with which you have had experience where you feel that power and politics played a significant role. How were you affected by those issues?

How have you been affected psychologically, socially, physically, and spiritually by your participation in this course? What changes have you noticed?

What do you see as the organizational structure of our university? How would you recommend its restructuring?

Asking such questions helps create an environment in which participants feel safe in bringing material of a more personal nature. We find that by modeling the use of real situations or by asking students to comment on a situation they share in common outside the classroom, they begin to work collaboratively on the solutions to other problems and situations they face throughout the course.

Developing Assignments Related to Real-Life Situations

Creating small-group assignments that deal with real-life situations is another means to achieve the same goal. These assignments can take the form of a problem the group is asked to solve together, the preparation and writing of a collaborative paper, or the completion of a simulation that can be processed with the larger group. The following are a few group assignments that we have used to promote collaborative work in our online classes:

Assignment for graduate level class in Management and Organizational Behavior:
You have all been asked to read the case study entitled, "Sunnyvale Youth Center," which was distributed in our face-to-face session. Once you have read it, begin an e-mail discussion with the partner you chose in class regarding the case. Your task is to come to consensus on the issues involved in the case and to present your thoughts and suggestions regarding the case to the large group during next week's discussion. Your team's position should take the form of a one to two page position paper which you will post to the course site.

Assignment for undergraduate level class in Organizational Behavior:
Doing Business in the GOOD OLE USA!!!!

Utilizing any resources you can (preferably the Internet) find a company from a country outside the U.S. that has a branch or subsidiary in the U.S. and do a one-page report/paper on the significance of that company. This is your first team project, so remember it will be graded. Guidelines for team grading will be posted tonight.

Simulation for graduate level course in Addiction Studies:
You have been formed into treatment teams consisting of 5 people. Each team will be given two actual cases, one adult and one adolescent, to work with. The material you will receive is an intake assessment completed at the time of admission to a treatment program. I will be sending each of you your case material via e-mail. It is in Word format. If you have difficulty accessing the material or opening the file, contact me immediately so that I can get the case material to you in another way. Once you have completed the work outlined below, submit the forms to me via e-mail. We will discuss the outcome next week. Feel free to contact me with any questions.

Your team is expected to do the following with the case material provided within one week:

a)   Come to consensus about the level of care at which you are working (outpatient or inpatient).

b)   Complete a collaborative problem list outlining the issues this client is facing in treatment. The form to use is included in the case material you have received. Please submit only one form per team.

c)   Complete an initial treatment plan based on the problem list you have generated. Please refer to your previous reading material on formulating goals, objectives, and action plans to assist you with this portion of the assignment. Again, you have received the form to use with your materials. Please submit only one form per team.

It is assumed that as groups work through collaborative assignments, they are likely to encounter conflict as they form a subgroup of the larger class group. Once again, the working through of this conflict assists with the learning process. If a group becomes stalled as the result of the conflict, the instructor needs to act as mediator to assist the group in moving through the problem and reaching a solution. Additionally, as the results of collaborative assignments are fed back to the larger group, a discussion of the process each of the smaller groups went through can be helpful to the rest of the group in learning about how to work collaboratively.

Dialogue as Inquiry

When students engage in discussions with each other rather than with the instructor, the possibilities for collaboration grow significantly. According to Boga (taken off Internet, n.d.):

A collaborative learning entails a skilled discussion and a dialogue. Dialogue, on the other hand, carries a flow of meaning between participants. In a dialogue all the participants are open to the idea of reconstructing their mental models. Discussion involves a volley of views between people. It is a ping pong conversation in which, as Covey (1989) puts it, each participant is either speaking or preparing to speak. In a discussion, according to Senge (1990), each participant advocates and defends a point of view. Every view is based on some observations, interpretations, assumptions, or generalizations. Skilled discussion involves a dynamic balance between advocacy of views and inquiry about the associated inferences [p. 5].

It is thus important for the instructor to be able to facilitate this dialogue without dominating it, so as to allow for the "volley of views" to occur. This can be done in several ways. First, instructors as well as participants must learn and develop the art of asking expansive questions. Next, the responsibility for the facilitation of discussion can be shared among the participants. And last, students should be encouraged—even required—to provide constructive feedback to one another throughout the course. The sharing of this responsibility among the participants is one way instructors learn to stretch their facilitative skills. Rather than being at the forefront of the discussion, the instructor is an equal player, acting only as a gentle guide. This is a new skill for many instructors. Therefore, as we develop our abilities in this area, we grow as instructors, just as our students grow as learners.

Encouraging Expansive Questioning

Questions posed in the online environment need to be the jumping-off point of a discussion promoting deep exploration of a topic and the development of critical-thinking skills. There are no right or wrong answers to these questions. They serve only to stimulate thinking and are a means by which to tackle what may be a large body of knowledge. The instructor in an online course needs to model this form of questioning so that students can learn to ask them of each other. A measure of whether a question has achieved these goals is the level of discussion and participation it creates. Poor or minimal response to a question indicates that it has not done the job of stimulating a level of thinking that excites the learners and compels them to respond. An instructor who is closely monitoring a discussion can jump in with another question when this occurs, thereby expanding the level of thinking on the original question. What is important is to provide a kernel or a nugget of a question that serves to begin a dialogue and empowers students to pursue the issue at hand.

When students become excited by the learning that expansive questions create, they can become adept at asking the same types of questions themselves. This serves to propel the learning of all involved to much higher levels. The following bits of dialogue are examples of where students can take a discussion by asking questions of the other participants. This first one was posted to a discussion about leadership:

It seems that mass media is quick to pounce on any story that could sell newspaper, magazines, or raise television ratings. My question is, if there was mass media in the early years of the country (Washington's term for instance), do you think today we would have a different view of our founding fathers? Also do you think it would be better for the American people to not know every aspect of the president's personal life? Somehow I bet that the first presidents did some questionable things in their lives. What do you think? *Jason*

The following was the first post to a discussion of "The Search for Soul and Spirit in the Workplace":

I had occasion to watch "Jerry Maguire" with Tom Cruise last nite on Showtime with some of my family members. Did anyone else see it then or previously? I couldn't help but think of how the protagonist tried to infuse meaning into his job and the result was that he was fired. Like Bolman and Deal portrayed in "Leading with Soul", – leading means giving – and when you give, you run the risk of your gift getting rejected, and unfortunately sometimes, "you" along with it. I thought the movie provided food for thought and some interesting discussion related to soul and spirit issues in the work place. Has anyone else experienced this in their work? *Sandra*

These posts not only illustrate good thinking and questioning but they bring the outside world into the online classroom. As we previously mentioned, the more we can do that, the more likely we are to stimulate the kind of interest in the course material that will expand the level of thinking and exploration occurring. Additionally, the posts illustrate the means by which one student can encourage others to work with him or her by opening themselves to possible challenge as well as support. This is the essence of collaborative work.

Sharing Responsibility for Facilitation

Because an active learning process is a desired outcome of distance learning, one way to ensure active participation is to share the responsibility for facilitation with the participants. Usually this is accomplished by assigning students responsibility for leading a portion of the discussion. The assignment can be made on the basis of a student's having expressed interest in a particular topic or a rotation of presentations to the group by individual members; or roles can be rotated throughout the duration of the course. For example, participants may be assigned dates by which to post a paper. The other members of the group would have the responsibility for reading that paper and posting feedback and a response. Or one participant might be asked to lead the discussion while another acts as an observer and commentator on process; yet another may record and summarize the process. If teams are assigned within the context of the larger group, these roles can be established and remain fixed throughout the duration of the course, or may be rotated. The roles that students might take in an online course include

- Facilitator of the discussion
- Process observer, commenting on group dynamics
- Content commentator, summarizing the group's learning over the previous week
- Team leader, with or without the additional responsibility of evaluating the work of the other members
- Presenter on a particular topic, book, or area of interest

Additionally, all students are responsible for providing feedback to each other—a topic we will explore in more detail in the next section of this chapter.

The following are examples of the ways students kicked off discussion in a graduate-level class on management and organizational behavior. The facilitation assignments were based on students' expressed interest in the books assigned for reading and discussion. Julie begins the discussion on Bolman and Deal's *Reframing Organizations* (1991):

For those of you who were able to get the book, I hope you have gained as much from the reading as I have. I would like to start the discussion with some feedback on what you are learning, what impact your reading has had on you, and which areas seem to resonate with you the most. I was particularly interested in the evolution of varied theories about how organizations work, and the authors' approach on consolidating these theories into the four frames. I agree, from my own experience, that a wise manager or leader will need to be able to pull from many theories or perspectives in order to be effective. Every management situation has a different twist to it and calls for a different combination of tools. The four frames discussed in the book offer a solid set of tools for understanding organizations. On page 19, the authors state that "an artist reframes the world to help us see new possibilities." They also say that "modern organizations rely too much on engineering and too little on art in their effort to foster such attributes as quality, commitment, and creativity." I agree wholeheartedly with these statements and cannot help but respond with a great big WHY?? I watched, at my most recent place of employment, how employee morale and spirit was crushed under the "leadership" of the bright, young engineering type who was given total authority by upper management to "manage" half of the company. This engineer had no understanding of how people think, feel, or create, and upper management seemed to think he was doing a great job. I heard just last week that this plant is currently in the process of being shut down. I would have liked to have the opportunity to work as a consultant with this company to help them reframe, to see what was really going on within the company. I probably would have started with the Human Resource Frame, since this one especially resonates with my own thinking. I agree with Argyris and McGregor that when employees are unproductive, it is the direct result of the inability or unwillingness of management to provide an environment that nurtures the needs of the employees. What do you think everyone?

Tonia begins the discussion on Morgan's *Images of Organization* (1997):

I am pleased with this book. It is open minded, interesting and thought provoking. It is invaluable for me, as a student to be assigned a book like Morgans Images of Organization. This is so because the scope of discussion is broad and easy to read. Some of the books we've been assigned in the program have been a bit trying to say the least. Usually I'm glad to glean whatever I can, but in this case I give thanks to Rena for introducing this book because I think it's substantial and we'll be well off for reading it. Having found myself bogged down and confused in the past within my real estate organization . . . Uncertain how to get a handle on the total chaos surrounding me, I am greatly comforted to finally see that the company was very mechanistic. There were two of us who were trying with all of our might, to figure out how to create an open system environment. Unfortunately, neither of us had the training to be able to recognize clearly what was happening . . . and what we were trying to do . . . anyone else been that confused? Luggage in hand with a ticket to quagmire? It is really empowering as Judie said in the last section, to know where WE are coming from first. That way we have a chance of getting past the filmy walls. I appreciated the discussion on contingency theory. This appeals to me personally as well as professionally because I think the need to control in a traditional sense is ultimately a dead end. Steel can be inflexible but humans?

Cindy begins the discussion on Janov's *The Inventive Organization* (1994):

I thought it would be interesting to begin our discussion of Janov's book around the subject of systems thinking. I thought this would be rich because it is one of our core program philosophies, it has been discussed in all of our books and many of us were in the Systems class last quarter. Janov states; "This increased turbulence [within organizations] will result in an increased need to think systematically about how our individual realities are mirrored in society and vice versa. We will be challenged to see the connection between individual actions and collective outcomes and, thereby, we will be challenged to create more interdependence rather than more independence-to find our common cause and not just recognize and respect our diversity. Janov p.367 Janov speaks about relationships as being key to inventive organizations, which again relates to interdependence/systems thinking. Her reflection that we need to "create more interdependence rather that more independence" is just so darn un-American. I have argued this point with many a person who tells me that at the core people are selfish and they care more about independence/the individual than they do about interdependence/the collective. Is it possible to create/inspire a systemic paradigm within a culture that has prided itself on its rugged individual paradigm? I wonder what all of your thoughts and reflections are on this in relation to your experiences and feelings, and Janov's thinking around this. How do we create a systemic paradigm? Is finding a common cause and respecting diversity enough to create interdependence? Have any of you worked with or for an Inventive Organization? If so what influence did it have on you as an individual and how did it inspire the culture of the organization? If you have not worked for an Inventive Organization, what was it about the organization/s you have worked for that related to one/some of the aspects of the Frameworks for Inventive Organizations (p.96 etc.)? We will start here and see where it goes-I hope to "see" you all soon . . .

In order for the facilitative role to be successfully shared, an instructor must be willing to give up control of the direction—even the content of the discussion—and act as a participating member, allowing the students to take the discussion wherever it might go. Certainly, if the discussion is straying too far from course objectives, the instructor should step in to set gentle limits and redirect the flow. However, for the most part, the instructor must control the urge to lead and become more like a follower, thus engaging in the type of collaborative work we have been discussing.

Promoting Feedback

An important element that should be built into an online course is the expectation that students will provide constructive and extensive feedback to each other. This may occur as part of an ongoing discussion or specifically related to the work submitted in fulfillment of the course requirements. The ability to give meaningful feedback, which helps others think about the work they have produced, is not a naturally acquired skill. It must be taught, modeled, and encouraged by the instructor. Students tend to give feedback that does not promote collaboration or enhanced learning. It is not uncommon to see students respond with "Good job" or "I agree with you" as their initial attempts at providing feedback. Therefore, the expectation of substantive feedback should be built into the course. Once again, this should be delineated in the guidelines posted at the beginning of the course and discussed and negotiated by all participants. If students "forget" about this responsibility, the instructor should gently remind them.

Because this is a new experience for many students, providing substantive feedback can be a source of conflict; the instructor may need to act as mediator and to reassure students that the feedback is on their ideas and presentation and is not to be taken personally. In one of our early online courses exploring systems theory, one student wrote a paper about family systems, which was posted to the course site for comment and discussion. Another student, who worked as a family therapist, took issue with some of the material in the paper. The writer became upset and felt as if a bond of friendship had been violated by the feedback she received. We stepped in and talked about good feedback and encouraged the students to work this out "in public," so to speak. The students were both able to expand on the points they were attempting to make, creating not only a broader understanding of the theories being studied for all participants but an understanding of how to resolve conflict in this medium as well.

Take the following exchange between two students as evidence of increasing competence with the art of giving good feedback.

Hello to everyone. Attached please find my response to the Perfection or Bust case. I had fun with this one and I hope you all have fun reading it too. *Sandra*

Hi Sandra, Rena has suggested that we discuss your paper, but I don't have much to discuss – I agree with most everything you have said. My paper is very similar in tone to yours and many of the same points were touched upon. The only area of difference might be in our interpretation of Klee. I think that he was a leader in the literal sense, but he is not the kind of leader I would want to follow. I don't know if you think of him as a leader or not. What do you think? I would be interested to hear what your opinion is of my paper, and if you agree that our ideas are similar. *June*

June, thanks for your input. Unfortunately Virus warnings have kept me from your paper to date but will read it for sure and respond As far as Klee goes, I really had to think about his motives. Did he genuinely believe that his workers could reach perfection or did he recruit them just to use them in such a questionable manner while promoting perfection as a selling point of inducement? It was a little difficult for me to read his heart clearly or should I say "perfectly" on this point. *Sandra*

The feedback exchanged through this bit of dialogue goes much deeper than just saying "Good job." It creates a point of connection between the two participants and allows them to look at their ideas in another light. Through the exploration of consensus as well as difference, the students are able to construct a collaborative view of the material being discussed that goes far beyond the ideas each held at the start. Stephen Covey (1989) talks about developing the ability to "seek first to understand, then be understood" as a means by which to promote interdependence. Without interdependence, there can be no collaboration, and ultimately no community.

Intergroup and Other Forms of Collaboration

The online environment is perfect for the development of collaborative skills. Students learn to work with and depend on each other to reach their learning objectives and enhance the outcome of the process. Other forms of collaboration, however, can be promoted in this environment—forms with the potential to expand the level of learning achieved. Some of those are *intergroup collaboration, resource sharing,* and *collaborative writing.*

Intergroup Collaboration

The vastness of the Internet allows us to connect with individuals and groups all over the world. Exposure to some of these individuals and groups can provide students with a deeper understanding of the subject they are studying, allow them to develop greater facility with online research, and create connections that can serve them long after a course ends. Instructors should include assignments in their courses that push students to explore the Internet as a resource. An example of this type of assignment would be to find a website that deals with a particular element or topic being discussed. In our class, "The Search for Soul and Spirit in the Workplace," we asked students to find a website dealing with spiritual issues, to write a paper about what they found, and to post that paper to the course site. One student got so excited about what she found "out there" that she ended up visiting seven or eight websites to complete the assignment. In an undergraduate class on organizational behavior, students were asked to visit a site that was related to power and politics and post the address of that site with a brief description to the course site. As the result of being given that assignment, one student commented that he now uses the Internet as a resource for doing research for his other classes as well.

What we are doing by encouraging students to explore the Internet is promoting collaboration with other learning communities around the globe. Instructors can also facilitate that type of collaboration by creating connections among groups of students enrolled in different courses. In other words, if two sections of the same course are operating at the same time, or if an instructor is teaching two courses that are interrelated, students enrolled in both can be given opportunities to interact. Perhaps one group could prepare and present to the other group on a topic of mutual interest and concern. Furthermore, instructors can promote collaboration with colleagues at other universities and the students in their classes. Some ways to facilitate this process include (1) providing a list of e-mail addresses of instructors or students in another university who are interested in receiving messages from members of the group; (2) creating a common discussion area that can be accessed by participants and visitors; (3) creating and posting a list of websites of interest; (4) presenting "guest speakers" to the group online. Involving the participants in developing these possibilities helps make this type of collaboration more meaningful to them. The possibilities are limitless and can greatly enhance the educational experience.

Resource Sharing

The assignments we just described have the additional component of allowing students to share resources—Internet resources as well as readings. In this way, a greatly expanded bibliography of readings can be developed to allow students to explore far beyond the confines of the readings assigned for the course. A separate area of the course site can be created to house this growing list so that students can add to it and refer back to it whenever they choose. Expanding the resources in this way encourages students to take greater responsibility for their own learning and allows the instructor to act as an equal participant.

Collaborative Writing

Electronic communication in its various forms makes the transmission of documents easy. Students can work together or with an instructor to complete course assignments, usually by sending documents between or among participants. E-mail, as well as the ability to attach documents to posts on a course site, has been extremely useful in composition courses conducted online, as well as in the completion of team learning assignments. Additionally, whiteboarding software in a course allows for brainstorming sessions and for completing collaborative work by simulating what might occur in a face-to-face session. Requiring students to complete papers collaboratively and evaluating that work on a group basis also promotes interdependence.

Final Thoughts

Collaboration and the ability to promote interdependence is a critical element in the formation of an electronic learning community. Consequently, it is important that the instructor in an online course pay close attention to ways collaboration can be incorporated and facilitated throughout the course. The inability to promote collaboration in this environment generally results in low levels of participation and in two-way interactions between the instructor and any given student. Collaborative work also forms the basis for the student's ability to engage in a transformative learning process—the topic of the next chapter. The questions that follow are designed to help instructors think about ways to incorporate collaboration into the planning for an online course.

Guiding Questions to Promote Collaborative Learning

The following questions are designed to assist in the development of a collaborative learning approach in online courses. Just as with all other aspects of an online class, collaborative learning must be planned and purposefully facilitated. These questions should help create a planning process whereby these goals can be achieved. Additionally, we are including questions for students to consider when engaging in collaborative activities.

Questions for Instructors

What is the content of this course? What aspects of the content lend themselves to collaborative group activities?

What are the goals of the small-group activities?

What size groups or teams should be formed in order to achieve those goals?

How should groups or teams be formed? By the instructor? By the students? Dependent on interests? Dependent on strengths?

Should the groups be heterogeneous?

Will the participants remain in the same groups throughout the course, or will new groups be formed for each activity?

How will activities be structured to ensure participation by all members of the group?

Should roles be assigned to various group members?

What rewards or motivations will be built into the process?

How will accountability be built into the process?

How will individual and group performance be evaluated? Who will evaluate this performance? The instructor? The participants themselves?

Is there an expectation that students will provide feedback to each other on their work? How will this be built into the course?

Questions for Students

How well did I participate in my group? Was I a team player?

Did I make a significant contribution?

Did I share my portion of the work load?

How comfortable do I feel with the group process?

Did I feel comfortable expressing any problems or concerns openly?

Did I provide substantive feedback to other group members?

How do I feel about the collaborative work produced by my group?

How well did the collaborative process contribute to my learning goals and objectives for this course?

CHAPTER NINE

TRANSFORMATIVE LEARNING

Thus far, we have discussed the process of establishing connections among participants in an online course and with the instructor. We have also described ways a group can carry on a dialogue throughout the course. It is now time to turn our attention to the "real" learning that takes place as the result of participation in an online course. We call this form of learning *transformative learning* because it represents a self-reflective process that occurs on several levels.

Jack Mezirow (1990, 1991) coined the term *transformative learning* to refer to learning that is based on reflection and on the interpretation of the experiences, ideas, and assumptions gained through prior learning. This type of learning is rooted in the meaning-making process that is central to constructivism, which we have already established as a major feature of the online classroom. The goal of transformative learning is to understand why we see the world the way we do and to shake off the constraints of the limiting perspectives we have carried with us into the learning experience. Patricia Cranton (1994) adds that in order for the questioning of personal assumptions and self-reflection to occur, the environment must provide the support and the ability to dialogue and critically reflect on the material presented and on the self.

Participants in an online course engage with and reflect on the course content. Parallel processes should also be in place that allow participants to consider the learning that comes out of this engagement. Participants should explore not only how learning in this medium is different but how engaging with the medium and the machine allows them to learn something about the technology itself (see Chapter Five). Another parallel process should be self-reflection. Participants should ask themselves, How am I growing and changing as a learner and as a person through all of these interactions?

We have previously referred to this element of online learning as a *double loop* in the learning process, based on a term coined by Chris Argyris (1992). This loop provides a means of self-reflection that fuels further inquiry. However, transformative learning is actually a complex series of interactions that is multidimensional. It is what Robert Hargrove (1998) calls *triple loop learning*, which he describes as "learning [that] involves altering the particular perspective, underlying beliefs, and assumptions (or old rules) that shape *who we are* as a human being—what we identify with" (p. 62).

In this process, learners do not complete one set of reflections and then move on to the next. Instead, they may visit the next level while returning to previous levels to further reflect on the learning contained there. It is a vibrant, dynamic process that is typically not completed when a course ends. Ideally, the first experience with this process creates a hunger for more and sets the stage for participants to become lifelong, reflective learners. It is, however, a process that needs nurturing along the way in order for it to continue. We have seen many students become frustrated when their attempts to continue their learning in this manner were thwarted by an instructor who preferred to teach using fairly traditional methods, either online or in the face-to-face classroom.

To tackle this complex topic and demonstrate its implementation in an online course, we first examine the process by which it occurs. We then explore each of the parallel processes previously mentioned: learning about new forms of learning by using technology, learning about technology by using it, and encouraging the self-reflective process.

The Process of Transformative Learning in the Online Classroom

Transformative learning is, to many participants, an unanticipated result of the online learning process. If students were informed in advance that a process of transformation would be the outcome of their participation in an academic course, is it likely that they would enroll? Intellectual growth is anticipated, but personal growth is not necessarily a reason students engage in a process of online learning.

Mezirow (1990) states that perspectives are transformed when learners encounter what he terms *disorienting dilemmas*—dilemmas that cause the learner to critically assess distortions in the areas of the nature and use of knowledge, belief systems related to power and social relationships, and *psychic distortions*—or presuppositions that cause anxiety and inaction. By simply getting involved in an online class, a learner immediately encounters a disorienting dilemma. This is a new medium in which participants interact differently and in which students are expected to engage with material, each other, and the instructor in a completely different way. Thus the online classroom is fertile territory for transformative learning.

Because this process is an unconscious one for the most part, it is important for an instructor to make space for transformative learning and to surface it as the course progresses. In so doing, an awareness of increasing competence and independence as a learner begins to emerge for the participants—an outcome they can carry with them to subsequent learning experiences. Thus personal growth becomes a companion to intellectual growth as the student assumes greater responsibility for the learning process, competence, authority, self-confidence, and an overall sense of mastery and power. We now review this process in more detail and provide examples of its emergence in online courses.

Reviewing the Process

The transformative learning process is one that moves a participant from student to reflective practitioner. It begins with the practice of acquiring knowledge. Students, by enrolling in an online course, commit to that process. They enter the online environment and begin to form new relationships, which deepen as students post material to the course site and are acknowledged for their ideas and their participation. As the result of acknowledgment and feedback, students perceive that value has been added to their contribution. Their contribution has been recognized and appreciated by the group. Consequently, their ideas may be supported and expanded, or they may begin to branch off in another direction of inquiry. They then begin to question why this has happened. Why should I begin to look at this idea in a new way? Do I need to? As a result, they begin to develop new ways of explaining their ideas and the material with which they are interacting. This creates a web of learning through which new ideas and means of reflection provide a feedback mechanism regarding the ideas being studied and the learning process itself. The diagram in Figure 9.1 illustrates this process.

The excerpt of dialogue that follows is an example of the effect of this process. A student posts material and receives feedback, which stimulates the process of questioning and reflecting on ideas and self. The result is movement to the next level of reflection. That next level is illustrated here.

At this point I'd like to approach this from a more personal inquiry. Joyce has done an impressive synthesis and an outstanding analysis of the book. I apologise for the less academic and the simplistic approach I'm capable of.

FIGURE 9.1. THE LEARNING WEB.

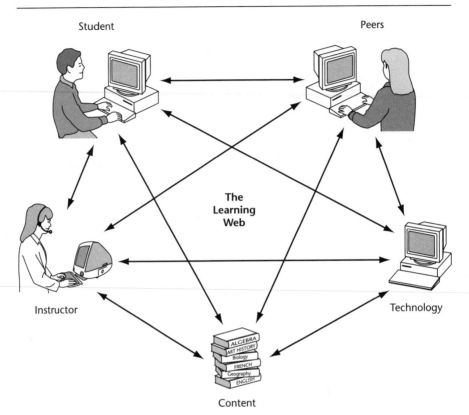

This is my favourite of the books so far, in that it has the most personal connection for me. Around about 3 months ago, before this class and before coming across this book, when people asked me what I was studying/doing at graduate school, I began to say "new paradigm business" instead of just "business". I did so to find a way, to find some way to convey that I wasn't studying business in the common definition of the term but something different. Always I would be asked what that was or I would take the initiative to elaborate. "It's not the typical business program" I would add. "It's about learning to do socially and environmentally responsible business, sustainable economics, spirituality in the workplace-as different from religion" would be my standard intro, for that's the longest I find one can push it to in the typical standard one minute intro time. So it was very reassuring and validating to come across the concepts and points put forward [in this book].

The chapter on new-paradigm thinking immediately drew me. Overall I think [the authors] put forward something valuable, and I tend to agree with a lot of their points.

However I did think they were overly concerned with style, and their chapter was a lot of stylish writing, and what they're actually saying can be condensed into half the size. I found myself going through the list on p6 of ch1 of the attributes of the New Paradigm Manager and assessing how many I make. Out of the 7 I would say I fit 4 (though I disagree with #4 in putting people ahead of the environment, the same way I get irritated when people say save the planet for our grandchildren kind of thing-the world does not belong to the human species, though we act like it does). I don't know that I "have the scope, range and power to manage the entire staircase of your own, of others', of your organisation's and of society's history," nor if I am "skilled at recognising and dealing with different levels of development, each in the process of change." And realised that though I do believe/know "that everything connects to everything else," I should always remind myself to remember that and be mindful of it all the time. So how about you? Do you agree with this definition and list of attributes of what a New-paradigm Manager is?

One thing that really struck me was a sentence in Ch 18: "Doing business in the new paradigm starts with managing yourself" (p347). I thought, well, how do I manage myself ?, and I thought, well, not very well, right?! No I don't manage myself very well at the moment; and I thought this simple statement has a lot of significance for me and is something I should be continually aware of and direct the changes I need to make in my life. *Jennifer*

While engaging with the course material being read, this student began a process of self-reflection. Not only does she explore the meaning the material has for her academically but she reflects on the meaning it has in her own life. The questions she asks throughout are, "Where do I fit? What does this mean to me personally and professionally? What changes do I need to make in my life to accommodate this new learning?" In addition, she questions the way the material is written and presented. Her inquiry is more than just a review of the book; it involves questioning where the ideas came from and where those ideas fit in her reality. The level of reflection in which this student is engaged goes well beyond trying to make sense of the book she just read for class, as it expands the relevance of the material for her, as well as for the others in the group. Because of its importance, this process needs to be initiated by the instructor and guided if it is not occurring spontaneously.

The expected outcome of the transformative process in the online environment, then, is significantly different. To frame it simply, the results of the transformative learning process are the student's ability to stay focused on a position or idea or to achieve a shift in paradigm, thereby adopting a new view of the same idea. Students may be able to develop new ways of explaining their ideas, or they may be able to enhance or expand upon those ideas; they may also be able to reflect on how the process itself has affected them. The example just presented illustrates this desired end result. Jennifer begins her post by stating that she now has a better way of explaining her idea of what *new-paradigm business* is by having engaged with the reading material for the course. She has not necessarily shifted that idea but has found new ways to explicate it. The process does not end there, however. She goes on to reflect on herself by seeing herself in the material and sharing that with the group.

Although it is certainly possible to see this type of reflection occurring in a traditional classroom, it is not necessarily encouraged. Students in a traditional setting are asked to reflect on the meaning and importance of the course material but are not expected to apply it to their own lives or to reflect on its potential impact on present or future behavior, attitudes, and actions. By encouraging students to engage in self-reflection related to the learning process, however, their ability to make meaning is greatly enhanced and the learning outcomes become deeper and more permanent.

Making Room for the Process in the Online Classroom

In order to encourage this level of inquiry, a space needs to be created in the learning process in which it can occur. As we have described, we deliberately create two streams in the course site for that purpose. One is the area for electronic reflection, which we will discuss in the next section of this chapter. The other is a place for self-reflection. These streams can be joined in one section of the course site to minimize the number of items to which participants need to pay attention, as long as the instructor is clear about how to use that area of discussion. For example, one of the authors, while teaching an online course, created an area he titled "Reflections on the Class." His explanation for using that area was, "This is a forum for discussing the impact, issues, problems and concerns or any other idea relevant to how this type of class (electronic) is affecting you in any way."

Another means by which to create space for this type of reflection is to ask questions that promote it as a part of the ongoing discussion. Questions that relate the course material to the interaction occurring in the online classroom will achieve the same result. The author, in the same course mentioned earlier, also asked questions that facilitated this type of thinking. To kick off a discussion on teamwork, he asked the following:

As you should well know this week's chapter is about "Group Behavior and Team Work." The material in the book mostly relates to things that happen in Face-to-Face (F2F) situations. Are any of these concepts, ideas, theories and viewpoints relevant in groups in "Cyberspace." If so tell me why? If not tell me what are the concepts, ideas, theories, viewpoints and issues that are important to look at when dealing with groups and this medium. (HINT) You may want to think about some of the issues that we have dealt with here.

The creation of this space opens the door to reflection. It conveys a message to the participants that says that this type of inquiry is expected and completely acceptable. Furthermore, by setting it apart from the discussion of content, participants are more likely to visit that section of the course site on a regular basis. This allows them to develop their skills in the area of self-reflection as the course progresses and does not limit their involvement with this process to the points during the course that call for self-evaluation. It is important, however, when students are being asked to evaluate their work or participation, to include a self-reflective piece in that evaluation. (We will discuss this concept further in Chapter Ten.)

Learning About Learning Through the Use of Technology

As students engage in the self-reflective process that is a part of transformative learning, it is important for the instructor to remind them that the medium they are working in allows this process to occur. In so doing, the instructor opens a new area of inquiry: What are we learning about learning by using technology? We have discussed the fact that the learning process occurring online is a learner-centered process. It is essentially directed by learners from the time the instructor posts guidelines that are open to negotiation and allows the process to go where it will, with only the gentlest of guidance and facilitation. As the learners begin to feel and acknowledge an increasing sense of empowerment, they will begin to make comments about how this type of learning differs from that of the face-to-face classroom. For some this is uncomfortable. For others it opens new vistas. Learning about the ways we learn is an important outcome of the online process that needs encouragement and support. It provides the participants with a foundation for future learning experiences. The following post illustrates this concept.

I have had several courses online. [I have noticed that] the students take a little time before becoming comfortable with the online courses. Of course the professors are challenged by the new style of teaching their course. Also, the computer software package can impact the transition for learning at a distance. Ideally, the learning would be nice if everything ran smoothly.

All the professors who I have had for distance learning have found a way to convey their passion [to] the students. Each professor has his or her unique style for ensuring that students are learning the course material. I am learning about distance learning and we are all learning about distance learning.

I was working with another student on a paper on distance learning and read a web site about the subject. The article I read indicated that by the year 2000 one in two students will be learning at a distance. Harvard University's entire business school

is connected on line. At Harvard the business students can talk with each other from
their dorms and I believe they retrieve lecture notes too.

Yes, we have suffered through some days in our class. However, in the end what
I am hearing is that the students haven't lost their Soul and Spirit. I've got to go
now. With Courage. With Compassion. *Greg*

As this post indicates, the ability to differentiate the type of learning that occurs online is important in the meaning-making process. Greg noted the differences in both learning and teaching that occur in this environment and became
interested enough in those differences to pursue research with another student
about it. Transformative learning is not easy; in fact, it may be somewhat painful
for some. Just recognizing that it is different and that "I function differently here"
is important to the learning process, allowing students to proceed with courage
and compassion, even though the going may be difficult.

Creating Opportunities to Encourage Reflection on the Differences

Once again, it is important to make space for this type of reflection in the learning
process. Instructors should ask, "How is this different for you? How are you different as a learner in this medium? How are you experiencing this process?" This ac-
knowledges the fact that the process is different and may be difficult, which can relieve
anxiety on the part of learners that they are not "doing it right." This response to
one author's question presented earlier illustrates that when the opportunity to reflect on these differences is created, participants will go to that level of reflection.

Okay, don't you think that everyone has a hard time accepting disagreement f2f. Only
a few people have the confidence to stick with their opinions without going back to
the book and looking. I know that we have all had some life experiences that can be
transferred to this medium but you still have to squirm a little when you are not real
sure. Cyberspace lets you squirm in peace. You are able to rethink without having people questioning you. . . . Is this making sense? Maybe we all need that time to realize
that we are full of ideas that we sometimes have to let grow. . . . Maybe some good
ideas too. *Rob*

We will discuss this element further when we talk about evaluation in Chapter Ten, as reflection on the differences in this type of learning frequently becomes
a part of the evaluation process that is so critical to an online course. The following are final posts from an online seminar that demonstrate the reflection on
new ways of learning as a result of learning electronically.

As I write this, my final note, I do so with a real sadness. The last few months have been personally transformative, in large part because of this seminar. The sharing, collaboration, and learning we have all experienced is boundless. Most interestingly, I note how many of us have experienced major life changes during this brief period. . . . And yet, the continuity of [this seminar] acted to provide stability and support during those difficult times. Not only have I suffered loss and pain, I have changed both my dissertation interests and knowledge area focus. Currently, I am investigating the proliferation of online learning programs globally as well as why, despite our illusory discomfort with telecommunications, we like it so much. *Cyd*

Thank you to each of you for what you have given me over the past several months. My view of the world has been expanded and challenged. You have shared your courage, sadness, frustration, support, and caring. You have asked dozens of hard questions and raised the important issues of the electronic transformations surrounding us. You have given me hope and some courage of my own – to keep asking the questions; to get more involved as our government, communities, and institutions grapple with the changes; and to focus my dissertation work in the area of Information Technology and Society. I wouldn't be here without your help. *Claudia*

We frequently have students who become so intrigued with the process of online learning that they choose to engage in further study about it. Noting the transformations that have occurred for them in the process, they seek to understand why. This is the essence of transformative learning.

Learning About Technology by Using It

In Chapter Five we discussed the importance of the technology being used for online courses and the fact that learning through the use of technology allows participants to explore its use in more general terms. Students participating regularly in an online course cannot help but improve their ability to use technology. As they engage with the machine, they learn more about word processing, logging on to the Internet, and using a browser. By the end of an online course, a complete novice is likely to have gained enough skill to continue to engage with technology with some degree of confidence. He or she may feel less threatened and intimidated by using more advanced forms of technology as well. Often, students who are new to the medium will begin to ask about having chat sessions and about how to use technology to collaborate on documents. As previously mentioned, however, in order for this to occur, the technology must be easily mastered and transparent within the course. Additionally, the instructor and the institution must be available to provide answers to questions regarding the technology as well as technical support. An instructor should not be put off by students posting questions to the course site that relate to the technology. This is not a way to detract from dealing with course material but is how students begin to learn about technology by using it.

Encouraging Questions and Comments About the Technology

As instructors allow students to ask questions about software use and other technical questions, we find that some of the best responses, encouragement, and advice are frequently supplied by students themselves. This promotes a feeling that everyone is in this thing together, as students support each other with their growing technical expertise. Additionally, we have found that more advanced students are patient with their less knowledgeable colleagues and are willing to provide instruction and support that is appropriate and easily understood. We once taught a web-based course using software in which an "edit" button appeared in each post, allowing students to change a post once it appeared if they were dissatisfied with it. However, some of the students found it confusing and began asking about it online. What is it? Can we get rid of it? Has anyone tried using it? Before we had a chance to respond, we found that they had supported each other in figuring out the button's use. As the less experienced students began to discover the button, the more advanced students very patiently explained again and again what it was for.

In another case, a virus warning appeared every time a student posted an attached document to the course site. A couple of students became nervous when they saw this and were reluctant to download the attached documents. They stated online: "I want to read your paper, but I get a virus warning every time I try to access it." In this case, we had to intervene to reassure students that this was simply a routine warning generated by the software and could, in fact, be turned off.

When a student has ongoing concerns that seem unresolvable online, it is important for the instructor to encourage phone or e-mail contact to resolve these concerns. The instructor must be familiar with the software or be willing to do what it takes to get the issue resolved. If the student is having difficulty obtaining satisfactory technical support from the source designated by the institution, the instructor may need to act as an intermediary in order to maintain the flow of the class and to instruct the students around technical issues. Face-to-face sessions may need to be set up to ensure that students can use the technology. Once the process of learning about technology has begun in whatever way necessary, students will begin to feel comfortable in acquiring additional learning about technology. If there are numerous issues and concerns about the use of the technology, or if students are interested in further exploring the use of technology as part of their involvement with the course, the instructor may want to consider setting up a separate discussion forum to deal with those issues. If a separate item is created, it is then important to direct students to use it. A gentle reminder about where to post what helps to keep this material separate from the discussion of course content.

Comfort in starting is the key, however. If early attempts are frustrating, a student may become reluctant to further explore their abilities in this area, and thwart further involvement with online learning. Consequently, learning about technology by using it becomes one of the desired learning outcomes for an online course.

Self-Reflection

Self-reflection is distinctly different from the types of reflection we have been discussing. It is not about how I learn or what I am learning about technology; it is instead about who I am as a person. Has that perception of myself changed as I have participated in an online course? Have I revealed a part of myself that has not been revealed in other settings? Again, it is a process that participants may or may not be conscious of. When an opening is created through which students can reflect on change, however, students are likely to note the changes.

Okay, I am going to jump right in this conflict. It seems to me that if we were to go back to f2f classroom situation we would have some conflict. It could be the type that helps or betters the group. We have become an organization. We have decided in a way that there are a lot of good things that come out of this bunch. We have some ideas that do help us all understand a little better what we are talking about and to also help jar our thoughts to think a bit farther. We have become so dependent on the ability to do this at our time and our own rate of thinking that the creative thinking is beginning to develop. I am afraid that the openness and the ease of typing would out weigh the f2f tension. We each one sit back and think over each posting before we join in. *Mason*

The changes in self being reflected here are the ability to connect to others, the ability to take time to think and thus think more deeply, and the emergence of creativity. This occurs through a constant process of looking back and taking stock. As the course progresses, participants cannot help but remember what things were like for them as they entered this new, perhaps previously unexplored realm and to comment on the differences. This process, then, is historical; it takes stock of our shared history and records it as we progress through the course. But the reflective process does not end with history taking. It is also a looking ahead as to how this process will affect the learner in the future. Mezirow (1991) refers to this component of learning as a process of using a prior interpretation to revise or create a new interpretation of one's experience as a means by which to guide future action.

The Reflective Process

When we incorporate this historical process into the online classroom, it is important to ask such questions as, How were you as a learner before you came into this course? How have you changed? How do you anticipate this will affect your learning in the future? As previously mentioned, this is an important component of the evaluation of a course, as it helps us know whether we have achieved our learning objectives. However, in order to promote the process of transformative learning, we must ask these questions throughout the course. The answers help us stay on target and provide additional support for the process of transformative learning as it occurs. The following final post illustrates the historical nature of transformative learning.

Uniqueness? Boy that is not the only word for it. This class was the first class that I have taken on a computer. This has allowed me to expand my paradigms of learning. I have used many different ways of studying from the Internet to just thinking in an unusual manner about what was said on-line. I have always been a listener and not much of a face to face interaction person or at least the interaction may not have a great deal of thought. But with this communication resource we have developed a method of feedback that has seemed very effective for a better learning base. . . . The openness gave us a chance to follow up on the postings, research the subject, develop empathy, trust in everyone's thoughts, simplify the language, and use our time effectively. Although we did not have the nonverbal traditional communication, we did have the personalities and the quirks of some come through the postings. I really feel that we have had a good group of people to work with and we have all come a long way . . . I really feel that this medium of an online class has given me the best opportunity to learn in the method that meets my learning style. . . . This class has been an opening into the confidence of tackling a business organization. On a scale of learning material from a class that will be useful in the business world——this class would receive a 9 to 9½. (10 being the best). . . . But I have found myself asking other people in the business world for input. That's new for me . . . I think you could say I have grown up some. I would love to see more classes like this . . . I know that I have not done well in the traditional classroom on several occasions but in this class I feel pretty good about my work. . . . It really got to the point that we (the participants) were all the teachers. *Rob*

This post illustrates that, as instructors, we were successful in initiating a process of transformative learning. Rob is able to reflect on how he has been as a learner, what he has gained, how he has reframed and reinterpreted his learning as the result of this learning experience. He has already begun to apply his new views of himself and of knowledge in the world outside the university. Rob will take this new view of himself into future learning experiences and will probably experience greater success as a learner, even in a traditional setting, because his sense of empowerment and confidence have grown.

Encouraging Conscious Reflection and Acknowledging the Unconscious

In Chapter Two, we discussed the concept of the *electronic personality* (Pratt, 1996), meaning that what is going on inside the learner inevitably shows up on the screen. As we encourage conscious, critical reflection of the material and self, this is far more likely to occur. As a course progresses and participants become more comfortable with the environment, as well as feel the increasing support from their colleagues, they may feel more comfortable with letting elements of their personalities, previously unrevealed, emerge on the screen. The following are examples of posts by an undergraduate student in a class on organizational behavior. At the beginning of the term, his posts typically looked like the one to follow; it appears exactly as it did in the online classroom:

I THINK ONE OF THE DRAWBACKS IS A TIME FACTOR WE DONT HAVE AS QUICK OF A DISCUSSION, WE AREN'T ALL ON AT THE SAME TIME AND THAT CAN MAKE THINGS A LITTLE DELAYED. ALSO IF YOU WANT TO SAY SOMETHING SOMETIMES YOUR FACIAL EXPRESSIONS AREN'T INVOLVED AND THERE COULD BE A BARRIER TO CROSS AND THIRD SOME PEOPLE CANT WRITE AND THIS COULD AFFECT THEM THE MOST CAUSE THEY Can't put their thoughts into words, but for the most part i am happy with this class overall! *Mike*

Mike was immediately given feedback about posting all in capital letters. In the online world, posting in capital letters generally means that one is screaming. He continued to experiment with the way he posted, and by the middle of the term he had discovered a way of posting that was comfortable for him. The following two posts illustrate the method he chose.

i think there are many issues which we have dealt with in our little cyberspace world and each person has had a different way of dealing with them. most of the people on here have went to dr. pratt when they have experienced some sort of problem, f2f that is. not many have emailed or tried to get in touch with dr. pratt on here though. i think that is because of the newness of all of this. we still feel a little uncomfortable dealing with everything on here. also the people who do not want to talk f2f do not do anything on here to communicate they just wait for someone to get a hold of them. *Mike*

to me conflict is a disagreement n beliefs or thought, it doesn't necessarily have 2 b verbalized, but it is known. if there is conflict btween 2 people n a group they each know it, but don't have 2 make it affect them. *Mike*

Although these posts might make a professor of composition shudder, we are thrilled to see posts like this. They are indications that students are attempting to express who they are textually. Mike is clearly expressing his uniqueness as a person while reflecting on the material being studied in the course. He switched from all capitals to all lowercase letters. Although this generally means that someone is diminishing their contribution in the online world, Mike is clearly not doing that. His posts are transformative in nature. He is looking at and commenting on the process of online learning as he is experiencing it, as well as how he sees the involvement of his student colleagues. In addition, he is clearly engaged with and reflecting on the course material. If Mike had submitted these posts as written material in a traditional classroom, he would likely have failed the assignment or been asked, at the very least, to revise it. In the online classroom, however, he is surfacing a part of him that others would not normally see—his electronic personality.

Final Thoughts: We Are the Experts When It Comes to Our Own Learning

Although it may seem daunting to an instructor in an online course to be far more than someone who imparts knowledge, there is no need to be fearful of the transformative process that this form of learning sets in motion. It is a process that will occur, whether or not an instructor purposefully facilitates it, when the course is designed to allow participants to explore beyond the confines of the course material. We have subtitled this section "We Are the Experts When It Comes to Our Own Learning"—truly a definition of the transformative learning process.

When students are empowered to become experts at their own learning, they cannot help but be transformed as people. Their self-esteem rises, as does their confidence in their abilities. They learn about areas they never thought possible before, one of which may be technology. The main task of instructors as facilitators of this process is to bring forth their best instructional practices and then get out of the way. If an instructor is willing and able to give up control of the process, amazing things can happen. Students who may sit quietly and not do well in the traditional classroom may emerge as the leaders in the online classroom, presenting thoughtful and knowledgeable material for others to consider. Rather than a process to be feared, the transformative learning process is one of the most exciting aspects of online learning. This process can also be purposefully integrated into the evaluation of individual performance within the course, as well as evaluation of the course itself—topics we will discuss in the next chapter. What follows are some questions to consider in order to welcome and facilitate the occurrence of transformative learning in an online course.

Guiding Questions to Promote Transformative Learning

The following questions are designed not only to allow for reflection on the transformative learning process as it occurs in an online course but to reflect on an instructor's level of comfort with the process. Stephen Brookfield (1995) notes that "those of us who are trying to get colleagues to identify and question their assumptions, or to look at their practice through different lenses, must do the same" (p. 205). If an instructor is uncomfortable with this aspect of online teaching, it will likely be missed or discouraged in the context of the course. Therefore, the questions that follow are self-reflective. We cannot encourage our students to engage in a transformative process if we are unwilling to do so ourselves.

How do I view myself as an instructor? Do I see myself as an expert? Am I open to the views and opinions of others? How do I process those views when I encounter them?

How much more do I feel I need to learn about teaching and about my subject matter?

How do I generally run a class? Do I rely on lecture and discussion methods?

In the traditional classroom setting, do I empower students to pursue knowledge on their own? Do I routinely incorporate collaborative exercises and assignments into my courses?

How do discussions generally go in my courses? Are they dominated by a few? Are my classes truly interactive?

How comfortable do I feel with the concept of promoting self-knowledge in learners? Do I honestly feel that this should be the work of someone other than a teacher, such as a counselor or therapist?

How comfortable am I when students disagree with my point of view? How would I feel if a student suggested that I read material they have discovered in their learning process?

Do I feel that I need to maintain control of the learning environment? How comfortable would I feel in giving over that control to the learners and being an equal participant?

How comfortable am I with receiving material from students that is not grammatically correct and well written but is nevertheless an expression of self?

How do I define learning? What do I hope to see as learning outcomes from an online class?

CHAPTER TEN

EVALUATION

In the previous chapter we discussed several places in an online course where the process of transformative learning logically connects to evaluation. When we refer to evaluation, we mean several different forms of evaluation that may occur throughout the course: student performance, including student self-evaluation; the course and the quality of instruction; and the technology being used, including its functionality and user friendliness. Finally, the total online program should be evaluated in terms of its usefulness in the overall institutional context. All of these forms of evaluation should lead to an ongoing process of planning and review so that online courses and programs can be continuously improved.

Evaluation Basics

Course and student progress evaluation generally take two forms: *formative* and *summative* evaluation. Formative evaluation is an ongoing process that can occur at any point throughout the course; it can surface gaps in course material or in learners' ability to grasp that material. Formative evaluation gives instructors a way to shift focus if the course is not proceeding according to plan. Summative evaluation assesses the completed course and is most often the model of evaluation used in academic institutions. Stephen Brookfield (1995), in commenting on the reliance on summative evaluation, states that this form of evaluation is really a measure of student satisfaction with the course and the instructor and not a measure of the dynamics and rhythms of student learning. He advocates for another form of evaluation when he states: "Knowing something of how students experience learning helps us build convincing connections between what we want them to do and their own concerns and expectations" (p. 93).

Evaluating an online course using only summative methods serves to ignore many of the important concepts we have been discussing that are related to this form of teaching and learning. If instructors are truly establishing a collaborative, transformative process, then formative as well as summative evaluation must be used. Formative evaluation helps determine to what extent instructors are successfully facilitating reflection on the course material under study, reflection on this means of learning, and reflection on self as a learner as the course progresses. Summative evaluation helps us know how well we have achieved the goals and learning outcomes we established going into the course. We will now look at each of these forms of evaluation and discuss ways to accomplish them in an online course. Additionally, we will explore the areas in need of evaluation and suggest ways to do so.

Student Performance

Harasim and others (1996), in reflecting on the evaluation of online courses, state: "In keeping with a learner-centered approach, evaluation and assessment should be part of the learning-teaching process, embedded in class activities and in the interactions between learners and between learners and teachers" (p. 167). They are describing an ongoing formative evaluation process that is built into the class structure.

If instructors have done a good job of establishing learning guidelines and outcomes, as well as the criteria for evaluating student performance, then establishing a formative process of student evaluation should be relatively easy. These evaluations should take multiple sources of data into account, such as the quantity of posts and the quality of participation in the online discussion. Performance on course assignments and other class exercises should also be considered. As can be noted by the examples of student posts used to illustrate various points throughout this book, we continuously scan the online dialogue for spontaneous comments related to learning objectives and the quality of the learning experience. The dialogue generated in an online course can be a rich source of evaluation material if an instructor remains alert to its presence, seeking examples as they appear.

Using the Dialogue as a Source of Evaluative Material

In addition to scanning the dialogue for spontaneous posts of evaluative material, instructors can post questions for students to consider that relate the material under study to the process of the online group. This can provide yet another source of data for evaluation. For example, in one author's undergraduate organizational behavior class, he related the material in the text on conflict in organizations to conflict in the group when he asked the following: "The book states that 'conflict between groups is inevitable' and that the conflict will be either positive or negative. Do you believe that if I put this group back into the face-to-face classroom that there would be conflict? If so what type of conflict? What could be done to prevent the conflict? What steps could I take to build a cohesive team if this happened?" By asking this type of question, we hope that, through their responses, group members will begin to look at and evaluate their own process, thus providing the instructor with important information. In this case, students were asked to compare their process online to what might occur if they were face to face. We were looking here for indicators of how well the group was coalescing online and whether or not the skills being learned in this medium were transferrable to the traditional face-to-face classroom. The following responses to the question posed indicate how well this process was occurring.

As a group I think the online students would have positive conflict with the traditional class. We would have different opinions, because we are different types of people. We had the choice to enter the online class. Like last week's discussion stated, we think that the advantages outweigh the need to be in the classroom. The people who chose the traditional class obviously felt the classroom would be better for them. There is conflict, but we could learn from each other about our experiences. I think the first step in building a cohesive team is to recognize and understand each individual's strengths and weaknesses. Consider a group working on a project, composed of traditional and online students. The traditional students might be more comfortable around people. It would make sense for them be the presenters. The online students might be more comfortable putting the ideas down on paper. *Jason*

I agree with Jason. I think that we are sensitive to each others feelings in the online class because we like to keep the conversation going and respect that the other people are posting. For example, when Stacy and I discussed that one week about [another professor], I saw her at track practice and she asked if I was offended by anything that she said. We were honest and just said we were only stating our opinions, no hard feelings. In the normal classroom, sometimes things are taken the wrong way when there is disagreement and one person may have hurt feelings or hold a grudge. *Carmen*

These posts indicate that students are reflecting on the process of the online classroom and offering ideas and opinions about why they feel it is working well for them. We can also tell that the group has coalesced and that this coalescence is extending beyond the online realm. They are seeking each other out in other situations and checking with each other about the nature and impact of their work online. Additionally, inferences are being made about how the participants might deal with issues in the face-to-face classroom differently, based on their experiences online. This material provides a part of the ongoing evaluation of the occurrence of collaborative and transformative learning—two desired learning outcomes for this course. Through asking this type of question, the instructor has contributed to the ongoing formative evaluation of student performance in this course.

Evaluating Student Assignments

One of the fears we frequently hear expressed by instructors as we present our workshops on distance learning has to do with cheating. Instructors want to know how to monitor or eliminate cheating in the online environment. We hope we have conveyed that when a course is well constructed, is learner-centered, and promotes learner empowerment and self-reflection, the notion of cheating should not become a concern. If the assignments promote the use of critical thinking and are designed to be shared with the remainder of the group, then participants gain a sense of responsibility for producing pieces of learning that will be useful for the others in the group. As one of our participants aptly put it, "We [the participants] were all the teachers for one another." Our experience has shown us that if we trust and empower our learners, they realize that they are the experts at their own learning. Cheating is irrelevant in this process because the participant would be cheating only him- or herself.

Grading student assignments can be accomplished in a number of ways. First, we frequently ask students to submit a self-evaluation as part of the closure process for the course. In it, we ask how well students feel they have met their learning goals for the course and how well they feel they performed overall. We often ask students in a graded course to determine what grade they think they have earned. In a large class that has been divided up into work teams, the group may be asked to appoint a leader who can, if the instructor feels comfortable with this, suggest grades for team members based on their level of contribution to the group. The group itself can also negotiate a group grade on collaborative assignments. Finally, we frequently refer to the guidelines established at the beginning of the class to determine the relative weight placed on each aspect. In a class that relies heavily on discussion, the quality and quantity of student posts become evaluative material. Assignments or exams are evaluated separately; all are averaged, along with participation, at the end of the class.

If an instructor wants to include examinations and quizzes in the evaluation of student performance, additional planning needs to occur. Some courseware allows for the creation of online tests and quizzes, with the added feature of allowing students to receive immediate feedback on correct answers. The results of these tests and quizzes are usually stored in an encrypted data file that is not accessible to students. Consequently, an instructor can be relatively assured that once students take an exam, they will be unable to alter the results. The instructor cannot be certain, however, that the student whose name appears on the exam is the person who actually took it. Consequently, some instructors have used proctored testing sites, either on campus or in remote locations, to gain some assurance that this form of cheating will not occur. Additionally, instructors have made arrangements to use remote facilities in courses where lab work is necessary. This allows for the online teaching of science courses, as well as courses that have a need for face-to-face contact such as courses in counseling techniques. Other techniques include laboratory exercises on videotapes or CD-ROMs that are sent to the participants, as well as computer-based simulations. Once again, however, we issue a caution: including such materials assumes that students can receive and work with them. Instructors must either make the use of these materials a condition of enrollment in the course or adapt them for those who, for whatever reason, cannot use them.

Using Collaborative Assessment

The evaluation of student assignments in an online course should not be the job of the instructor alone. Students should be asked to evaluate their own performance and to receive feedback from each other throughout the course. Developing skills in giving effective feedback and in self-assessment can be useful in the promotion of collaborative and transformative learning. Greg Wiggins (1998), in his book *Educative Assessment*, gives further credence to the use of ongoing feedback when he states: "The receipt and use of feedback must be an ongoing, routine part of assessment. The reason for making feedback concurrent with performing is that this is the only way students can learn to self-assess continually and then self-adjust their intellectual performance, just as musicians, artists, athletes, and other performers continually self-assess and self-adjust" (pp. 59–60).

We are describing a form of *360-degree feedback*, as it is termed in the business world (London and Beatty, 1993). In a business organization, an employee receiving such feedback compares anonymous feedback from a superior, subordinates, and peers with self-perception of performance. In the online course, self-perception is compared against feedback from the instructor and peers—feedback that may be private but not anonymous. This feedback can be delivered to a participant privately, through the use of e-mail, or posted on the course site for the group to see and review. If the latter approach is used, the instructor needs to feel comfortable that adequate trust exists within the group, that feedback is professionally delivered, and that it will promote continuous quality improvement and enhancement of the learning process.

Brookfield (1995) discusses the importance of taking into account the students' perception of their own progress. What seems like minimal progress to an instructor may be a major leap in a student's eyes. Consequently, students' self-assessment regarding the amount of learning gained and the achievement of their learning objectives is often just as important, or more so, than the instructor's evaluation of their work. The following is an example of the type of self-assessment we seek.

I thought teaching in this setting was a great learning experience. It was convenient to complete the work at whatever time I wished. If I was busy one day I could do it the next. If I knew I would be busy I could do the work ahead of time. That's not possible in traditional classes. Sometimes students are not given the opportunity to express their views fully. I am not the type of person that stereotypically should excel in an online class. I like to express my views in class. I am usually not the guy sitting in the corner who might have something intelligent to say if only someone asked him. As early as grade school I found out that the only way I was going to understand anything was to ask questions. I thrive on immediate feedback and information. I think that I adjusted to this class rather well. It provided me with new views and opinions and also with the feedback I need. Reading someone's response to my post, whether they agree or disagree, is what made this class rewarding. . . . Overall this class was a success for me. I learned some things about myself that I didn't know before. I now realize the importance of budgeting time. I also realize that some of my crazy ideas don't seem so crazy when shared by others. I enjoyed the class immensely and look forward to the availability of more online classes. *Jason*

Additional Assessment Considerations

Additional considerations in evaluating student assignments in the online course are the needs and learning objectives students identified at the start of the course, their educational level, their familiarity with technology and online learning (and any problems that may have occurred as they adjusted to the use of technology), and issues related to writing. Finally, the assessment of participation is critical.

Because we are using a learner-centered approach in the online classroom, evaluation of student assignments needs to take into account how well the assignment met the learning needs of the participant. Requesting that students give us feedback on the utility of an assignment in their learning process assists us with ongoing evaluation of the course as well. We have received feedback such as, "This was a great case to work with. It stimulated my thinking." However, receiving feedback such as "I didn't find the question of the week very interesting and I really had to push myself to say anything" also gives us a great deal of information about how well we are meeting the learning objectives of a particular student and what kinds of adjustments need to be made in order to make the class more challenging.

As feedback is provided to students, it is important to consider their level of experience educationally and in the online environment. Some students may take longer to become involved in the online discussion if they are experiencing technical difficulties or adjusting to the use of technology for the first time. These students should be encouraged through feedback about the progress they are making in this regard and not penalized in their evaluations because they are not as technologically adept as others in the group.

Except in the submission of assignments, we usually do not comment on the mechanics of writing as they pertain to online posts. Because students frequently compose their posts while online, they are likely to make spelling and grammar errors. Students for whom English is not their primary language may have numerous writing errors in their posts. We have found that encouraging students to post without editing promotes spontaneity and liveliness in the discussion. When students are concerned about being corrected for the spelling and grammar contained in their posts, they may not post as often or may become uncomfortable and discouraged with the medium.

Significant weight must be placed on the level and quality of participation in an online course, which is not true in a traditional face-to-face course. We have discussed the importance of establishing participation guidelines at the onset. Having established guidelines, then, we have a responsibility to follow up—to evaluate the quantity and quality of participation at the close of the course when we award grades, if that is an institutional requirement. Many courseware applications allow an instructor to request reports of how many times and when students have accessed the course site, whether they posted or not. If this is not built into the software, an instructor may choose to count the number of posts per student as a means of evaluating attendance and level of participation. These measures are particularly useful in academic institutions requiring attendance reports from instructors at the close of a term.

Good participation should be recognized and subsequently rewarded, and instructors must feel comfortable with the added weight that must be placed on this element of the course. A department chair, who had taught only one course online and whose responsibility was to review all course syllabi in his department, established a requirement for all instructors that the maximum weight permitted for the grading of class participation be 10 percent. Discussion with him revealed that he thought it was punitive to quieter students to demand more participation. He had a difficult time understanding that in the online classroom, posting to the course site represents the bulk of the course. He also admitted that his first online course had been a dismal failure due to lack of participation. The "quieter students" in an online course are simply not there. Following our conversation, he agreed to reconsider his decision and allow online instructors the leeway to establish participation guidelines that make sense for that medium.

Course Evaluation

Many academic institutions require the use of a course evaluation format that is standardized across the organization. These evaluation forms rarely address whether or not a class has supported students in achieving their learning objectives. Instead, they tend to evaluate whether the student liked the instructor or the course (Brookfield, 1995). Particularly in the case of adjunct instructors, these evaluations are used to determine whether or not the instructor will be retained to teach again and are more a measure of popularity than of learning achievement.

Given the nature of the online course and the myriad of goals it is attempting to achieve, this type of course evaluation form is not very useful in determining whether the course was successful in achieving the objectives set forth at the start of the course. However, it will tell us whether or not students enjoyed learning in this fashion. Additionally, the interpretation of the data received is at issue because of the technology being used to deliver the course. We now turn our attention to the elements of good course evaluation in the online environment, as well as the elements that need to be taken into account as that evaluation is interpreted.

Elements of Course Evaluations in the Online Classroom

At the beginning of this chapter, we discussed the importance of using formative evaluation in the online classroom. Questions need to be asked throughout to determine how students are experiencing the course, the mode of instruction, and the online environment. At a minimum, these types of questions need to be asked of students midway through the course and again at the end. Based on the answers, instructors need to be prepared to alter the direction of the course in order to make it more responsive to the needs of the learners.

Many times, participants are unwilling to be completely honest about their evaluation of a course or an instructor due to fear of repercussions (Brookfield, 1995). Consequently, the willingness of participants to be honest will relate to whether a trusting, cohesive community among the learners has been established— one that includes the instructor as an equal member. The following responses to questions evaluating an online course at its conclusion are indicative that trust has been developed and that students are willing, at least to some degree, to be honest about their experience in the course.

I loved this class! It gave me the freedom to come to class when I wanted and not have to look at that ugly teacher for another class. I think that teaching a class through this medium forces people to learn to communicate through words, and gives them confidence in what they are saying. In a classroom some people are afraid to speak because of the thought of being wrong, but here they have no choice, saying nothing is wrong. For me this class allowed me to sleep when I wanted to and study when I wanted. At a university that is as controlling as [ours] is this class was the complete opposite. We all had the freedom that [our university] does not want us to have, to come and go as we please. *Mason*

Another shortcoming I saw in the class was the actual work itself. It was difficult to discuss one question for a whole week. Sometimes an expression of our views was all that was required. Once my thoughts were posted, there wasn't much more to say. With that, I would like to express my thanks to the instructors for trying to keep the ball rolling every week. More variety would have made for a more interesting class. I liked the group work. It was different to collaborate to achieve a common goal instead of expressing individual opinions. I realize that this medium has certain limitations but other group projects would have been fun. . . . I didn't like the confusion we experienced when choosing teams. I know that it was mostly the students' fault but that was one situation where it would have been easier to have everyone together in a room. . . . I was also disappointed with the user interface. I thought it was a bit outdated. That is a tedious complaint and should receive no real attention, but I thought I would share my view. *Jason*

At times in the face-to-face classroom, when students are given the opportunity to provide course and instructor feedback anonymously, they feel comfortable being painfully honest about their experiences in the class. The difference here is that the feedback is being owned and shared by the participants. Clearly, these students felt that their opinions and feedback would be used in the spirit in which they were delivered—to work toward continuous improvement of the class and instructional methods they had just experienced. The honesty with which these thoughts are delivered indicates that trust has developed in the group and with the instructor. The comments demonstrate the achievement of the more important learning objectives for the class.

Interpretation of the Feedback

The difficulty with receiving feedback such as that presented in the previous section lies in its reception. The instructor and the institution should receive and interpret it without assuming that the course has been a failure. Stephen Brookfield (1995) comments on this phenomenon.

Many teachers take an understandable pride in their craft wisdom and knowledge. They want to be good at what they do, and consequently, set great store by students' evaluations of their teaching. When these are less than perfect—as is almost inevitable—teachers assume the worst. All those evaluations that are complimentary are forgotten, those that are negative assume disproportionate significance. Indeed, the inference is often made that bad evaluations must, by definition, be written by students with heightened powers of pedagogic discrimination. Conversely, good evaluations are thought to be produced by students who are half-asleep [p. 17].

As we think about the receipt of feedback, it is important to consider the additional constraints that the online classroom provides. In the face-to-face classroom, an instructor can fairly easily establish a sense of presence. Students can see them and interact with them. One instructor may be active and lively. Another may tell lots of stories and jokes; yet another may be more somber and serious. When students evaluate a course in which they see the instructor in action, they cannot help but take these factors into account. In the online classroom, however, the instructor is represented predominantly by text. Just as with their students, an instructor's engagement with the material and the course is demonstrated through the number, length, and quality of his or her posts. In many cases, the students and instructor may never meet. The physical manifestation of the instructor may be a photograph on a homepage. Although this creates a difficult evaluation process, it also serves, on some level, to make the feedback received from students more valuable, as it relates directly to their experience of the course and the material they have studied rather than reflecting the personality of the instructor.

Program Evaluation

The last but certainly not the least important area in need of evaluation is the online program itself. Ideally, good planning and thinking have gone into the creation of an online program. But even when this is not the case, it is important to receive feedback from participants on their overall experience of working online through the institution. It is important to determine how well the technology worked for them and whether they received the technical support they needed, as well as any suggestions they might have for additional courses to be offered online. Not only do participants need to be involved in this level of evaluation but faculty need to provide feedback on their experience of teaching in the online environment and what they feel is needed to improve it.

Program evaluation begins with the planning phase of an educational program and concludes with follow-up studies to determine the program's effectiveness. At its core is an attempt to determine the value of the educational program being offered (Caffarella, 1994). Given this, all constituents involved with the program need to be involved with its evaluation. In the case of the online program, the constituents include the participants, the faculty, and the institution through which the program was delivered. The three groups, however, have different needs and concerns that should be reviewed.

For participants, ease of access to the program, smooth, seamless delivery, and availability of immediate support are generally of greatest concern. In addition, the breadth of the program, meaning the numbers and types of courses available, are important.

Faculty are also concerned with the ease of access and smooth delivery of the course. They too expect to receive support when needed. However, the greatest need for faculty in the distance learning arena is the availability of training to support their work online. The training they receive should not be limited to the technology used for course delivery but should include electronic pedagogy. Institutions offering distance learning programs need to ask faculty what their needs are in order to improve their work and offer courses that are of high quality. Which courses would faculty like to see offered in this medium? Is there a need to assess student appropriateness for online courses? If so, how will this occur?

Currently, institutions are taking all students who express an interest in or desire to participate in online work, as long as they meet internal academic requirements. Few institutions are assessing the appropriateness of a given student to participate in this medium. The following self-assessment appears on the website of De Anza College to help students determine whether they should participate in online learning. It is the only one we have encountered.

How well would Distance Learning courses fit your circumstances and lifestyle? Circle an answer for each question and score as directed below. Answer honestly—no one will see this but you! (Adapted from "Are Telecourses For Me?" and printed in the PBS-Adult Learning Service The Agenda, Spring, 1994, this questionnaire was developed by the Northern Virginia Community College Extended Learning Institute.)

1. My need to take this course now is:
   a. High—I need it immediately for a specific goal.
   b. Moderate—I could take it on campus later or substitute another course.
   c. Low—it could be postponed.
2. Feeling that I am part of a class is:
   a. Not particularly necessary to me.
   b. Somewhat important to me.
   c. Very important to me.

3. I would classify myself as someone who:
   a. Often get things done ahead of time.
   b. Needs reminding to get things done on time.
   c. Puts things off until the last minute or doesn't complete them.
4. Classroom discussion is:
   a. Rarely helpful to me.
   b. Sometimes helpful to me.
   c. Almost always helpful to me.
5. When an instructor hands out directions for an assignment, I prefer:
   a. Figuring out the instructions myself.
   b. Trying to follow the directions on my own, then asking for help as needed.
   c. Having the instructions explained to me.
6. I need faculty comments on my assignments:
   a. Within a few weeks, so I can review what I did.
   b. Within a few days, or I forget what I did.
   c. Right away, or I get very frustrated.
7. Considering my professional and personal schedule, the amount of time I have to work on a Distance Learning course is:
   a. More than enough for an on campus course.
   b. The same as for a class on campus.
   c. Less than for a class on campus.
8. Coming to campus on a regular schedule is:
   a. Extremely difficult for me—I have commitments (work, family, or personal) during times when classes are offered.
   b. A little difficult, but I can rearrange my priorities to allow for regular attendance on campus.
   c. Easy for me.
9. As a reader, I would classify myself as:
   a. Good—I usually understand the text without help.
   b. Average—I sometimes need help to understand the text.
   c. Slower than average.
10. When I need help understanding the subject:
    a. I am comfortable approaching an instructor to ask for clarification.
    b. I am uncomfortable approaching an instructor, but do it anyway.
    c. I never approach an instructor to admit I don't understand something.

Scoring

Add 3 points for each "a" that you circled, 2 for each "b," and 1 for each "c." If you scored 20 or over, a distance learning course is a real possibility for you. If you scored between 11 and 20, distance learning courses may work for you, but you may need to make a few adjustments in your schedule and study habits to succeed. If you scored 10 or less, distance learning may not currently be the best alternative for you; talk to your counselor.

Explanations

1. Distance Learning students sometimes neglect their courses because of personal or professional circumstances. Having a compelling reason for taking the course helps motivate the student to stick with the course.
2. Some students prefer the independence of Distance Learning; others find the independence uncomfortable and miss being part of the classroom experience.
3. Distance Learning courses give students greater freedom of scheduling, but they can require more self-discipline than on-campus classes.
4. Some people learn best by interacting with other students and instructors. Others learn better by listening, reading and reviewing on their own. Some Distance Learning courses provide less opportunity for group interaction than most on-campus courses.
5. Distance Learning requires you to work from written directions.
6. It may take as long as two to three weeks to get comments back from your instructor in Distance Learning classes.
7. Distance Learning requires at least as much time as on-campus courses. Students surveyed say that Distance Learning courses are as hard or harder than on campus courses.
8. Most people who are successful with Distance Learning find it difficult to come to campus on a regular basis because of their work/family/personal schedules.
9. Print materials are the primary source of directions and information in Distance Learning courses.
10. Students who do well in Distance Learning courses are usually comfortable contacting the instructor as soon as they need help with the course.

Not all students will be successful in the distance learning arena. This self-assessment is one attempt at helping students look at whether or not this medium is for them. Another way to establish appropriateness is to empower faculty to make that decision early in the course and enable them to move the student to a face-to-face situation should that be in the student's best interest. Furthermore, as students apply for admission to an online program or course, someone should discuss with them the rigors involved with this form of study, as well as the orientation to the demands of the medium. It should not be assumed that all students can succeed in an online course; not all students succeed in a face-to-face environment. Institutional investment in this type of screening and orientation will provide benefits down the line. A continuous lack of success in an online program can reflect on the institution, resulting in lower enrollments and a perception that the online program is of poor quality. Therefore, these types of considerations are critical to the institutional planning of online coursework, as well as the evaluation of the effectiveness of the program.

Finally, institutions may want to consider the use of focus groups and strategic thinking with the students and the facilitators of online classes; focus groups should be conducted by someone outside the participating group. The use of this type of evaluative technique can provide the institution with valuable information from all sectors that can be used for the purpose of continuous quality improvement.

Final Thoughts

We cannot place enough emphasis on the importance of evaluating all aspects of the online course, from the performance of individual students to the effectiveness of the course and instructor to the effectiveness of the overall program. The ongoing use of good evaluation assists in expanding online programs and course offerings in a more deliberate way and helps attract students to this medium. Evaluation is an important component of good planning. It provides a feedback loop in the planning process that enables us to "walk our talk." As we ask our participants to reflect on the ways they have changed through their involvement in an online course, so should we ask ourselves how we might transform and improve our teaching and delivery of online classes and programs. This medium does not allow us to become complacent. It is developing much too rapidly for instructors and institutions to become too comfortable with their existing online programs. Therefore, we owe it to our students and ourselves to keep abreast of the changes as they occur, be prepared to accept feedback, both positive and negative, and adapt our approaches and programs to the needs of our learners. In this learner-centered environment, this is the only approach that makes sense.

Questions to Consider in Student, Course, and Program Evaluation

The following is a sample of evaluation questions that might be used both midway and at the end of an online course to evaluate course effectiveness, the experience of online learning for the participants, and self-evaluation of the participants' perceptions of how well they achieved their learning objectives. This is not meant to be an exhaustive list but rather to stimulate thinking regarding the types of questions that might be asked in order to move beyond the traditional forms of evaluation. Many authors have written on the topics of course, student, and program evaluation. Three have, in part, inspired this list of questions: Stephen Brookfield (1995), Rosemary Caffarella (1994), and Grant Wiggins (1998). We encourage readers interested in moving in new directions with evaluation to review their work.

Student Evaluation

What was most useful to me in my learning process? What was least useful?

Did I achieve my learning objectives in this course? If yes, what did I achieve? If no, what got in the way of achieving those objectives?

What did I learn about my own learning process by taking this course? How did I change as a learner through my involvement with this course?

Do I feel that what I learned in and through this course will have application in other areas of my life? If so, where will I apply this knowledge?

How well did I participate in this course? Am I satisfied with my level and quality of participation?

Did I see myself as an active member of the group? Did I contribute adequately to collaborative assignments?

How would I evaluate my performance in this class overall?

Course and Instructor Evaluation

How well did the class meet your needs as a student?

How did you feel about the mode of instruction?

Did you feel that the instructor was responsive to you and the rest of the group?

How do you feel overall about online learning?

What did you see as the strengths of this class?

What recommendations would you make to the instructor of this course to improve it?

What advice would you give to future students who will take this course online?

Program Evaluation

How easy was it to access the course site?

How easy was it to navigate the course site once it was accessed?

Did you have any concerns about the software used?

Were you able to receive technical support when needed? How would you evaluate the quality of that support?

Do you feel that the online program should be expanded? Reduced? Kept about the same?

If you think the program should be expanded, what additional courses would you like to see offered?

Are you enrolled in an online degree program? How well is that program meeting your learning needs? What suggestions would you make to improve the quality of the program?

CHAPTER ELEVEN

LESSONS LEARNED AND A LOOK AHEAD

Computer-mediated distance learning is a growing phenomenon. Some people are dismayed by this fact; they believe this signals the end of traditional classroom education as we know it. Others fear that once a course has been converted for use online the need for faculty will disappear. We have attempted to dispel some of those fears through the presentation of a new form of pedagogy—electronic pedagogy.

We do not believe that distance learning will replace the traditional classroom. However, it continues to appeal to nontraditional students for a number of reasons, the main one being that the structure and confines of the traditional classroom simply do not work.

Electronic pedagogy does not advocate the elimination of faculty in the delivery of online courses. In fact, just the opposite is true. We are promoting the development of new approaches and skills for faculty so that their teaching in this medium might be more effective. Electronic pedagogy is not about fancy software packages or simple course conversion. It is about developing the skills involved with community building among a group of learners so as to maximize the benefits and potential that this medium holds in the educational arena. In this final chapter, we summarize and review the important lessons we have learned through our experience of teaching electronically. We highlight the unanswered questions with which institutions continue to struggle as this phenomenon grows. Finally, we take a look ahead, suggesting implications and potential future directions for this work.

The Keys to Success in Distance Learning—Revisited

At the conclusion of Chapter One, we offered six elements that we feel are critical to the success of distance learning: *honesty, responsiveness, relevance, respect, openness, and empowerment.* Although these are simple concepts, without any one of them, a virtual learning community cannot function. We now discuss each of these in terms of its importance in the creation of a learning community and the contribution each makes to a successful outcome in an online learning experience.

Honesty

In order for participants to connect with each other, there must be a sense of safety and trust. Participants must feel comfortable that the others in the group are who they say they are and that they will post messages that provide open, honest feedback. In addition, participants must feel that their posts will be received in an atmosphere of caring, connection, and trust. If all of this is to occur, members of the online group must be honest with each other, and with the instructor or facilitator as well. If members of the group sense that the instructor is not being honest with them, they will have difficulty being honest with each other. Although honest feedback is sometimes difficult to hear, it is critical to the development of an online learning community and to the transformative nature of this type of learning.

Responsiveness

An online learning community simply cannot exist unless members respond to each other and the instructor responds quickly to the other participants. Unlike the face-to-face educational environment, learning in the online classroom only occurs when the participants interact with each other and with the instructor. Through interactions with each other, the members of the group create understanding of the material they are struggling with together. They are mutually responsible for the acquisition of knowledge.

Additionally, the importance of collaboration in achieving learning outcomes hinges on the group's ability to work with and respond to each other. Two-way interaction with a given student and the instructor simply is not enough. Faculty members who have never taught an online course have asked us, "Isn't this just like a correspondence course?" The interaction between and collaboration with other members of the group significantly distinguishes computer-mediated distance learning from a correspondence course, even though distance learning derives its roots from there.

The responsiveness of the instructor to the needs and concerns of the participants is also a crucial element. If participants are struggling with the technology or with each other, the instructor needs to be prepared to intervene and to do so quickly. While an online course is in process, an instructor is on duty seven days a week. This is not a responsibility to be taken lightly, either by faculty or by their institutions.

Relevance

The beauty of distance learning is its ability to bring life in the outside world into the classroom. In order for students to get their hands around the topic they are studying, it must have some relevance for them. Relating the subject matter to their life experiences and being encouraged to seek out and share real-life examples to illustrate it only enhances the learning outcome. This practice also begins to promote a sense of being an expert when it comes to the learning process. Every participant has something relevant to share with the group, whether it be a story from their workplace or family life or a pertinent case example. Encouraging students to bring their experiences into the online classroom helps the entire group in the meaning-making process.

Respect

In order to coalesce as a learning community, members need to feel as though they are being respected as people. This begins with an initial welcome to the group and continues through the respectful receipt of their posts and the receipt of constructive and expansive feedback on the material they present. Students need to feel as if they are equal participants in the learning process. The instructor holds no more power in the learning process than they do. Even the assessment, evaluation, and grading processes can be shared with the group. The creation and maintenance of an online learning community works best when the instructor relinquishes power to the group and, as we like to state it, gets into the sandbox and plays as an equal. This demonstrates that the instructor understands that students are learners who will, given the opportunity, pursue knowledge and meaning with only gentle guidance. If we demonstrate this type of respect for our students, they will respond in kind.

Another indicator of respect is the willingness of the members of the group to preserve its sanctity. In other words, members of the group keep confidential any information of a personal nature that a member may choose to share online. Every effort is made to keep "lurkers" from entering the group without the members' consent. Postings made by one member will not be shared in another forum without consent. Members agree to maintain a code of ethics, including an agreement not to harass or stalk another member. Issues of basic respect for other human beings are magnified in this environment and must not be assumed. Guidelines negotiated by the group need to include the requirement that everyone show respect for the other participants.

Openness

Although related to the topic of honesty, openness relates more to the environment created within the group and is a product of the ability to be honest with and have respect for each other. In an atmosphere of openness, students can feel free to share their thoughts and feelings without fear of retribution. In an open, online classroom, students should not be afraid that their grade will be affected by the nature of their opinions. Again, this represents the ability of all participants to give and receive feedback with respect and the confidence that it will be received in the spirit with which it was sent. If an atmosphere of safety and trust has been successfully created, members can feel confident that, if they are open with one another, only positive outcomes will result.

Empowerment

A sense of empowerment is both a crucial element and a desired outcome of participation in an online learning community. In a learner-centered environment, the learner is truly the expert when it comes to his or her own learning. Consequently, participants in the online learning community take on new roles and responsibilities in the learning process and should be encouraged to pursue knowledge wherever that path takes them. We hope that, once students experience this form of learning, it will follow them and provide them with a new foundation from which to experience other forms of learning. In the construction of a transformative learning environment, the participants gain a new view of themselves and a new sense of confidence in their ability to interact with knowledge.

One of our participants summed up the importance of all of these elements in the formation of a successful learning community:

We find honesty, responsibility, trust and mutually respective behavior—traits that are all too rare in our increasingly paranoid and hostile culture. This medium, then, is where we can turn the tide. Through computer communication, we quickly evolved from individuals embedded in their separateness into community. [This seminar] celebrates the community spirit of wholeness and connection. *Cyd*

Not only are these traits rare in our culture, they are rarely related to our educational experiences. As we hope that students will carry these elements with them into other learning experiences, we also hope faculty will do the same; electronic pedagogy is the use of our best teaching practices.

The Essence of Distance Learning: Community

Without the purposeful formation of an online learning community in distance learning, we are doing nothing new and different. In giving us feedback on our earliest electronic seminar, Don MacIntyre, president of the Fielding Institute, commented: "In talking about distance learning, I keep stressing that our focus is on the learning process and not the technology. Many institutions are jumping on the technology bandwagon so as to become a part of the information superhighway. In doing so, their goal is to use the technology to transmit a tired and stale pedagogy over fiber optic cable—as if the fiber optic cable will somehow transform the pedagogy."

The development of a learning community in the distance education process involves developing new approaches to education and new skills in its delivery. Many times when we present this concept to faculty members, they comment that this is not new information to them—that they are familiar with these practices. Why, then, do we see so many distance learning programs and classes that rely on the technology to create a new environment for learning rather than employing the skills of community building in the classroom? We believe the answer lies in the fact that many instructors have not looked closely at the distance learning environment and what it demands in order to create a successful learning outcome. Our efforts to incorporate community building into the process cannot be assumed but need to be much more purposeful in this medium.

The creation of a learning community supports and encourages knowledge acquisition. It creates a sense of excitement about learning together and renews the passion involved with exploring new realms in education. The collaboration involved in learning together in this way truly creates a sense of synergy, as Stephen Covey (1989) describes it, or a chemistry between people that creates an atmosphere of excitement and passion for learning and working together. The total outcome of knowledge acquired and shared is far greater than what would be generated through independent, individual engagement with the material. The bonus is the newly developing sense of self and sense of empowerment that accompanies the process. The power of community is great. The power of a learning community is even greater, as it supports the intellectual as well as personal growth and development of its members.

However, because this is a new and developing area of education with almost daily technological changes, as well as rapid growth and expansion, there continue to be many issues that surface in distance education and remain unresolved and unanswered. Some of these issues relate to the work required to develop a learning community in cyberspace; others relate to the infrastructure required to support it. By the time this book is published, some of these issues may be resolved. However, we are certain that, as this field continues to develop, others will emerge to take their place. In the next section, we discuss some of the issues as we see them currently. In so doing, we are striving to create points for further discussion rather than offering solutions.

Unresolved Issues and Unanswered Questions

Many institutions have entered the distance learning arena because it makes economic sense for them. The hope has been to attract nontraditional students, as defined by age, marital status, or employment status, to the academic market. The attempt has been to capture a group of students who might not otherwise attend classes in a traditional setting. However, what we are finding through our own classes, and what universities are noting, is that this form of education also attracts students in residence on campuses who may also be attending traditional face-to-face classes. They are younger and may be attracted to these classes for very different reasons. An article in the *Chronicle of Higher Education* (Guernsey, 1998) that discusses this trend notes that many residential students enroll in computer-mediated distance learning courses for convenience. But others, the article notes, "would rather learn over the Internet. They get more individual attention from instructors in online courses, and they can spend more time thinking about, and responding to, whatever questions instructors pose" (p. 4).

The phenomenon being described here is one we have discussed. The introverted student who may not feel comfortable speaking out or asking for help in a face-to-face setting may flourish in the online setting, and all students gain the luxury of control over their time while attending classes and the ability to be more thoughtful about their interactions within those classes (Pratt, 1996). This creates a set of dilemmas with which academic institutions must grapple. How will institutions come to terms with the needs of the student who prefers online learning? How will online courses be offered without jeopardizing face-to-face offerings? Will faculty need to make a choice between offering one or the other, or will departments and institutions make it possible for those faculty who prefer the online environment and who are adept at this form of teaching to offer both types of classes? What will the impact of these decisions be on such issues as faculty compensation, faculty recruitment, department and school budgets, and current marketing efforts to attract the nontraditional student, as currently defined, to the online environment? Institutions must answer these questions and more as they move solidly into computer-mediated distance learning.

Perhaps institutions will need to devise means by which to assess which courses and programs will be appropriate for online delivery. And there may be a need to develop student assessments, such as the one offered by De Anza College, to determine which students would do best in online courses as opposed to face-to-face instruction. Clearly, the old distinctions between market segments are blurring. As a result, institutions need to rethink their strategies for attracting students to the online environment and develop ways to attract students based on their learning needs rather than their life status.

Because of the need to rethink our educational strategies, Carol Twigg (1994a), then of Educom (now known as Educause), an organization devoted to looking at the transformation of education through information technology, talks about the need to rethink our current system of education for the purpose of developing a new learning infrastructure. She states:

> Our current system was developed to serve a different student population and is based on old assumptions about teaching (e.g., viewing the teacher and the classroom as the only delivery method) and learning (mastery of a body of knowledge as the way to prepare for life.) What was once the most effective and efficient way to teach and learn—the research university model of faculty who create knowledge and deliver it to students via lectures—now cracks under the strain of meeting new learning demands. As an old technology, the traditional classroom suffers from severe limitations, in both its on-campus and off-campus versions. We need a better system of learning to enable students to acquire knowledge. We need to create a support system for faculty who want to teach in this new way [p. 4].

She further states that "our understanding of how people learn is growing, suggesting that increased individualization of the learning process is the way to respond to the diverse learning styles brought by our students as they enter and re-enter the world of higher education" (Twigg, 1994b, p. 1).

Perhaps the answers to the questions and challenges posed here lie in a change of focus. In order to successfully accommodate the needs of a diverse body of learners and to make room for both traditional, nontraditional, and online approaches that may encompass both, institutions should concentrate their efforts on what learners need and are demanding, as well as what our society is demanding of our graduates. It is, as one instructor told us, "the Nordstrom approach"—a customer-service orientation to education. When academic institutions truly begin to acknowledge that students are our customers and that their service needs come first, they will be able to focus on allowing several forms of knowledge delivery to exist side by side without a sense that one is competing with the other. It is a broadening of our thinking about education in general that is needed, as institutions move into an increasingly technological future.

Lessons Learned and a Look to the Future

One of the basic requirements for education in the twenty-first century will be to prepare students for participation in a knowledge-based economy; knowledge will be the most critical resource for social and economic development. Curricular content and the approaches to twenty-first-century society are being forged through discussion and debate in the public, business, and academic sectors. It becomes increasingly clear that current educational models, structures, and approaches are inadequate. Students need new and different information resources, skills, roles, and relationships. The traditional educational model, based primarily on the concept of the school and the teacher in a classroom as islands, standing alone and not interconnected with society or other educational institutions, will not generate competence in a knowledge society (Harasim and others, 1996).

The educational opportunities that are created should be responsive to the demands of students and the world in which they work and live. As globalization and the rapid exchange of information required become more of a reality, the need for our faculty, institutions, and students to respond to that reality expands. Increasingly, the corporate sector is attempting to shape education by offering incentives to academic institutions to provide educational opportunities that are more responsive to corporate need. Although computer-mediated distance learning is not the sole response to this reality, it certainly offers a means by which students can practice and acquire the skills needed to compete. In addition to knowledge acquisition, students learn about technology through its use. They learn about themselves and their own learning styles, and about how to collaborate with others in geographically distributed teams. They learn what it takes to pace themselves in order to get the job done. As this is occurring, they become increasingly confident in their abilities, feel empowered to work in a manner that best suits them, and seek out the information they need for the task at hand. All of these skills are transferrable to the world of work and gained through participation in an online learning community.

As we stated at the beginning of this chapter, the traditional face-to-face classroom is not likely to disappear. It continues to serve the needs of many students and will do so in the future. However, what we have learned from our experience of facilitating online classes is that regardless of the setting, the creation of community greatly enhances the learning experience and the likelihood of successful learning outcomes.

Implications for Instructor Training

This work also has implications for the training and development of faculty. As students who intend to teach become more involved in successful online classes where the development of a learning community is intentionally built into the process, their experiences should translate into their own teaching. It is also important for institutions to include training for their faculty in the process of online learning as they move into this arena.

Too often, faculty training involves an introduction to the hardware and software being used to deliver classes, with no emphasis on process. Just as the technology used to deliver an online class should become transparent in the learning process, so should it become transparent in faculty training. Once again, the technology should only be used as a vehicle to convey the ability to create a collaborative, transformative process. It is only the means by which instructors and students can connect to form community. By focusing on electronic pedagogy in faculty training rather than on technology, faculty will become excited about the potential and power of this medium in the educational arena.

Online education is not the panacea that will cure the ills of education today. However, if facilitated in a way that incorporates community into the process, it is a way to promote a generation of empowered learners who can successfully navigate the demands of a knowledge society. As Don MacIntyre stated in observation of our first seminar and the work of the Fielding Institute involving distance learning:

> We are trying to do what no one else in higher education has done to date: create a true virtual academic community. . . . You have grappled sensitively and openly with many of the key issues of a virtual community. You have

brought together "high tech" with "high touch." You have demonstrated caring, concern, love, and support for one another. I doubt if you could find your kind of interchanges taking place in any other graduate program around the country. It was really beautiful to behold.

We find that we are touched and moved by our students in every electronic seminar we conduct. We feel that we learn as much or more than they do. Not only are we helping to shape the creation of empowered, lifelong learners, our participation as equal members of a group of learners supports us in our own quest for lifelong learning. For us, this is the power of online distance learning.

EXAMPLES OF COURSE SYLLABI

Instructor: Rena M. Palloff, Ph.D.
Quarter: Spring
Year: 1997
Course Title: *Management and Organizational Theory: A Global Perspective*
Units: 3

Level of Instruction: M.A.
Enrollment Limitations: Open to all Masters and Doctorate students
Maximum Class Size: 20 students
Grading Options: Student's option

Summary of Educational Purpose:

The purpose of this course is to introduce learners to post-modern philosophy as applied to management and organizations, to provide examples of new paradigm thinking in business, and to introduce one or more methodologies for applying new paradigm theories in the everyday, real world operation of businesses, non-profits, and government agencies. The course also provides a grounding in the history and theory of management and organizations in America. Finally, the course is intended to encourage learners to increase their exposure to and application of emergent management practices and organization designs that are humane, socially responsible, and ecologically sound.

Description of Course Content:

This course intends to build knowledge of and capacities in management and organization theories and practices. The course begins by building a foundation of the theory of mainstream management and organization. A deepening perspective will be provided by investigating post-modern philosophy as it applies to management and organizations. An additional alternative perspective is provided by an in-depth study of one type of post-modern organization, the "inventive organization." Finally, as a means of pulling all of this together, new paradigm leadership from a holistic perspective will be explored. All of these studies will be enhanced by application of the learnings to cases, the study of an existing organization of the learner's choice, and experiential exercises.

Learning Objectives:

After completing this course, learners will be able to:

1. Understand the historical and cultural foundations of mainstream American management;
2. Articulate the strengths and weaknesses of the old paradigm;
3. Understand the historical and cultural reasons for a new paradigm;
4. Build awareness of what the new paradigm looks like and might include;
5. Appreciate when and how elements of the old paradigm need to be applied, and
6. Apply elements of new paradigm theory and practice.

Learning Activities:

Learning Activities	Percent of Class Time
1. Facilitation of and participation in online dialogue	30 percent
2. Experiential exercises and case studies	10 percent
3. Participation in face-to-face meetings	30 percent
4. Final integrative paper based on application of material generated in class to an organization in the community	30 percent

In general, learning activities consist of reading, learner reflections on the reading, discussion, experiential exercises, analysis of cases, application of the materials to an organization in the community, and integration through a final paper.

Readings: Learners will complete all reading assignments in timely fashion in order to facilitate group learning and discussion, which requires full and equal participation from each individual. Each learner will take responsibility for facilitating two weeks of the online discussion during the quarter, thus assisting the learning group in sharing the reading load. However, each learner is accountable for enough familiarity with the material to adequately reflect on the readings' impact on group discussion.

Learner Reflections: As learners complete the readings, they are expected to identify a list of key concepts, ideas, and questions. These should comprise the basis for online discussion. Learners may choose to enhance these thoughts and questions through reading additional material and sharing those readings online with the learning group.

Experiential Exercises/Cases: During the face-to-face meetings, learners will participate in exercises and will complete case studies designed to stimulate and enhance learning. These will be completed as a small group. In addition, each learner will be asked to write up and turn in two case studies. One will be due at the second face-to-face meeting and one at the last face-to-face meeting.

Final Integrative Paper: At the beginning of the quarter, learners will be expected to choose an organization in the community with which they wish to form a relationship and study. During the course of the quarter, students will be encouraged to visit the organization and explore the application of the concepts discussed through the readings, online, and in the face-to-face meetings with members of that organization. At the completion of the course, learners will write a 7–10 page paper integrating the readings, discussion, and the study of this organization, illustrating the presence or absence of new paradigm thinking within this organization.

Criteria for Evaluation:	Facilitation of and participation in online dialogue	30 percent
	Case studies and experiential exercises	30 percent
	Final integrative paper	40 percent

Required Texts:

Bennis, W., Parikh, J., and Lessem, R. (1995/96), *Beyond Leadership: Balancing Economics, Ethics, and Ecology.* Cambridge, MA: Blackwell Press.

Bolman, L. and Deal, T. (1991), *Reframing Organizations: Artistry, Choice, and Leadership.* San Francisco: Jossey-Bass.

Janov, J. (1994), *The Inventive Organization: Hope and Daring at Work.* San Francisco: Jossey-Bass.

Morgan, G. (1997), *Images of Organization.* Thousand Oaks, CA: Sage Publications.

Recommended Readings:

Learners are strongly encouraged to add to a list of recommended readings as they encounter information during the course of the quarter. The following is a starting point only.

Bolman, L. and Deal, T. (1995), *Leading with Soul: An Uncommon Journey of Spirit.* San Francisco: Jossey-Bass.
Helgesen, S. (1995), *The Web of Inclusion.* New York: Currency/Doubleday.
Vaill, P. (1989), *Managing as a Performing Art.* San Francisco: Jossey-Bass.
Wheatley, M. and Kellner-Rogers, M. (1996), *A Simpler Way.* San Francisco: Berrett-Koehler.
Whyte, D. (1994), *The Heart Aroused: Poetry and the Preservation of the Soul in Corporate America.* New York: Currency/Doubleday.

Specific Assignments:

Specific assignments for this course will be posted online beginning the first week of the quarter. We will begin by reading Bolman and Deal's *Reframing Organizations* and discussing their ideas online.

WINTER, 1998

COURSE: BUS5010 E9 Quantitative Methods

INSTRUCTOR: Suzanne Thornton Garrett, MBA

TEXT: Render and Stair, Quantitative Analysis for Management, 6th edition, 1997. Prentice Hall. Required. (QM for Windows Software should be with the text.)

COURSE PREREQUISITES: BUS3180 Math for Managers and BUS3041 Statistics & Research Applications for Managers. Passing both sections of the QRT (Quantitative Reasoning Test) will waive these requirements.

COURSE OBJECTIVES:

1. To help students formulate, use and interpret mathematical models commonly used in business.
2. To see and use computerized models demonstrated in the text software and others.

COURSE REQUIREMENTS:

Students must read the assigned chapters and complete weekly assignments. Homework will be collected for grading. Quizzes will be given online and will be based on material covered in the preceding week. These will be timed from when you download to when you send an answer. These can be taken at the JFKU campus instead.

GRADING CRITERIA:

Homework and computer problems	40 percent
Cases (2 written)	25 percent
Quizzes (at least 5)	25 percent
Participation online	10 percent

Cases will be assigned from the text or from supplemental materials found in the library. The homework problem assignments will be distributed online. Participation requires involvement in the discussions online and logging on at least twice per week. I will be online almost every day.

COURSE OUTLINE:

DATE	TOPIC(S)	READING ASSIGNMENT(S)
Week of Jan. 12	Introduction to course and probability concepts	Chapters 1, 2
Week of Jan. 19	Probability distributions, decision theory	Chapters 3, 5
Week of Jan. 26	Decision trees, utility theory, quality control	Chapters 6, 7

DATE	TOPIC(S)	READING ASSIGNMENT(S)
Week of Feb. 2	Inventory models	Chapters 8, 9
Week of Feb. 9	Linear programming and applications	Chapters 10, 11
Week of Feb. 16	Linear programming continued with sensitivity analysis	Chapter 12 (skim) Chapter 13
Week of Feb. 23	Transportation models and assignment problems	Chapter 14 (sects 1–3, 7,10, 12–15) and 15
Week of Mar. 2	Queuing theory, waiting lines, simulation	Chapters 16, 17
Week of Mar. 9	Continuation of simulation; Network models	Chapter 18
Week of Mar. 16	Markov analysis; Wrap-up	Chapter 19
Week of Mar. 23	Case studies due	

Students should feel free to contact me if questions or problems arise.

Topics in Business Administration 5906S:
The Search for Soul and Spirit in the Workplace
Syllabus—Winter Quarter, 1998

Instructors: Rena M. Palloff, Ph.D., LCSW
Keith Pratt, Ph.D.

Introduction, Course Overview, and Objectives:

Writers in the area of organizational change talk about the constant change that besieges today's organizations as "turbulence" or "permanent whitewater." Right-sizing, re-engineering, and globalization are but a few of the changes having significant effect on the people who work in organizations. Jack Canfield and Jacqueline Miller (1996) in their book *Heart at Work* state, "The work environment in modern organizations leads to a parching of the human spirit. In reaction against this, people are speaking out for 'heart at work,' for 'spirit in the workplace.' We find a growing insistence that every part of society—especially the workplace where so many spend so large a portion of their lives—be conducive to the fullest development of the human being" (p. xi). Organizational writers have begun to pay attention to this growing demand and have begun to explore not only the importance of soul and spirit in the workplace, but also their implications for leadership and organizational transformation. This course will explore recent writings regarding the search for soul and spirit in the workplace, as well as how it impacts the notions of meaningful work, leadership, and organizational change.

Methods to Achieve Objectives:

1. This course will be taught online. All students are required to participate actively in the online discussion. *(Please see the guidelines attached to this syllabus.)*

2. Required Reading:
    Bolman, Lee and Deal, Terrence (1995), *Leading with Soul,* San Francisco: Jossey-Bass.
    Canfield, Jack and Miller, Jacqueline (1996), *Heart at Work,* New York: McGraw-Hill.
    Conger, Jay (1994), *Spirit at Work,* San Francisco: Jossey-Bass.
    Covey, Stephen (1990), *The 7 Habits of Highly Effective People,* New York: Simon & Schuster.
    Whyte, David (1994), *The Heart Aroused,* New York: Currency Doubleday.

3. Written Assignments:
    There are 3 written assignments for this course. They are:

a. Visit a website devoted to issues of soul and spirit at work (there are many, trust us!) and write a brief paper evaluating the site and the information contained therein. This paper will be posted online by the due date contained in the schedule which follows.
b. Complete a case study evaluation. The case will be provided by the instructors. Your evaluation will be posted online by the due date contained in the schedule which follows.
c. Complete a final paper on one of the following:
   Write a 5 to 7 page paper on any topic related to soul and spirit in the workplace that has been touched on in this class. In order to complete this assignment, please read at least 2 additional sources besides those assigned in class.

   Complete an evaluation of the organization for which you work, addressing issues related to soul and spirit in the workplace. How are they manifested in your place of work, or are they absent? Please read at least 2 additional sources besides those assigned in class to support your work.

4. Attend 1 face-to-face meeting of the class. It will be held on Friday, January 16, 1998. The place of the meeting is to be announced.

Evaluation:

Evaluation of student performance in this course will be conducted as follows:

Number, content, and relevancy of online postings	40 percent
Website evaluation and case study	30 percent
Final Paper	30 percent

Please note: *Students will not be able to pass this class without participating in the online discussion. Consequently, if you are having technical or other difficulties with your participation, please contact the instructors immediately.*

"Schedule of Classes"

Please note that reading assignments are for the following week.

Week 1 (January 12–18):
• Students will post introductions online including hopes and expectations for the course
   Reading Assignments: Bolman and Deal, entire book

Week 2 (January 19–25):
• Soul, Spirit, Organizational Change and Transformation
   Reading Assignments: Conger, Chapters 1–3; Whyte, Chapters 1 and 2

Week 3 (January 26–February 1):
- Defining soul and spirit
  Reading Assignments: Conger, Chapters 4–6; Whyte, Chapters 3 and 4

Week 4 (February 2–8):
- Finding soul and spirit in the workplace
  Reading Assignments: Conger, Chapters 7 and 8; Whyte, Chapters 5 and 6

Website Assignment Due This Week

Week 5 (February 9–15):
- Leadership, motivation, soul, and spirit
  Reading Assignments: Canfield, Parts 1 and 2; Whyte, Chapters 7 and 8

Week 6 (February 16–22):
- Soul, spirit, and self-esteem
  Reading Assignments: Canfield, Parts 3 and 4

Week 7 (February 23–March 1):
- Soul, spirit, and the bottom line
  Reading Assignments: Canfield, Parts 5 and 6

Week 8 (March 2–8):
- Meaningful work
  Reading Assignments: Covey, Parts 1 and 2

Case Study Due This Week

Week 9 (March 9–15):
- "New paradigm" organizations and their relationship to soul and spirit
  Reading Assignments: Covey, Parts 3 and 4

Week 10 (March 16–21):
- Avoiding burnout through spiritual practice in the workplace

Week 11 (March 21–28):
- Summing up—What have we learned? How can we apply what we've learned?

Final Paper Due

OAD 30063—Behavior in Organizations
Spring Term—January 13ᵗʰ-May 13ᵗʰ 1998

Instructor: Keith Pratt, Ph.D.

Textbook: *Organizations: Behavior, Structure, Processes, by Gibson, Ivancevich, Donnelly, 9ᵗʰ Edition.*

> I will be available for appointments any time I am not scheduled to teach a class. Please schedule the appointment as far in advance as possible. My office is located in the Behan Hall Room 15. (See Page 3 for my schedule.)

Course Description:

This course is designed as a study of human behavior in organizational settings; the organization's effect on employee perceptions, feelings, and actions; and the employee's effect on the organization. Emphasis is placed on the attainment of organizational goals through the effective utilization of people.

Course Objectives:

Upon successful completion of this course the student will be able to discuss, analyze and critically reflect upon:

- Cultural influences on organizational behavior.
- Group behavior and its effect or organizations and their structure.
- Effective utilization of motivation and the theoretical constructs supporting it.
- Team concepts within and outside the organization.
- Processes and systems within and outside organizations that influence their structure and behavior.
- The concept and constructs of organizational change and how to manage it.

Evaluation:

1. *Class Participation.* Assessment of the student's class performance will be based on the frequency, relevance, and quality of his/her participation in the discussion and other activities.
2. *Case Studies.* Each student is required to complete three case studies. These case studies will follow the format outlined in the attached guide (see Attachment A). Two case studies will be completed individually and one will be completed as a team project.
3. *Written Work.* The quality of written work, whether a case study or essay questions on an exam, will be graded according to content, context and spelling. All written assignments, with the exception of in class work, will be presented in typewritten form.

The students enrolled in the online version of this class will be required to be present in the classroom during the first week of class, a week (to be determined by the instructor) in the middle of the term and the last week of the class.

All students will be given the option of taking the mid-term and final exam either online or in the classroom.

Case studies will be assigned weekly on Monday or on the first day of class for that week. Response to these case must be posted to the "Virtual Classroom" prior to midnight on Thursday. Students will be allowed to work on the case studies collaboratively and post their response as such.

Evaluation will be conducted in the following manner:

Number, content, and relevancy of postings — 20 percent
Case Studies — 30 percent
Exams, Quizzes and other written assignments — 50 percent

Grades will be assigned using the following standard:
90 percent to 100 percent = A
80 percent to 89 percent = B
70 percent to 79 percent = C
60 percent to 69 percent = D
Less than 60 percent is an "F"

Spring Term Schedule for Behavior in Organizations:

Week One:
January 14   Introductions
                    Syllabus

Week Two:
January 21, 23   Chapter 1: The Study of Organizations

Week Three:
January 26, 28, 30 Chapter 2: Cultural Influences on Organizational
                    Behavior

Week Four:
February 2, 4, 6   Chapter 3: Globalization
                    Chapter 4: Individual Behavior and Differences

Week Five:
February 9, 11, 13 Chapter 5: Motivation: Content Theories and Applications
                    Chapter 6: Motivation: Process Theories and Applications

Week Six:
February 16, 18, 20   Chapter 7: Rewarding Organizational Behavior

Week Seven:
February 23, 25, 27   Chapter 8: Group Behavior and Team Work

Week Eight:
March 2, 4, 6   Chapter 9: Intergroup Behavior, Negotiation, and
                       Team Building

Week Nine:
March 9, 11, 13   Chapter 10: Realities of Power and Politics

Week Ten:
March 16, 18   **Review for Mid-Term Exam**
March 20   **Mid-Term Exam**

Week Eleven:
March 21–March 29   Spring and Easter Break

Week Twelve:
March 30   Chapter 11: Leaders: Born, Made, or Responsive to
                       the Situation?
April 1, 3   Chapter 12: Leadership: Emerging Concepts and
                       Approaches

Week Thirteen:
April 6, 8, 10   Chapter 13: Organization Structure

Week Fourteen:
April 13, 15, 17   Chapter 14: Designing Productive and Motivating Jobs
                       Chapter 15: Designing Effective Organizations

Week Fifteen:
April 20, 22, 24   Chapter 16: Managing Effective Communication Processes

Week Sixteen:
April 27, 29
May 1   Chapter 17: Managing Effective Decision-Making
                       Processes

Week Seventeen:
May 4, 6   Chapter 18: Managing Organizational Change and
                       Development
May 8   **Review for Final Exam**

May 12   **3:00 P.M.—Final Exam**

Course: **Treatment and Recovery in Chemical Dependency**
              Cal-State Hayward Extension
Instructor: **Rena M. Palloff, Ph.D., LCSW**

Goals & Objectives of this course:

At the conclusion of the course the student should:

1. Know the background of society's historical responses to abuse and addiction.
2. Identify the role denial plays in the assessment, intervention, and treatment process and can develop appropriate strategies to address this.
3. Know the probable effects of chemical dependency of the family system and can appropriately engage the family in the identification, intervention, and treatment process.
4. Know the basic approaches to identification, intervention, and treatment of chemical dependency.
5. Know the importance of the 12 Step programs in the recovery process for both the chemically dependent and their families.
6. Be able to identify the salient issues involved in chemical dependency treatment as they relate to issues of gender, lifestyle, culture, and life span.
7. Know case management principles, techniques, and standards of practice for the treatment of chemical dependency, utilizing the development model of recovery in social and/or medical settings.
8. Can apply the essential elements of chemical dependency case management in assessment practices, treatment planning, progress documentation, discharge, and aftercare planning.
9. Know a variety of approaches and modalities effective in treating chemical dependency and its related problems, can implement preferred approaches, and apply appropriate counseling strategies and techniques.

Course Structure:

The course will take place over the span of an academic quarter (11 weeks). It will be conducted completely online. Guidelines for participation and completion of course assignments will be posted online.

Required Reading:

Perkinson, Robert (1997), *Chemical Dependency Counseling.* Thousand Oaks, CA: Sage Publications.

Evaluation:

Methods used to measure your goal attainment are:

A. Case studies:

Students are expected to respond to 5 assigned case vignettes that will be posted online

B. Online participation

C. Brief report posted online regarding a visit to a chemical dependency treatment program

D. Completion of treatment planning simulation in online teams

The relative weight of these assignments is as follows:

Online Participation	(35 percent)
Case Studies	(20 percent)
Program Review	(20 percent)
Online Treatment Planning Exercise	(25 percent)

Discussion Schedule:

The instructor will introduce the topic of the week by posting some material regarding that topic. The following is the list of topics to be discussed:

Week 1:	The importance of treatment; the "Continuum of Care" concept; and outpatient vs. inpatient treatment
Week 2:	The developmental model of recovery; intervention-review of skills; and prospective patient placement
Week 3:	12-Step Programs; relapse, recovery, and aftercare; and treatment outcome
Weeks 4 and 5:	Adjustment of the family system to the crisis of alcoholism/addiction; codependency; approaches to family treatment; adult children of alcoholics
Week 6:	Treatment issues and complications: Shame; grief; ambivalence, resistance, denial
Week 7:	Multimodal Care
Week 8:	Professional Ethics and Survival
Week 9:	Principles and practices of case management
Week 10:	Psychosocial assessment; treatment techniques
Week 11:	Work in online treatment teams to complete treatment plans for assigned cases; summary and wrap-up

ONLINE SYLLABUS
Human Behavior in the Management of Organizations

INSTRUCTOR: Arlene Hiss, Ph.D.

WELCOME TO ORGANIZATIONAL BEHAVIOR

I hope that this will not only be a learning experience for you but will be FUN in the process. If you need to talk to me, you will find me at my desk during the day (Pacific Time). I'm usually teaching on-ground at night so it is a bit harder to catch me in during the evening. However, I have an answering machine and I will get back to you if I'm not in.

This course is going to cover such subject areas in organizational behavior as Theories of Motivation; Job Design; Group Behavior; Power, Politics, and Conflict; Leadership; Decision Making; Communication; Performance Appraisal and Evaluation; Rewards; Organizational Design; and Organizational Change, Employee Development, and Legal Issues and Current Trends.

Now for the SECOND week. . . . Just kidding. How's that for an action packed six weeks? So, hang on to your hats, grab your PC's and jump right in.

COURSE DESCRIPTION

This course is designed to provide the student with a basic understanding of organizations and how people fit into them in order to lead and manage more effectively. The purpose of this course is to combine theory with application of organizational behavior and human resource topics.

COURSE TEXT

REQUIRED TEXT

Robbins, Stephen P. (1998) Organizational behavior: concepts, controversies, applications. Eighth Edition. Englewood Cliffs, NJ: Prentice Hall.

Publication Manual of the American Psychological Association. Fourth Edition. (1994)

SPECIAL ATTENDANCE GUIDELINES

The student is expected to attend the virtual classroom by dialing in at least 5 out of 7 days of each week. The standard is that an average participant should "attend" class 5 of 7 days per week. This is measured by recording the date of each entry you make to the system—whether it be a response to one of the assignments, a comment on the work of another, or a question to the group or to your faculty.

An absence does not excuse the student from the responsibility of participation, assigned work, and/or testing. Students may be dropped for poor attendance after two consecutive weeks of absences are accumulated.

ASSIGNMENT SUMMARY

DISCUSSION QUESTIONS: There will be a few discussion questions at the end of each lecture. Send these to the main meeting room (Virtual Classroom) and they should be roughly 2 pages (4 screens).

REPORTS: You will be asked to write a short report on a topic that will be assigned at the beginning of each week. Reports should be roughly 2 pages (4 screens single-spaced). These will all go to the branch meeting that is set up for "reports."

LESSONS LEARNED: The Lessons Learned should relate to how the concepts of the course relate to your workplace. Comment on problems or successes encountered, deficiencies of style in management and/or leadership, or other ideas related to the "Topics for the Week". It is not enough to identify a list of problems. You should be able to demonstrate that you have thought through the issues and can propose solutions in keeping with the discussions in the meeting rooms. These will be approximately 2 screens in length (one page). These should be sent to the branch meeting set up for lessons learned.

TERM PROJECT: The term project will be spelled out and sent in a separate note.

PARTICIPATION: It is extremely important to generate and participate in class discussion. The understanding and application of concepts is best reinforced by "lessons learned" of others. You should strive to participate in the meeting rooms and branches at least five out of every seven days. I would like to see you comment on your classmates' discussion questions, reports, and lessons learned. Besides commenting on other students' work, you will be given a final overall participation grade of 10 points. All discussion questions, comments to each other, or just plain 'ole rapping will be done in the Virtual Classroom. The Virtual Classroom is your "student lounge" so you should keep your "chatting" there. You may comment on each other's Reports, and Lessons Learned right in the same "Branch Meeting" where it was sent and this should all be topic related. I will be the observer/facilitator of this process and will be assessing your contributions to the topic related discussions. From time to time I will interject comments but for the most part, the discussions will be left to you. I will also be throwing out some "goodies" that you can hash over. I send handouts every day and you may comment on any of those. There will be plenty to talk about so you don't have to fear that you will run out of things to say. I would also like to mention that it is our online policy that you log on and *participate* 5 of the 7 days in the week minimum. Of course, since you will be so excited about this class, more than likely you will be logging on 7 of the 7 days ;-). Remember that just logging on is not the same as logging on and *participating*.

MISCELLANEOUS

A page that would be double spaced ordinarily on-ground, would be considered the same as one screen single spaced online. We don't double space anything online, therefore, 2 screens = 1 single spaced page.

GRADES

You will receive weekly grades and feedback no later than Monday night of the following week. However, I usually have them out prior to that time.

COURSE OUTCOMES

After studying Organizational Behavior, you should be able to:

Seminar One
1. Define organizational behavior (OB), describe what managers do, and identify the contributions made by major behavioral science disciplines to OB.
2. Understand how learning theories provide insights into changing behavior.

Seminar Two
3. Explain what role perception, judgments, and ethics play on decision making.
4. Explain the source of an individual's value system and how these values and behavior affect job satisfaction.
5. Define motivation and describe the motivation theories.
6. Identify the ingredients common to MBO programs.

Seminar Three
7. Understand, define, and classify group structure, processes, tasks, and decision making.
8. Explain and contrast teams and groups.
9. Define and identify the communication process.

Seminar Four
10. Summarize the leadership theories and contrast with recent approaches to leadership.
11. Define power and contrast with leadership.
12. Define conflict and describe the negotiation process.

Seminar Five
13. Identify an organization structure.
14. Identify work redesign and work schedule options.
15. Contrast job descriptions with job specifications.

Seminar Six

16. Describe organizational culture.

17. Explain forces for change and approaches to manage organizational change and stress.

SEMINAR OUTLINES

Description of Assignments/Participation Requirements:

ASSIGNMENTS:

(Note: Check in parentheses and at the end of each lecture for the destination of each assignment. All branches will begin with your class number).

SEMINAR 1—COs 1–2

   Read: Appendix A, Chapters 1, 2
   Chapter 1–What is organizational behavior?
   Chapter 2–Foundations of individual behavior
   Complete the "Learning About Yourself" Exercises on pages 32 and 84
   All week: Class discussion and what you "learned about yourself."
   Due Day 1–2 (Thurs.-Fri.) Send in your bio. Please include such things as where you work, why you are getting your degree, family, pets, hobbies, leisure activities, etc. (Virtual Classroom)
   Due Day 3 (Sat)–Discussion Questions (found at the end of the weekly lectures)–5 points (VC)
   Due Day 5 (Mon)–Report–(found at the end of the weekly lectures)–5 points (Reports Branch)
   Due Day 7 (Wed)–Lessons Learned–3 points (Lessons Learned Branch)

SEMINAR 2—COs 3–6

   Read: Chapters 3, 4, 5, 6
   Chapter 3–Perception and individual decision making
   Chapter 4–Values, attitudes, and job satisfaction
   Chapter 5–Basic motivation concepts
   Chapter 6–Motivation: From concepts to applications
   Complete the "Learning About Yourself" Exercises on pages 125, 162, 198, 230.
   All Week: Class discussion and what you "learned about yourself."
   Due Day 3 (Sat)–Discussion Questions–5 points (VC)
   Due Day 5 (Mon)–Report–5 points (Reports)
   Due Day 7 (Wed)–Lessons Learned–3 points (Lessons Learned)

SEMINAR 3—COs 7–9

   Read: Chapters 7, 8, 9
   Chapter 7–Foundations of group behavior

Chapter 8–Understanding work teams

Chapter 9–Communication

Complete the "Learning About Yourself" Exercises on pages 279, 305, 340.

All week: Class discussion and what you "learned about yourself."

Due Day 3–Discussion Questions–5 points (VC)

Due Day 5–Report–5 points (Reports)

Due Day 7–Lessons Learned–3 points (Lessons Learned)

SEMINAR 4—COs 10–12

Read: Chapters 10, 11, 12

Chapter 10–Leadership

Chapter 11–Power and politics

Chapter 12–Conflict, negotiation, and intergroup behavior

Complete the "Learning About Yourself" Exercises on pages 389, 427, 469.

All Week: Class discussion and what you "learned about yourself."

Due Day 3–Discussion Questions–5 points (VC)

Due Day 5–Report–5 points (Reports)

Due Day 7–Lessons Learned–3 points (Lessons Learned)

SEMINAR 5—COs 13–15

Read: Chapters 13, 14, 15

Chapter 13–Foundations of organization structure

Chapter 14–Work design

Chapter 15–Human resource policies and practices

Complete the "Learning About Yourself" Exercises on pages 509, 545, 588.

All Week: Class discussion and what you "learned about yourself."

Due Day 3–Discussion Questions–5 points (VC)

Due Day 5–Report–5 points (Reports)

Due Day 7–Lessons Learned–3 points (Lessons Learned)

SEMINAR 6—COs 16–17

Read: Chapters 16, 17

Chapter 16–Organizational culture

Chapter 17–Organizational change and stress management

Complete the "Learning About Yourself" Exercises on page 617, 668

All Week: Class discussion and what you "learned about yourself."

Due Day 3–Discussion Questions–5 points (VC)

NO Report this week

Due Day 7–Final Project–20 points (my personal mailbox)

Due Day 7–NO Lessons Learned this week. Instead, please send a note to
my personal mailbox telling me what you thought of the class, material, the

text, my teaching, or anything else. What did you like the most? What did you like the least? What can I do to make it better?

Overall participation for 6 weeks–10 points

TOTAL POINTS FOR THE COURSE–100 Points

<u>GRADING</u>

A   = 100–95
A- = 94–90
B+ = 89–88
B   = 87–82
B- = 81–80
C+ = 79–78
C   = 77–72
C- = 71–70
D+ = 69–68
D   = 67–62
D- = 61–60
F   = 59

Arlene Hiss

GLOSSARY OF TERMS USED IN COMPUTER-MEDIATED DISTANCE EDUCATION

Asynchronous: A type of communication that can occur at any time and at irregular intervals, meaning that people can communicate online without a pattern of interaction. It is the predominant mode of communication used in e-mail, in usenet groups, and on bulletin boards and websites.

Chat/IRC (Internet Relay Chat): A chat system that was developed by Jarkko Oikarinen in Finland in the late 1980s. IRC allows people connected anywhere on the Internet to join in on a live discussion that is not limited to just two people. In order to participate in an IRC chat, participants need IRC Client software and Internet access. The client software runs on the participant's computer and sends and receives messages from an IRC server. The IRC server, in turn, broadcasts all messages to everyone participating in the discussion.

Client-Server Application: A network architecture in which each computer or process on the network is either a client or a server. Servers are computers or processes dedicated to managing disk drives (file servers), printers (print servers), network traffic (network servers), or other processing services. Clients are PCS or workstations on which users run applications. Clients rely on servers for resources such as files, devices, communications, or processing power. Client-server architectures are sometimes called two-tier architectures.

Computer Conferencing: Conducting a conference between two or more participants at different sites by using computer networks to transmit any combination of text, static pictures, audio and/or motion video. Multipoint conferencing allows three or more participants to sit in a virtual conference room and communicate as if they were sitting right next to each other.

Course Authoring Software: Software specifically designed to assemble and electronically publish educational and training courses. The courses may be interactive in nature, wherein several students can interact, or may involve only the interaction of the student and computer.

Courseware: Software that is designed to be used in some type of educational process.

Desktop Video Conferencing: A video conference that occurs between two or more participants located at different sites by using personal computers to transmit and receive audio and video.

Extranet: A secure network that allows for the exchange of information between a group and its customers. An extranet might be set up, for example, as a means by which to register students for courses and provide them with ongoing information.

FTP (File Transfer Protocol): Provides the ability to transfer files to and from remote computer systems on the Internet.

Groupware: Software designed to allow groups of colleagues to organize their activities. The group must be connected electronically, whether it be through the Internet, an intranet, or an extranet. The software usually facilitates such things as scheduling meetings and allocating resources; it also facilitates e-mail, telephone utilities, file distribution, and password protection for shared documents.

Intranet: A private Internet operating within an organization. Both require the same network protocols and both use e-mail and World Wide Web standards for communication.

ISP (Internet Service Provider): A company that provides access to the Internet for a monthly fee.

Netiquette: Contraction meaning *Internet etiquette.* These are the guidelines for etiquette in the posting and sending of messages to online services and to Internet news groups. Netiquette not only covers rules for maintaining civility in interactions but also guidelines unique to the electronic nature of forum messages. For example, the special formatting of text is discouraged because some people would not be able to see the special formatting.

Network: A group of two or more computers linked together electronically.

Real Time Audio/Video: Audio and video that is broadcast and received with very little time delay.

Server: A computer or device on a network that manages network resources. For example, a file server is a computer and storage device dedicated to storing files. Any user on the network can store files on the server. A print server is a computer that manages one or more printers, and a network server is a computer that manages network traffic. A database server is a computer system that processes database queries. Servers are often dedicated, meaning that they perform no other tasks besides their server tasks. On multiprocessing operating systems, however, a single computer can execute several programs at once. A server in this case could refer to the program that is managing resources rather than the entire computer.

Synchronous: A type of communication in which those communicating do so at the same time. An example is a chat room where people are all typing at the same time.

URL (Uniform Resource Locator): The global Internet address of documents and other resources on the World Wide Web. The first part of the address—ftp or http—indicates the protocol to use, and the second part specifies the Internet Protocol (IP) address or the domain name where the resource is located.

Usenet Groups: Groups formed around numerous topics that are located or housed on the Internet. The usenet is a worldwide bulletin board system that can be accessed through the Internet or the online server.

Video Conferencing: Conducting a conference between two or more computers at different locations by the use of networks to transmit and receive audio and video data.

Web-Based Application: Software that is designed specifically to be used with the Internet. Frequently, this term is used to describe software through which courses might be delivered, wherein a student interacts only with the computer and not with other participants.

Whiteboard/Whiteboarding: An area on a display screen that multiple users can write or draw on that other remote users can see simultaneously. Whiteboards are often a principal component of computer conferencing applications because they enable shared visual communication.

INTERNET RESOURCES FOR DISTANCE EDUCATION

The following is a collection of websites, Internet journals, and courseware for use in and assistance with computer-mediated distance learning. It is not exhaustive but should give readers a place to start in researching additional resources in computer-mediated distance education. Inclusion of course resources on this list is for the information of our readers only and does not constitute endorsement of a particular software application. We invite our readers to visit our website at *http://www.xroadsgroup.com* for additional information about our work.

Websites of Interest:

These sites contain interesting information regarding computer-mediated distance learning, as well as links to other sites on the Internet:

De Anza College: http://dadistance.fhda.edu

University of Colorado, School of Education – "Teaching and Learning on the Internet": http://www.cudenver.edu/~mryder/itc_data/net_teach.html

Computer-Mediated Communication in Education: http://www.tec.hkr.se/~chen/webresources/cmcined.html

Educational Technology Resources and Policy Committee, Northern Michigan University: http://www.nmu.edu/ETRPC/etrpc-pedagogy.html

Indiana University Distance Learning Resources: http://www.indiana.edu/~iudisted/dlresources/

The California Distance Learning Project: http://www.otan.dni.us/cdlp/cdlp.html

avinfo – Distance Learning Technology: http://www.avinfo.com/distlern.htm

Educom: http://educom.edu/

Pennsylvania State University—The American Center for the Study of Distance Education: http://www.cde.psu.edu/ACSDE/

Resources for Distance Education: http://webster.commnet.edu/HP/pages/darling/distance.htm

Electronic Journals

These are but a sample of the numerous electronic journals now found on the Internet:

The Journal of Computer Mediated Communication: http://www.ascusc.org/jcmc/

The Journal of Critical Pedagogy: http://www.lib.wmc.edu/pub/jcp/jcp.html

T.H.E.–Technological Horizons in Education: http://www.thejournal.com

Educom Review: http://www.educom.edu/web/pubs/review/

CMC Magazine: http://www.december.com/cmc/mag/

Courseware, Course Hosting Services, and Comparisons of Course Resources

These sites not only represent courseware but also some sites where the attributes of various courseware applications are compared to assist readers in choosing courseware:

Learnability: http://www.learnability.com

Web Course in a Box: http://www.madduck.com

The Node—Technologies for Learning: http://node.on.ca/tfl/integrated/details/

Online Educational Delivery Applications: A Web Tool for Comparative Analysis: http://www.ctt.bc.ca/landonline/techinfo.html

PC Week Online—PC Week Lab's Comparison of Popular Web-Based Course Systems: http://www8.zdnet.com/pcweek/reviews/0818/18chart.html

TopClass: http://www.wbtsystems.com/

WebCT: http://aslnx1.asb.uah.edu:8900/

Virtual U: http://www-distlearn.pp.asu.edu/chih/webtool/virtualu.html

Convene International: http://www.convene.com

BIBLIOGRAPHY

Abrami, P., and Bures, E. M. "Computer-Supported Collaborative Learning and Distance Education." *The American Journal of Distance Education,* 1996, *10*(2) pp. 37–42.

Argyris, C. *On Organizational Learning.* Oxford, UK: Blackwell, 1992.

Baiocco, S. *Successful College Teaching: Problem Solving Strategies of Distinguished Professors.* Needham Heights, Mass.: Allyn & Bacon, 1998.

Baker, B., Harvell, T., and Yuan, Z. "A Collaborative Class Investigation into Telecommunications in Education: Chapter One—Teaching via Telecommunications," Spring 1997. [http://disted.tamu.edu/~kmurphy/chapter1.htm].

Baylor, D., Pavel, S., and Smith, N. "A Collaborative Class Investigation into Telecommunications in Education: Chapter Four—Constructivism," Spring 1997. [http://disted.tamu.edu/~kmurphy/chapter4.htm].

Berenfeld, B. "Telecommunications in Our Classroom: Boondoggle or Powerful Teaching Tool?," 1996. [http://balsa.cetp.ispl.fr/inet96papers/cl/cl_2.htm].

Boga, S. "Systems Approach to Collaborative Learning." n.d. [http://print.cps.nl/calgary/1.html].

Bolman, L., and Deal, T. *Reframing Organizations.* San Francisco: Jossey-Bass, 1991.

Bolman, L., and Deal, T. *Leading With Soul.* San Francisco: Jossey-Bass, 1995.

Brookfield, S. D. *Becoming a Critically Reflective Teacher.* San Francisco: Jossey-Bass, 1995.

Brooks, J., and Brooks, M. *In Search of Understanding: The Case for Constructivist Classrooms.* Alexandria, Va.: Association for Supervision and Curriculum Development, 1993.

Brown, J. "You'll Never Learn Alone Again." *Wired News,* Nov. 19, 1997. [http://www.wired.com/news/news/culture/story/8641/html].

"Building an Understanding of Constructivism." *Classroom Compass,* Winter 1995, *1*(3). [http://www.sedl.org/scimath/compass/v01n03/understand.htm.].

Caffarella, R. *Planning Programs for Adult Learners.* San Francisco: Jossey-Bass, 1994.

California Distance Learning Project, "What is Distance Education?" 1997. [http://www.otan.dni.us/cdlp/distance/whatis.html].

Catalfo, P. "America Online." In S. Walker (ed.), *Changing Community.* St. Paul, Minn.: Greywolf, 1993.

Christiansen, E., and Dirckinck-Holmfeld, L. "Making Distance Learning Cooperative," 1995. [http://www-cscl95.indiana.edu/cscl95/chritia.html].

Collins, M., and Berge, Z. "Facilitating Interaction in Computer Mediated Online Courses," 1996. [http://star.ucc.nau.edu/~mauri/moderate/flcc.html].

Conrad, L. D., and Crowell, P. W. "E-mail Addiction." *Business Officer,* National Association of College and University Business Officers, 1997. [http://www.nacubo.org/website/members/bomag/1097_conrad.html].

"The Core and the Cloud." *The Economist Newspaper Limited,* May 10, 1997. [http://www.economist.com/editorial/freeforall/5–10–97/uni4b.html].

Covey, S. *The Seven Habits of Highly Effective People: Powerful Lessons in Personal Change.* New York: Fireside, 1989.

Cranton, P. *Understanding and Promoting Transformative Learning: A Guide for Educators of Adults.* San Francisco: Jossey-Bass, 1994.

Daley, B. "Transformative Learning: Theory to Practice Links." Presented at the Midwest Research-to-Practice Conference in Adult, Continuing, and Community Education. Michigan State University, Oct. 15–17, 1997. [http://www.canr.msu.edu/aee/research/daley.htm].

David, J. "Restructuring and Technology: Partners in Change." In K. Sheingold and M. Tucker (eds.), *Restructuring for Learning with Technology.* New York: Center for Technology in Education at Bank Street College and the National Center on Education and the Economy, 1990.

De Anza College Distance Learning Center. "Are Distance Learning Courses for You?" n.d. [http://dadistance.fhda.edu/DLCQuestionnaire.html].

December, J. "Searching for Meaning Online." *CMC Magazine,* Mar. 1997. [http://www.december.com/cmc/mag/1997/mar/ed.html].

Dede, C. "Distance Learning to Distributed Learning: Making the Transition." *NLII Viewpoint,* Fall/Winter 1997. [http://educom.edu/program/nlii/articles/dede.html].

Dixon, D., and Stone, A. "Electronic Communication and Collaborative Work in the Field of Psychology." Unpublished paper, Fielding Institute, July 13, 1997.

Duchastel, P. "A Web-Based Model for University Instruction." *Journal of Educational Technology Systems,* 1997, *25*(3), 221–228. [http://www.nova.edu/~duchaste/unimodel.html].

"ED Study Documents Growth of Distance Learning." *NACUBO News,* Oct. 6, 1997. [http://www.nacubo.org/website.hl100697.html].

Ehrmann, S. "The Bad Option and the Good Option." *Educom Review,* Sept./Oct. 1995, *30*(5). [http://educom.edu/web/pubs/review/reviewArticles/30541.html].

Felder, R. M., and Brent, R. "Cooperative Learning in Technical Courses: Procedures, Pitfalls, and Payoffs." ERIC Document Reproduction Service Report, 1994. (ED 377038.) [http://www2.ncsu.edu/unity/lockers/...elder/public/Papers/Coopreport.html].

Fleming, J. "How Learning in Residence Fosters Transformative Learning and Connected Teaching." Conference in Adult, Continuing, and Community Education, Michigan State University, Oct. 15–17, 1997. [http://www.canr.msu.edu/aee/research/fleming.html].

Floyd, B. "Scholar Says Internet's Unique Qualities Foster the Growth of On-Line Friendships." *Chronicle of Higher Education,* Apr. 2, 1998. [http://chronicle.com/che-data/internet.dir/itdata/1998/04/t98040201.htm].

Gergen, K. *The Saturated Self: Dilemmas of Identity in Contemporary Life.* New York: Basic Books, 1991.

Green, K., and Gilbert, S. "Content, Communications, Productivity, and the Role of Information Technology in Higher Education," July 25, 1996. [http://www.aahe.org/technology/tltr-ch4.htm].

Gubernick, L., and Ebeling, A. "I Got My Degree Through E-Mail." *Forbes,* June 19, 1997. [http://207.87.27.10/forbes/97/0616/5912084a.htm].

Guernsey, L. "Colleges Debate the Wisdom of Having On-Campus Students Enroll in On-Line Classes." *Chronicle of Higher Education,* Mar. 27, 1998. [http://chronicle.com/data/articles. . .rt-44.dir/issue–29.dir/29a02901.htm].

Hackett, T. "From Pedagogy to Netagogy: Observations about Resources and Instruction on the Internet." *Impact,* Spring 1994. [http://bliss.berkeley.edu/impact/students/timothy/timothy_final.html].

Hammonds, K, Jackson, S., DeGeorge, G., and Morris, K. "The New University: A Tough Market is Reshaping Colleges." *BusinessWeek,* Dec. 11, 1997. [http://www.businessweek.com/1997/51/b3558139.htm].

Harasim, L. "On-Line Education: A New Domain." *Mindweave,* 1989. [http://www.icdl.open.ac.uk/mindweave/chap4.html].

Harasim, L., Hiltz, S. R., Teles, L., and Turoff, M. *Learning Networks.* Cambridge, Mass.: MIT Press, 1996.

Hargrove, R. *Mastering the Art of Creative Collaboration.* New York: McGraw-Hill, 1998.

Horgan, B. "Transforming Higher Education Using Information Technology: First Steps." *Microsoft in Higher Education,* Jan. 1998. [http://microsoft.com/education/hed/vision.htm].

Janov, J. *The Inventive Organization.* San Francisco: Jossey-Bass, 1994.

Jonassen, D., Davidson, M., Collins, M., Campbell, J., and Haag, B. "Constructivism and Computer-Mediated Communication in Distance Education." *The American Journal of Distance Education,* 1995, *9*(2), 7–26.

Jones, S. *Cybersociety.* Thousand Oaks, Calif.: Sage, 1995.

Jones, B., Valdez, G., Nowakowsi, J., and Rasmussen, C. "Designing Learning Technology for Educational Reform." *NCREL,* 1994. [http://www.ncrel.org/sdrs/areas/issues/content/cntareas/math/ma2tvisi.htm].

Jones, D., and Robin, J. "A Collaborative Class Investigation into Telecommunications in Education: Chapter Two–Learning via Telecommunications," Spring 1997. [http://disted.tamu.edu/~kmurphy/chapter2.htm].

Keasley, G. "The Virtual Professor: A Personal Case Study," Oct. 28, 1997. [http://fcae.nova.edu/~kearsley/virtual.html].

Kiernan, V. "An Engineering Professor Uses the Web to Run a 'Virtual Laboratory.'" *Chronicle of Higher Education,* Oct. 10, 1997. [http://chronicle.com/].

Kiernan, V. "Some Scholars Question Research Methods of Expert on Internet Addiction." *Chronicle of Higher Education,* May 29, 1998. [http://chronicle.com/free/v44/i38/38a02501.htm].

Killian, C. "F2F—Why Teach Online?" *Educom Review,* July/Aug. 1997, *32*(4). [http://educom.edu/web/pubs/review/reviewArticles/32431.html].

Kolderie, T. "How Structural Change Can Speed the Introduction of Technology." In K. Sheingold and M. Tucker (eds.), *Restructuring for Learning with Technology.* New York: Center for Technology in Education at Bank Street College and the National Center on Education and the Economy, 1990.

London, M., and Beatty, R. W. "360-Degree Feedback as a Competitive Advantage." *Human Resource Management*, Summer/Fall 1993, 353–372.

Macduff, I. "Flames on the Wires: Mediating from an Electronic Cottage." *Negotiation Journal*, Jan. 1994, *10*(1), 5–15.

Martin, R. "Constructivism and Adult Education." Mar. 31, 1997. [http://inspiredinside.com/learn. . .ticles/Constructivism1/1–warmup.htm].

McCollum, K. "Accreditors Are Urged to Prepare to Evaluate Distance Learning." *Chronicle of Higher Education*, May 15, 1998. [http://chronicle.com/che-data/arctic. . .rt–44.dir/issue-36.dir/36a03402.html].

McDonald, S. "The Laws of Cyberspace: What Colleges Need to Know." *Chronicle of Higher Education*, Oct. 31, 1997.

McGrath, J., and Hollingshead, A. *Groups Interacting with Technology.* Thousand Oaks, Calif.: Sage, 1994.

McWilliams, B. "Dataholics Scourge of the Modern Workplace?" *PC World Online*, Dec. 8, 1997. [http://www.pcworld.com/cgi.bin/database/body.pl?ID=971208172606].

Mezirow, J. *Fostering Critical Reflection in Adulthood: A Guide to Transformative and Emancipatory Learning.* San Francisco: Jossey-Bass, 1990.

Mezirow, J. *Transformative Dimensions of Adult Learning.* San Francisco: Jossey-Bass, 1991.

Morgan, G. *Images of Organization.* Thousand Oaks, Calif.: Sage, 1997.

Myers, C., and Jones, T. *Promoting Active Learning: Strategies for the College Classroom.* San Francisco: Jossey-Bass, 1993.

Nipper, S. "Third Generation Distance Learning and Computer Conferencing." *Mindweave*, 1989. [http://www-icdl.open.ac.uk/mindweave/chap5.html].

Oakes, P. "Incorporating Electronic Technology into a Distance Learning Course." *Microsoft in Higher Education*, Oct. 1997. [http://www.microsoft.com/education/hed/action.htm].

Ornstein, R. *The Roots of the Self.* San Francisco: Harper, 1995.

Palloff, R. "Confronting Ghosts: Lessons in Empowerment and Action." Unpublished dissertation, Human and Organizational Systems, Fielding Institute, 1996.

Palloff, R., and Pratt, K. "Playing in the Cyberspace Sandbox: The Intersection of the Human and Electronic Communities." Paper presented at the ACE/Alliance Conference, San Francisco, Oct. 7, 1994.

Palloff, R., and Pratt, K. "Playing in the Cyberspace Sandbox: The Importance of Community in Distance Learning." Paper presented at and published in the proceedings of the Eastern Adult Continuing and Distance Education Research Conference, Pennsylvania State University, Oct. 1996.

Palloff, R., and Pratt K. "Playing in the Cyberspace Sandbox: The Intersection of the Human and Electronic Communities." Paper presented virtually at the Cybermind Conference, Perth, Australia, Nov. 1996. [http://www.curtin.edu.au/conference/cybermind/papers/index.html].

Palloff, R., and Pratt, K. "Facilitation in Cyberspace: New Approaches, New Skills." Paper presented at and published in the proceedings of the International Association of Facilitators Conference, Santa Clara, Calif., Jan. 1998.

Palloff, R., and Pratt, K. "Effective Teaching and Learning in the Virtual Classroom." Paper presented at and published in the proceedings of the Teleteaching Conference of the International Computer Congress, Vienna, Austria, and Budapest, Hungary, Sept. 1998.

Peck, M. S. "The Fallacy of Rugged Individualism." In C. Whitmyer (ed.), *In the Company of Others.* Los Angeles: Jeremy P. Tarcher/Perigree, 1993.

Pratt, K. "The Electronic Personality." Unpublished doctoral dissertation, Human and Organizational Systems Program, Fielding Institute, 1996.

Rheingold, H. "A Slice of Life in my Virtual Community." *Whole Earth Review,* June 1992.

Rheingold, H. *The Virtual Community.* Reading, Mass.: Addison-Wesley, 1993.

Salomon, K. D., and others. "Distance Learning Course Ownership and Compensation Policies." *Education Securities, Inc. Newsletter,* July/Aug. 1997, *1*(2).

Schmidt, P. "2-Year Colleges See Promise and Peril in Today's Rapid Technological Change." *Chronicle of Higher Education,* Apr. 27, 1998. [http://chronicle.com/che-data/news.dir/dailarch.dir/9804.dir/98042704.html].

Selingo, J. "Small, Private Colleges Brace for Competition from Distance Learning." *Chronicle of Higher Education,* May 1, 1998. [http://chronicle.com/data/articles. . .rt–44.dir/issue-34/34a03301.html].

Senge, P. *The Fifth Discipline: The Art and Practice of the Learning Organization.* New York: Doubleday Currency, 1990.

Shaffer, C., and Anundsen, K. *Creating Community Anywhere.* New York: Jeremy P. Tarcher/Perigee Books, 1993.

Shaw, M., and Gaines, B. "Comparing Constructions through the Web." *Knowledge Science Institute,* 1995. [http://ksi.cpsc.ucalgary.ca/articles/CSCL95WG/].

Shell, B. (ed.). "Shaping Cyberspace into Human Space." *CSS Update,* 1995, *6*(3), [http://fas.sfu.ca/css/update/vol6/6.3–harasim.main.html].

Sherry, L. "Issues in Distance Learning, *International Journal of Educational Telecommunications,* 1995, *1*(4). [http://www.cudenver.edu/public/education/sherry/pubs/issues.html].

Sproull, L., and Kiesler, S. *Connections.* Cambridge, Mass.: MIT Press, 1991.

Strickland, C. "A Personal Experience with Electronic Community." *CMC Magazine,* June 1998. [http://www.december.com/cmc/mag/1998/jun/strick.html].

Strommen, E., and Lincoln, B. "Constructivism, Technology, and the Future of Classroom Learning." 1992. [http://www.ilt.columbia.edu/k12/livetext/docs/construct.html].

Sumner, M. R. "Ethics Online." *Educom Review,* Jul./Aug. 1996, *31*(4). [http://educom.edu/web/pubs/review/reviewArticles/3142.html].

Tuckman, B. W. "Developmental Sequence in Small Groups." *Psychological Bulletin,* June 1965, pp. 384–399.

Turkle, S. *Life on the Screen: Identity in the Age of the Internet.* New York: Simon & Schuster, 1995.

Twigg, C. "The Changing Definition of Learning." *Educom Review,* July/Aug. 1994a, *29*(4). [http://educom.edu/web/pubs/reviewArticles/29422.html].

Twigg, C. "The Need for a National Learning Infrastructure." *Educom Review,* Sept./Oct. 1994b, *29*(5). [http://educom.edu/web/pubs/review/reviewArticles/29516.html].

Twigg, C. "Navigating the Transition." *Educom Review,* Nov./Dec. 1994c, *29*(6). [http://educom.edu/web/pubs/review/reviewArticles/29620.html].

Twigg, C. "Putting Learning on Track." *Educom Review,* Sept./Oct. 1997, *32*(5). [http://educom.edu/web/pubs/review/reviewArticles/32560.html].

University of Idaho, "Guide #4: Evaluation for Distance Educators." *Distance Education at a Glance,* Oct. 1995. [http://www.uidaho.edu/evo/dist4.html].

University of Idaho. "Guide #9: Strategies for Learning at a Distance." *Distance Education at a Glance,* Oct. 1995. [http://www.uidaho.edu/evo.dist9.html].

University of Idaho. "Guide #10: Distance Education: Research." *Distance Education at a Glance,* Jan. 1996. [http://uidaho.edu.evo.dist10.html].

Walker, S. (ed.). *Changing Community.* St. Paul, Minn.: Greywolf, 1993.

Whitesel, C. "Reframing Our Classrooms, Reframing Ourselves: Perspectives from a Virtual Paladin." *Microsoft in Higher Education,* Apr. 1998. [http://www.microsoft.com/education/hed/vision.htm].

Whitmyer, C. (ed.). *In the Company of Others.* Los Angeles: Jeremy P. Tarcher/Perigree, 1993.

Wiggins, G. *Educative Assessment.* San Francisco: Jossey-Bass, 1998.

Wolcott, L., and Haderlie, S. "Institutional Support for Distance Teaching: A Study of Reward Practices." In F. Saba (ed.), *Defining Concepts in Distance Education.* Madison, Wis.: Magna, 1997.

Wright, D. "Active Learning: Rationale and Strategies." *Teaching at UNL,* 1993, *15*(3).

Young, K. *Caught in the Net.* New York: Wiley, 1998.

INDEX